SO-BIJ-994

FEB 2 5 2022

Microsoft Excel
Step by Step
(Office 2021 and Microsoft 365)

Joan Lambert
Curtis Frye

Microsoft Excel Step by Step (Office 2021 and Microsoft 365)
Published with the authorization of Microsoft Corporation by:
Pearson Education, Inc.

Copyright © 2022 by Pearson Education, Inc.

All rights reserved. This publication is protected by copyright, and permission must be obtained from the publisher prior to any prohibited reproduction, storage in a retrieval system, or transmission in any form or by any means, electronic, mechanical, photocopying, recording, or likewise. For information regarding permissions, request forms, and the appropriate contacts within the Pearson Education Global Rights & Permissions Department, please visit www.pearson.com/permissions.

No patent liability is assumed with respect to the use of the information contained herein. Although every precaution has been taken in the preparation of this book, the publisher and author assume no responsibility for errors or omissions. Nor is any liability assumed for damages resulting from the use of the information contained herein.

ISBN-13: 978-0-13-756427-9
ISBN-10: 0-13-756427-9

Library of Congress Control Number: 2021949813

1 2021

Trademarks
Microsoft and the trademarks listed at http://www.microsoft.com on the "Trademarks" webpage are trademarks of the Microsoft group of companies. All other marks are property of their respective owners.

Warning and Disclaimer
Every effort has been made to make this book as complete and as accurate as possible, but no warranty or fitness is implied. The information provided is on an "as is" basis. The author, the publisher, and Microsoft Corporation shall have neither liability nor responsibility to any person or entity with respect to any loss or damages arising from the information contained in this book or from the use of the programs accompanying it.

Special Sales
For information about buying this title in bulk quantities, or for special sales opportunities (which may include electronic versions; custom cover designs; and content particular to your business, training goals, marketing focus, or branding interests), please contact our corporate sales department at corpsales@pearsoned.com or (800) 382-3419.

For government sales inquiries, please contact governmentsales@pearsoned.com.

For questions about sales outside the U.S., please contact intlcs@pearson.com.

Editor-in-Chief
Brett Bartow

Executive Editor
Loretta Yates

Sponsoring Editor
Charvi Arora

Development Editor
Kate Shoup

Managing Editor
Sandra Schroeder

Senior Project Editor
Tracey Croom

Project Editor/Copy Editor
Dan Foster

Technical Editor
Laura Acklen

Indexer
Valerie Haynes Perry

Proofreader
Susan Festa

Editorial Assistant
Cindy Teeters

Cover Designer
Twist Creative, Seattle

Compositor
Danielle Foster

Pearson's Commitment to Diversity, Equity, and Inclusion

Pearson is dedicated to creating bias-free content that reflects the diversity of all learners. We embrace the many dimensions of diversity, including but not limited to race, ethnicity, gender, socioeconomic status, ability, age, sexual orientation, and religious or political beliefs.

Education is a powerful force for equity and change in our world. It has the potential to deliver opportunities that improve lives and enable economic mobility. As we work with authors to create content for every product and service, we acknowledge our responsibility to demonstrate inclusivity and incorporate diverse scholarship so that everyone can achieve their potential through learning. As the world's leading learning company, we have a duty to help drive change and live up to our purpose to help more people create a better life for themselves and to create a better world.

Our ambition is to purposefully contribute to a world where:

- Everyone has an equitable and lifelong opportunity to succeed through learning.

- Our educational products and services are inclusive and represent the rich diversity of learners.

- Our educational content accurately reflects the histories and experiences of the learners we serve.

- Our educational content prompts deeper discussions with learners and motivates them to expand their own learning (and worldview).

While we work hard to present unbiased content, we want to hear from you about any concerns or needs with this Pearson product so that we can investigate and address them.

Please contact us with concerns about any potential bias at https://www.pearson.com/report-bias.html.

Contents

Part 1: Create and format workbooks

Part 2: Analyze and present data

10   Create PivotTables and PivotCharts

Part 3: Collaborate and share in Excel

11   Print worksheets and charts

Part 4: Perform advanced analysis

Acknowledgments

Every book represents the combined efforts of many individuals. Curt Frye wrote the original versions of this book and provided a solid starting point for this edition. I'm thankful to Loretta Yates for the opportunity to provide readers with information about Excel 2021 and Excel for Microsoft 365, and to Charvi Arora for keeping things on track. Kate Shoup and Laura Acklen provided valuable developmental and technical feedback. It was a pleasure to work once again with Dan Foster, who did so much more than simply copyedit this book and contributed greatly to the quality of the content. Thanks also to Danielle Foster for laying out the content, Scout Festa for proofreading it, and Valerie Haynes Perry for indexing it.

As always, many thanks and all my love to my divine daughter, Trinity Preppernau.

About the author

 **Joan Lambert** has worked closely with Microsoft technologies since 1986, and in the training and certification industry since 1997, guiding the translation of technical information and requirements into useful, relevant, and measurable resources for people seeking certification of their computer skills or who simply want to get things done efficiently. She has written more than 50 books about Windows, Office, and SharePoint technologies, including dozens of *Step by Step* books and five generations of *Microsoft Office Specialist* certification study guides. Students who use the GO! with Microsoft Office textbook products may overhear her cheerfully demonstrating Office features in the videos that accompany the series.

A native of the Pacific Northwest, Joan has had the good fortune to live in many parts of the world. She currently resides with her family—one daughter, two dogs, two cats, and seven chickens—in the Beehive State, where she enjoys the majestic mountain views every day...from her office chair.

Introduction

Welcome! This *Step by Step* book has been designed so you can read it from the beginning to learn about Excel for Microsoft 365 (or Microsoft Excel 2021) and then build your skills as you learn to perform increasingly specialized procedures. Or, if you prefer, you can jump in wherever you need guidance for performing tasks. The how-to steps are delivered crisply and concisely—just the facts. You'll also find informative graphics that support the instructional content.

Who this book is for

Microsoft Excel Step by Step (Office 2021 and Microsoft 365) is designed for use as a learning and reference resource by people who want to use Excel to manage data, perform calculations, create useful analyses and visualizations, generate forecasts, and discover insights into their operations. The book content is designed to be useful for people who are upgrading from earlier versions of Excel and for people who are discovering Excel for the first time.

The *Step by Step* approach

The book's coverage is divided into parts representing general Excel skill sets. Each part is divided into chapters representing skill set areas, and each chapter is divided into topics that group related skills. Each topic includes expository information followed by generic procedures. At the end of the chapter, you'll find a series of practice tasks you can complete on your own by using the skills taught in the chapter. You can use the practice files available from this book's website to work through the practice tasks, or you can use your own files.

Features and conventions

This book has been designed to lead you step by step through tasks you're likely to want to perform in Excel. The topics are all self-contained, so you can start at the beginning and work your way through all the procedures or reference them independently. If you have worked with a previous version of Excel, or if you complete all the exercises and later need help remembering how to perform a procedure, the following features of this book will help you locate specific information:

- **Detailed table of contents** Browse the listing of the topics, sections, and sidebars within each chapter.

- **Chapter thumb tabs and running heads** Identify the pages of each chapter by the thumb tabs on the book's open fore edge. Find a specific chapter by number or title by looking at the running heads at the top of even-numbered (verso) pages.

- **Topic-specific running heads** Within a chapter, quickly locate the topic you want by looking at the running heads at the top of odd-numbered (recto) pages.

- **Practice tasks page tabs** Easily locate the practice tasks at the end of each chapter by looking for the full-page stripe on the book's fore edge.

- **Detailed index** Look up coverage of specific tasks and features in the index at the back of the book.

You can save time when reading this book by understanding how the *Step by Step* series provides procedural instructions and auxiliary information and identifies on-screen and physical elements that you interact with. The following table lists content formatting conventions used in this book.

Convention	Meaning
TIP	This reader aid provides a helpful hint or shortcut to simplify a task.
IMPORTANT	This reader aid alerts you to a common problem or provides information necessary to successfully complete a procedure.
SEE ALSO	This reader aid directs you to more information about a topic in this book or elsewhere.
1. Numbered steps	Numbered steps guide you through generic procedures in each topic and hands-on practice tasks at the end of each chapter.

Convention	Meaning
■ Bulleted lists	Bulleted lists indicate single-step procedures and sets of multiple alternative procedures.
Interface objects	In procedures and practice tasks, semibold black text indicates on-screen elements that you should select (click or tap).
User input	Light semibold formatting identifies specific information that you should enter when completing procedures or practice tasks.
Ctrl+P	A plus sign between two keys indicates that you must select those keys at the same time. For example, "press **Ctrl+P**" directs you to hold down the Ctrl key while you press the P key.
Emphasis and *URLs*	In expository text, italic formatting identifies web addresses and words or phrases we want to emphasize.

Download the practice files

Before you can complete the practice tasks in this book, you must download the book's practice files to your computer from *MicrosoftPressStore.com/Excel365stepbystep/downloads*. Follow the instructions on the webpage.

> ⚠ **IMPORTANT** Excel 2021 and other Microsoft 365 apps are not available from the book's website. You should install Excel before working through the procedures and practice tasks in this book.

You can open the files that are supplied for the practice tasks and save the finished versions of each file. If you want to repeat practice tasks later, you can download the original practice files again.

> **SEE ALSO** For information about opening and saving files, see "Create workbooks" in Chapter 1, "Set up a workbook."

The following table lists the files available for use while working through the practice tasks in this book.

Chapter	Folder	File
Part 1: Create and format workbooks		
1: Set up a workbook	Excel365SBS\Ch01	CreateWorkbooks.xlsx
		CustomizeRibbonTabs.xlsx
		MergeCells.xlsx
		ModifyWorkbooks.xlsx
		ModifyWorksheets.xlsx
2: Work with data and Excel tables	Excel365SBS\Ch02	CompleteFlashFill.xlsx
		CreateExcelTables.xlsx
		EnterData.xlsx
		FindValues.xlsx
		MoveData.xlsx
		ResearchItems.xlsx
3: Perform calculations on data	Excel365SBS\Ch03	AuditFormulas.xlsx
		BuildFormulas.xlsx
		CreateArrayFormulas.xlsx
		CreateConditonalFormulas.xlsx
		NameRanges.xlsx
		SetIterativeOptions.xlsx
4: Change workbook appearance	Excel365SBS\Ch04	AddImages.xlsx
		CreateConditionalFormats.xlsx
		DefineStyles.xlsx
		FormatCells.xlsx
		FormatNumbers.xlsx
		ModifyTableStyles.xlsx
		ModifyThemes.xlsx
		phone.jpg

Chapter	Folder	File
Part 2: Analyze and present data		
5: Manage worksheet data	Excel365SBS\Ch05	FilterData.xlsx
		SummarizeValues.xlsx
		ValidateData.xlsx
6: Reorder and summarize data	Excel365SBS\Ch06	CustomSortData.xlsx
		OutlineData.xlsx
		SortData.xlsx
7: Combine data from multiple sources	Excel365SBS\Ch07	ConsolidateData.xlsx
		CreateDataLinks.xlsx
		FleetOperatingCosts.xlsx
		LookupData.xlsx
8: Analyze alternative data sets	Excel365SBS\Ch08	CreateScenarios.xlsx
		DefineDataTables.xlsx
		PerformGoalSeekAnalysis.xlsx
9: Create charts and graphics	Excel365SBS\Ch09	CreateCharts.xlsx
		CreateComboCharts.xlsx
		CreateSparklines.xlsx
		CreateSpecialCharts.xlsx
		CustomizeCharts.xlsx
		IdentifyTrends.xlsx
		InsertShapes.xlsx
		InsertSmartArt.xlsx
10: Create PivotTables and PivotCharts	Excel365SBS\Ch10	CreatePivotCharts.xlsx
		CreatePivotTables.xlsx
		EditPivotTables.xlsx
		FilterPivotTables.xlsx
		FormatPivotTables.xlsx

Chapter	Folder	File
Part 3: Collaborate and share in Excel		
11: Print worksheets and charts	Excel365SBS\Ch11	AddHeaders.xlsx
		ConsolidatedMessenger.png
		PrepareWorksheets.xlsx
		PrintCharts.xlsx
		PrintParts.xlsx
		PrintWorksheets.xlsx
12: Automate tasks and input	Excel365SBS\Ch12	AssignMacros.xlsm
		ExamineMacros.xlsm
		InsertFormControls.xlsm
		RecordMacros.xlsm
13: Work with other Microsoft 365 apps	Excel365SBS\Ch13	CreateHyperlinks.xlsx
		EmbedWorkbook.xlsx
		LevelDescriptions.xlsx
		LinkCharts.xlsx
		LinkFiles.xlsx
		LinkWorkbooks.pptx
		ReceiveLinks.pptx
14: Collaborate with colleagues	Excel365SBS\Ch14	CreateTemplate.xlsx
		DistributeFiles.xlsx
		FinalizeWorkbooks.xlsx
		ManageComments.xlsx
		ProtectWorkbooks.xlsx

Chapter	Folder	File
Part 4: Perform advanced analysis		
15: Perform business intelligence analysis	Excel365SBS\Ch15	AnalyzePowerPivotData.xlsx
		CreateQuery.xlsx
		DefineModel.xlsx
		DefineRelationships.xlsx
		DisplayTimelines.xlsx
		ManagePowerQueryData.xlsx
16. Create forecasts and visualizations	Excel365SBS\Ch16	CreateForecastSheets.xlsx
		CreateKPIs.xlsx
		CreateMaps.xlsx
		DefineMeasures.xlsx

Adapt exercise steps

This book contains many images of the Excel user interface elements (such as the ribbon and the app window) that you'll work with while performing tasks in Excel on a Windows computer. Unless we're demonstrating an alternative view of content, the screenshots shown in this book were captured on a horizontally oriented display at a screen resolution of 1920 × 1080 and a magnification of 100 percent. If your settings are different, the ribbon on your screen might not look the same as the one shown in this book. As a result, exercise instructions that involve the ribbon might require a little adaptation.

Simple procedural instructions use this format:

- On the **Insert** tab, in the **Illustrations** group, select the **Chart** button.

If the command is in a list, our instructions use this format:

1. On the **Home** tab, in the **Editing** group, select the **Find** arrow and then, in the **Find** list, select **Go To**.

If differences between your display settings and ours cause a button to appear differently on your screen than it does in this book, you can easily adapt the steps to locate the command. First select the specified tab, and then locate the specified group. If a group has been collapsed into a group list or under a group button, select the list or button to display the group's commands. If you can't immediately identify the button you want, point to likely candidates to display their names in ScreenTips.

Multistep procedural instructions use this format:

1. To select the paragraph that you want to format in columns, triple-click the paragraph.

2. On the **Layout** tab, in the **Page Setup** group, select the **Columns** button to display a menu of column layout options.

3. On the **Columns** menu, select **Three**.

On subsequent instances of instructions that require you to follow the same process, the instructions might be simplified in this format because the working location has already been established:

1. Select the paragraph that you want to format in columns.

2. On the **Columns** menu, select **Three**.

The instructions in this book assume that you're selecting on-screen content and user interface elements on your computer by clicking (with a mouse, touchpad, or other hardware device) or tapping a touchpad or the screen (with your finger or a stylus). Instructions refer to Excel user interface elements that you click or tap on the screen as *buttons*, and to physical buttons that you press on a keyboard as *keys*, to conform to the standard terminology used in documentation for these products.

When the instructions tell you to enter information, you can do so by typing on a connected external keyboard, tapping an on-screen keyboard, or even speaking aloud, depending on your computer setup and your personal preferences.

E-book edition

If you're reading the e-book edition of this book, you can do the following:

- Search the full text
- Print
- Copy and paste

You can purchase and download the e-book edition from the Microsoft Press Store at *MicrosoftPressStore.com/Excel365stepbystep/detail*.

Get support and give feedback

We've made every effort to ensure the accuracy of this book and its companion content. We welcome your feedback.

Errata and support

If you discover an error, please submit it to us at *MicrosoftPressStore.com/ Excel365stepbystep/errata*. We'll investigate all reported issues, update download-able content if appropriate, and incorporate necessary changes into future editions of this book.

For additional book support and information, please visit *MicrosoftPressStore.com/ Support*.

For assistance with Microsoft software and hardware, visit the Microsoft Support site at *support.microsoft.com*.

Stay in touch

Let's keep the conversation going! We're on Twitter at *twitter.com/MicrosoftPress*.

Part 1

Create and format workbooks

Set up a workbook

When you create a new Excel workbook, the app presents a blank workbook that contains one worksheet. You can add or delete worksheets, hide worksheets within the workbook without deleting them, and change the order of your worksheets within the workbook. You can also copy a worksheet to another workbook or move the worksheet without leaving a copy of the worksheet in the first workbook. If you and your colleagues work with a lot of workbooks, you can define property values to make them easier to find when you attempt to locate them by using the Windows search box.

Another way to make Excel easier to use is by customizing the Excel app window to fit your work style. If you find that you use a command frequently, you can add it to the Quick Access Toolbar so it's never more than one click away. If you use specific commands frequently, you can create a custom ribbon tab to make them easy to find. You can also hide, display, or change the order of the tabs on the ribbon.

This chapter guides you through procedures related to creating and modifying workbooks, creating and modifying worksheets, merging and unmerging cells, and customizing the Excel app window.

In this chapter

- Create workbooks
- Modify workbooks
- Modify worksheets
- Merge and unmerge cells
- Customize the Excel app window

Create workbooks

Any time you want to gather and store data that isn't closely related to any of your other existing data, you should create a new workbook. A workbook is the basic Excel file, comparable to a Microsoft Word document or Microsoft PowerPoint presentation. The default new workbook in Excel has one worksheet, which is like a page in a Word document or a slide in a PowerPoint presentation. You can add more worksheets to help organize your data more effectively.

When you start Excel without opening a specific file, the app displays the Start screen.

Create new workbooks from the Start screen, which is part of the Backstage view

The Start screen is part of the Backstage view (which you can display from an open workbook by selecting the File tab on the ribbon), where you can manage your Excel workbooks and account settings and perform operations such as printing. You can select one of the built-in templates available in Excel for Microsoft 365 or create a new blank workbook. You can then begin entering data into the worksheet's cells or open an existing workbook. After you enter information, you can save your work.

When you save a file, you overwrite the previous copy of the file. If you have made changes that you want to save, but you also want to keep a copy of the file as it was before you saved it, you can save your file under a new name or in a new folder.

> ⚠ **IMPORTANT** Readers frequently ask, "How often should I save my files?" You might save your changes every half hour or even every five minutes, but the best time to save a file is whenever you make a change that you would rather not have to make again. Excel for Microsoft 365 automatically saves files that are stored in OneDrive folders or SharePoint document libraries. In a locally stored workbook, you can toggle this function on and off by selecting the control in the upper-left corner of the Excel window. You can also turn off the AutoSave function for online workbooks by clearing the AutoSave OneDrive And SharePoint Online Files By Default On Excel checkbox on the Save page of the Excel Options dialog.

When saving a file, you can specify a different format for the new file and a different location in which to save the new version of the file. For example, if you work with a colleague who requires data saved in the Excel 97–2003 file format, you can save a file in that format from within the Save As dialog.

After you create a file, you can add information to make the file easier to find. Each category of information, or property, stores specific information about your file. In Windows, you can search for files based on the author or title or by keywords associated with the file.

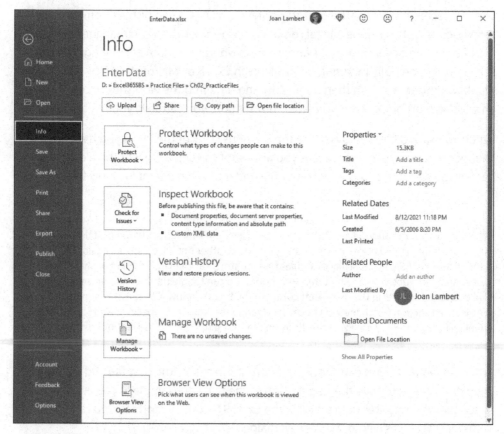

Assign properties to help Windows locate workbooks

You can set property values on the Info page of the Backstage view. Alternatively, you can display the Properties dialog to select one of the existing custom categories or create your own. You can also edit workbook properties or delete any that you no longer want to use.

When you're finished modifying a workbook, save your changes and then close the file.

To display the Backstage view

■   On the ribbon, select the **File** tab.

To display a page of the Backstage view

1. Display the Backstage view.

2. In the left pane, select **Home**, **New**, **Open**, **Info**, **Save**, **Save As**, **Print**, **Share**, **Export**, or **Publish**.

Or

- To display the **New** page of the Backstage view, press **Ctrl+N**.

- To display the **Open** page of the Backstage view, press **Ctrl+O**.

- To display the **Print** page of the Backstage view, press **Ctrl+P**.

- To display the **Save As** page of the Backstage view, press **Alt+F+A**. (In a read-only workbook, this keyboard shortcut displays the Save A Copy page.)

To create a new workbook

- If Excel is not running:

  a. Start Excel (without opening a specific workbook).

  b. On the **Start** screen, select **Blank workbook**.

- If Excel is running, display the **New** page of the Backstage view, and then select **Blank workbook**.

To create a workbook based on an existing template

1. Display the **New** page of the Backstage view.

2. If necessary, enter a search term in the **Search for online templates** box and press **Enter**.

3. Select the template you want to use, and then select **Create**.

To save a copy of a workbook

1. Do either of the following:

   - Display the **Save As** page of the Backstage view.

   - Press **F12** to open the original **Save As** dialog.

2. Navigate to the folder in which you want to save the workbook.

3. In the upper-right corner of the **Save As** page or dialog, in the **File name** box, enter a new name for the workbook.

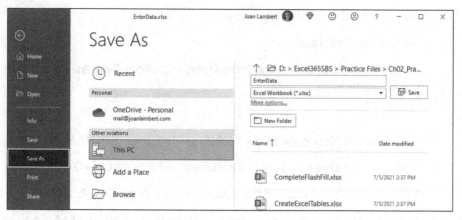

Save a new version of your file using the Save As page

4. To save the file in a different format, in the **Save as type** list, select a new file type.

> ✅ **TIP** The Save As Type list contains an extensive list of file formats, including older Excel formats used in Excel 97–2003, macro-enabled workbooks, Comma Separated Value (CSV), and XML Spreadsheet 2003. Some Excel for Microsoft 365 features are not available when working in file formats other than Excel Workbook (*.xlsx).

5. Select **Save**.

To open an existing workbook

1. Display the **Open** page of the Backstage view.

2. Locate the file you want to open by doing one of the following:

   - Select the file in the **Recent** list.

   - Select another location in the navigation list and select the file.

   - Select the **Browse** button, and then use the **Open** dialog to find the file you want to open, select the file, and then select **Open**.

To define values for document properties

1. Display the **Info** page of the Backstage view.

2. On the right side of the page, in the **Properties** group, select the **Add a** *property* text next to a label.

3. Enter a value or series of values (separated by commas) for the property.

4. Select outside the text box to add the property values.

To create a custom property

1. Display the **Info** page of the Backstage view.

2. In the right pane above the basic properties, select **Properties**, and then select **Advanced Properties**.

3. In the *file name* **Properties** dialog, select the **Custom** tab.

Define custom properties for your workbooks

4. Do either of the following:

   - In the **Name** list, select an existing property name.

   - In the **Name** box, enter a name for the new property.

5. Select the **Type** control arrow, and then select a data type.

6. In the **Value** box, enter a value for the property. Then select **Add**.

7. Repeat steps 4–6 to add more properties. When you're finished, select **OK**.

To close a workbook

- Display the Backstage view, and then select **Close**.

- Press **Ctrl+W**.

- Press **Ctrl+F4**.

Modify workbooks

You can use Excel workbooks to record information about specific business activities. Each worksheet within that workbook should represent a subdivision of that activity. To display a specific worksheet, select the worksheet tab (also called a sheet tab) on the tab bar (just below the grid of cells). You can also create new worksheets when you need them.

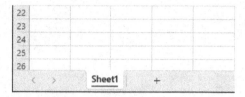

Display and create worksheets without leaving the main program window

Within an existing workbook, you can add a blank worksheet or a worksheet based on a template. From the General tab of the Insert dialog, you can insert a blank worksheet, a chart sheet, and other general worksheets. The Spreadsheet Solutions tab contains a set of useful templates for a variety of financial and personal tasks.

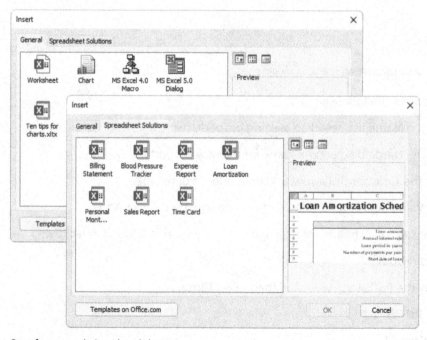

Start from a predesigned worksheet

TIP The other two options on the General tab, MS Excel 4.0 Macro and MS Excel 5.0 Dialog, help users incorporate solutions created in earlier versions of Excel into Excel 2019 workbooks.

When you create a worksheet, Excel assigns it a generic name such as *Sheet2*, *Sheet3*, or *Sheet4*. After you decide what type of data you want to store in a worksheet, you should change the worksheet's name to something more descriptive. You can also move and copy worksheets within and between workbooks. Moving a worksheet within a workbook changes its position, whereas moving a worksheet to another workbook removes it from the original workbook. Copying a worksheet keeps the original in its position and creates a second copy in the new location, whether within the same workbook or in another workbook.

TIP Selecting the Create A Copy checkbox in the Move or Copy dialog leaves the copied worksheet in its original workbook, whereas clearing the checkbox causes Excel to delete the worksheet from its original workbook.

Move or copy worksheets within and among workbooks

You can change a worksheet's position within a workbook, hide its tab on the tab bar without deleting the worksheet, unhide its tab, or change the sheet tab's color.

TIP If you copy a worksheet to another workbook and the destination workbook uses the same Office theme as the active workbook, the worksheet retains its tab color. If the destination workbook uses a different theme, the worksheet's tab color changes to reflect that theme. For more information about Office themes, see Chapter 4, "Change workbook appearance."

If you no longer need a specific worksheet, such as one you created to store some figures temporarily, you can delete the worksheet from the workbook.

To display a worksheet

- On the tab bar below the worksheet content, select the tab of the worksheet you want to display.

To create a blank worksheet

- To the right of the existing sheet tabs, select the **New Sheet** button (+).

To insert a predesigned worksheet into a workbook

1. Right-click any sheet tab and, on the context menu that appears, select **Insert**.

 TIP To display a context menu, right-click or long-press (tap and hold) the element.

2. In the **Insert** dialog, on the **General** or **Spreadsheet Solutions** tab, select the worksheet template you want to insert, and then select **OK**.

To rename a worksheet

1. Double-click the tab of the worksheet you want to rename.

2. Enter a new name for the worksheet.

3. Press **Enter**.

To move a worksheet within a workbook

- On the tab bar below the worksheet content, drag the sheet tab to the new position in the worksheet order.

Or

1. Right-click the sheet tab of the worksheet you want to move, and then select **Move or Copy**.

2. In the **Move or Copy** dialog, use the items in the **Before sheet** area to indicate where you want the new worksheet to appear.

3. Select **OK**.

To move a worksheet to another workbook

1. Open the workbook to which you want to move a worksheet from another workbook.

2. In the source workbook, right-click the sheet tab of the worksheet you want to move, and then select **Move or Copy**.

3. In the **Move or Copy** dialog, select the **To book** arrow and select the open workbook to which you want to move the worksheet.

4. In the **Before sheet** area, indicate where you want the moved worksheet to appear.

5. Select **OK**.

To copy a worksheet within a workbook

■ Hold down the **Ctrl** key and drag the worksheet's tab to the desired position in the worksheet order.

Or

1. Right-click the sheet tab of the worksheet you want to copy, and then select **Move or Copy**.

2. In the **Move or Copy** dialog, select the **Create a copy** checkbox.

3. In the **Before sheet** area, indicate where you want the new worksheet to appear.

4. Select **OK**.

To copy a worksheet to another workbook

1. Open the workbook to which you want to add a copy of a worksheet from another workbook.

2. In the source workbook, right-click the sheet tab of the worksheet you want to copy, and then select **Move or Copy**.

3. In the **Move or Copy** dialog, select the **Create a copy** checkbox.

4. Select the **To book** arrow and select the open workbook in which you want to create a copy of the worksheet.

5. In the **Before sheet** area, indicate where you want the new worksheet to appear.

6. Select **OK**.

To hide a worksheet

■ Right-click the sheet tab of the worksheet you want to hide, and then select **Hide**.

To unhide a worksheet

1. Right-click any visible sheet tab, and then select **Unhide**.

2. In the **Unhide** dialog, select the worksheet you want to redisplay.

3. Select **OK**.

To change a sheet tab's color

1. Right-click the sheet tab whose color you want to change and point to **Tab Color**.

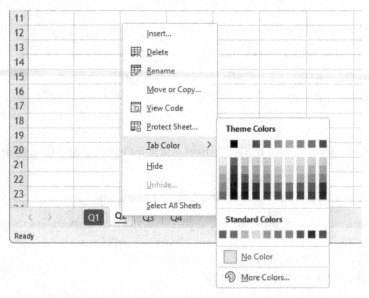

Change the sheet tab color to make it stand out or indicate a grouping

2. Do either of the following:

    • In the **Theme Colors** or **Standard Colors** palette, select a color.

    • Select **More Colors**, pick a color from the **Colors** dialog, and then select **OK**.

To delete a worksheet

1. Right-click the sheet tab of the worksheet you want to delete, and then select **Delete**.

2. If Excel displays a confirmation dialog, select **Delete**.

 TIP Excel displays a confirmation dialog when you attempt to delete a worksheet that contains data.

Modify worksheets

Excel identifies worksheet rows by number, and columns by one or more letters. Each row has a header at the left edge of the worksheet and each column has a header at the top of the worksheet. You can change the width of a column or the height of a row in a worksheet by dragging the column header's right edge or the row header's bottom edge to the position you want. Increasing a column's width or a row's height increases the space between the content within adjacent cells, making the data easier to read and work with.

 TIP You can apply the same change to more than one row or column by selecting the rows or columns you want to change and then dragging the border of one of the selected rows or columns to the location you want. When you release the mouse button, all the selected rows or columns change to the new height or width.

Modifying column width and row height can make a workbook's content easier to work with, but you can also insert a row or column between cells that contain data to make your data easier to read. Adding space between the edge of a worksheet and cells that contain data, or perhaps between a label and the data to which it refers, makes the workbook's content less crowded.

 TIP Inserting a column adds a column to the left of the selected column or columns. Inserting a row adds a row above the selected row or rows.

When you insert a row, column, or cell in a worksheet that has had formatting applied, the Insert Options button appears. Selecting this button displays a list of choices that pertain to how the inserted row or column should be formatted. The following table summarizes these options.

Option	Action
Format Same As Above	Applies the formatting of the row above the inserted row to the new row
Format Same As Below	Applies the formatting of the row below the inserted row to the new row
Format Same As Left	Applies the formatting of the column to the left of the inserted column to the new column
Format Same As Right	Applies the formatting of the column to the right of the inserted column to the new column
Clear Formatting	Applies the default format to the new row or column

You can also delete, hide, and unhide columns and rows. Deleting a column or row removes it and its content from the worksheet entirely, whereas hiding a column or row removes it from the display without deleting its content.

> ⚠ IMPORTANT If you hide the first row or column in a worksheet and then want to unhide it, you must select the Select All button in the upper-left corner of the worksheet (above the first row header and to the left of the first column header) or press Ctrl+A to select the entire worksheet. Then, on the Home tab, in the Cells group, select Format, point to Hide & Unhide, and select either Unhide Rows or Unhide Columns to make the hidden data visible again.

Just as you can insert rows or columns, you can insert individual cells into a worksheet. After you insert cells, you can use the Insert dialog to choose whether to shift the cells surrounding the inserted cell down (if your data is arranged as a column) or to the right (if your data is arranged as a row).

> TIP The Insert dialog also includes options to insert a new row or column; the Delete dialog has similar options for deleting an entire row or column.

If you want to move the data in a group of cells to another location in your worksheet, select the cells you want to move and then point to the selection's border. When the pointer changes to a four-pointed arrow, you can drag the selected cells to the target location on the worksheet. If the destination cells contain data, Excel displays a dialog asking whether you want to overwrite the destination cells' content. You can choose to overwrite the data or cancel the move.

To change row height

1. Select the row headers for the rows you want to resize.

2. Point to the bottom border of a selected row header.

3. When the pointer changes to a double-headed vertical arrow, drag the border until the row is the height you want.

Or

1. Select the row headers for the rows you want to resize.

2. Right-click any of the selected row headers, and then select **Row Height**.

The Row Height dialog displaying the default row height

3. In the **Row Height** dialog, enter a new height for the selected rows.

> ✓ **TIP** The default row height is 15 points.

4. Select **OK**.

To change column width

1. Select the column headers for the columns you want to resize.

2. Point to the right border of a selected column header.

3. When the pointer changes to a double-headed horizontal arrow, drag the border until the column is the width you want.

Or

1. Select the column headers for the columns you want to resize.

2. Right-click any of the selected column headers, and then select **Column Width**.

3. In the **Column Width** dialog, enter a new width for the selected columns.

 TIP The default column width is 0.72" or 8.43 characters when using the default 11-point Calibri font.

4. Select **OK**.

To insert a column

- Right-click a column header, and then select **Insert**.

To insert multiple columns

1. Select the number of column headers equal to the number of columns you want to insert.

2. Right-click any selected column header, and then select **Insert**.

To insert a row

- Right-click a row header, and then select **Insert**.

To insert multiple rows

1. Select a number of row headers equal to the number of rows you want to insert.

2. Right-click any selected row header, and then select **Insert**.

To delete one or more columns

1. Select the column headers of the columns you want to delete.

2. Right-click any selected column header, and then select **Delete**.

To delete one or more rows

1. Select the row headers of the rows you want to delete.

2. Right-click any selected row header, and then select **Delete**.

1

To hide one or more columns

1. Select the column headers of the columns you want to hide.

2. Right-click any selected column header, and then select **Hide**.

To hide one or more rows

1. Select the row headers of the rows you want to hide.

2. Right-click any selected row header, and then select **Hide**.

To unhide one or more columns

1. Select the column headers to the immediate left and right of the column or columns you want to unhide.

2. Right-click either selected column header, and then select **Unhide**.

Or

1. Press **Ctrl+A** to select the entire worksheet.

2. Right-click anywhere in the worksheet, and then select **Unhide**.

To unhide one or more rows

1. Select the row headers immediately above and below the row or rows you want to unhide.

2. Right-click any selected column header, and then select **Unhide**.

Or

1. Press **Ctrl+A** to select the entire worksheet.

2. Right-click anywhere in the worksheet, and then select **Unhide**.

To insert one or more cells

1. Select a cell range the same size as the range you want to insert.

2. Do either of the following:

   • On the **Home** tab of the ribbon, in the **Cells** group, select **Insert**.

   • Right-click a cell in the selected range, and then select **Insert**.

3. If necessary, use the controls in the **Insert** dialog to tell Excel how to shift the existing cells.

Indicate how Excel should move existing cells when you insert new cells into a worksheet

4. Select **OK**.

To move one or more cells within a worksheet

1. Select the cell range you want to move.

2. Point to the edge of the selected range.

3. When the pointer changes to a four-headed arrow, drag the cell range to its new position.

4. If necessary, select **OK** to confirm that you want to delete data in the target cells.

Merge and unmerge cells

When worksheet data is longer than the cell that contains it, you can widen the column, wrap the text within the cell, or merge multiple cells to make one larger cell.

For example, consider a worksheet in which the label text *Distribution Center Hubs* appears to span three cells, A1:C1, but is in fact contained within cell A1. If you select the cell and change its fill color, Excel fills only the first cell.

	A	B	C
1	Distribution	Center Hubs	
2	By region and city		
3	Northeast	Boston	
4	Atlantic	Baltimore	
5	Southeast	Atlanta	
6	North Central	Cleveland	
7	Midwest	St. Louis	
8	Southwest	Albuquerque	
9	Mountain West	Denver	
10	Northwest	Portland	
11	Central	Omaha	

Labels provide important context to worksheet data

You can solve this problem by merging cells A1:C1 into a single cell. Depending on the worksheet content, you can merge the cells and center the content at the same time, or simply merge them.

	A	B	C	D
1	Distribution Center Hubs			
2	By region and city			
3	Northeast	Boston		
4	Atlantic	Baltimore		
5	Southeast	Atlanta		

A worksheet with the label contained within a merged cell

You can merge cells either horizontally or vertically. When you merge two or more cells by using the Merge & Center or Merge Cells command, Excel retains only the content in the range's upper-left cell and deletes the rest of the text. You can split a merged cell back into individual cells, but you can't recover the deleted content (other than by immediately using the Undo command).

The Merge & Center option is popular for label text because the labels look nice and allow you to autofit other column content without the longer label affecting that operation. Note, however, that merged cells can cause difficulty for screen readers, so if you're designing your worksheet with accessibility in mind, you should avoid this.

You can also merge the cells in multiple rows at the same time by using Merge Across.

Merge cells on multiple rows by using Merge Across

To merge cells and center the content

1. Select the cells you want to merge.

2. On the **Home** tab, in the **Alignment** group, select the **Merge & Center** button.

To merge cells and retain the original alignment

1. Select the cells you want to merge.

2. On the **Home** tab, in the **Alignment** group, select the **Merge & Center** arrow (not the button), and then select **Merge Cells**.

To merge cells in multiple rows at the same time

1. Select the first range of cells that you want to merge.

2. Hold the **Ctrl** key and select each additional cell range. Then release the **Ctrl** key.

3. On the **Home** tab, in the **Alignment** group, select the **Merge & Center** arrow (not the button), and then select **Merge Across**.

To split merged cells into individual cells

1. Select the cells you want to unmerge.

2. On the **Home** tab, in the **Alignment** group, select the **Merge & Center** arrow (not the button), and then select **Unmerge Cells**.

Customize the Excel app window

How you use Excel depends on your personal working style and the type of data collections you manage. The Excel product team at Microsoft interviews customers, observes how differing organizations use the app, and sets up the user interface so

1

that many users won't need to change it to work effectively. However, if you want to change aspects of the Excel app window, including the user interface, you can. You can zoom in on worksheet data; change how Excel displays your worksheets; add frequently used commands to the Quick Access Toolbar; hide, display, and reorder ribbon tabs; and create custom ribbon tabs to make groups of commands you commonly use readily accessible.

Manage the ribbon

In Excel, you can customize the ribbon. For example, you can hide and display ribbon tabs, reorder tabs displayed on the ribbon, customize existing tabs (including tool tabs, which appear when specific items are selected), and create custom tabs.

The commands for managing the display of the ribbon are available from the Ribbon Display Options menu at the right end of the ribbon. New menu options let you customize your workspace more than ever before.

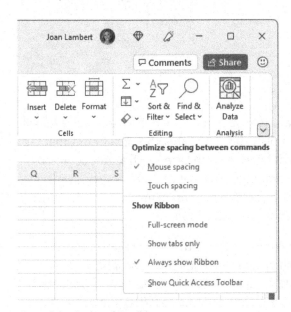

Control the display of the ribbon

In the Optimize Spacing Between Commands section, you can tighten up the spacing between commands by selecting mouse spacing or loosen it up by selecting touch spacing. In the Show Ribbon section, you can hide the ribbon entirely, hide all but the tabs, or show the entire ribbon as usual.

The tools to customize the ribbon content are on the Customize Ribbon page of the Excel Options dialog.

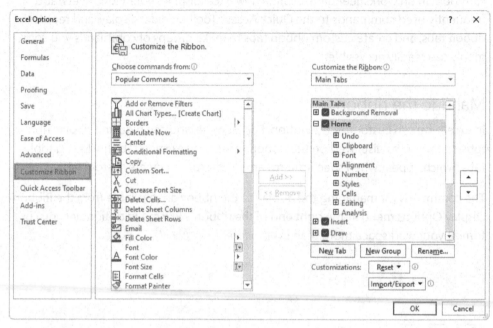

Control the display and content of commands on the ribbon

From this page, you can specify the tabs that appear on the ribbon and their order. A checkbox precedes the name of each ribbon tab. If the checkbox is selected, that tab appears on the ribbon. If programs that interface with Excel (such as Adobe Acrobat or QuickBooks) are installed on your computer, tabs that contain commands specific to those programs might be in this list. If you don't intend to use these commands, you can hide the tabs to reduce clutter on the Excel ribbon.

Just as you can change the order of the tabs on the ribbon, with Excel for Microsoft 365 you can change the order in which groups of commands appear on a tab. For example, the Page Layout tab contains five groups: Themes, Page Setup, Scale to Fit, Sheet Options, and Arrange. If you use the Themes group less frequently than the other groups, you could move that group to the right end of the tab.

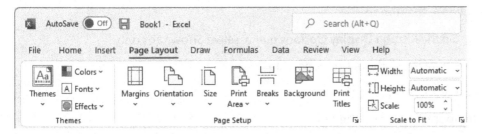

Change the order of tabs on the ribbon

You can also remove groups from a ribbon tab. If you remove a group from a built-in tab and later decide you want to restore it, you can restore it.

The built-in ribbon tabs are configured efficiently, so adding new command groups might crowd the other items on the tab and make those controls harder to find. Rather than adding controls to an existing ribbon tab, you can create a custom tab and then add groups and commands to it. The default New Tab (Custom) name doesn't tell you anything about the commands on your new ribbon tab, so you can rename it to reflect its contents.

You can export your ribbon customizations to a file that can be used to apply those changes to another Excel for Microsoft 365 installation. When you're ready to apply saved customizations to Excel, import the file and apply it. And, as with the Quick Access Toolbar, you can always reset the ribbon to its original state.

The ribbon is designed to use space efficiently, but you can hide it and other user interface elements such as the formula bar and row and column headings if you want to increase the amount of space available inside the app window.

To open the Excel Options dialog

1. Display the Backstage view.

2. Do either of the following:

   - At the bottom of the left pane, select **Options**.

   - If the window isn't tall enough to display all the links in the left pane (from **Home** to **Options**), select **More** and then select **Options**.

To display the Ribbon Display Options menu

- With the ribbon in its default expanded state, select the **Ribbon Display Options** button (v) in the lower-right corner of the ribbon.

To collapse the ribbon

- On the **Ribbon Display Options** menu, select **Show tabs only**.
- Double-click the active ribbon tab.
- Press **Ctrl+F1**.

To temporarily expand the ribbon

- Select any ribbon tab.

To expand the ribbon

- On the **Ribbon Display Options** menu, select **Always show ribbon**.
- Double-click any ribbon tab.
- Press **Ctrl+F1**.

To maximize the worksheet area

- On the **Ribbon Display Options** menu, select **Full-screen mode**.

To hide a ribbon tab

1. In the **Excel Options** dialog, select **Customize Ribbon**.
2. In the tab list on the right side of the dialog, clear the checkbox next to the name of the tab you want to hide.
3. Select **OK**.

To reorder command groups on the ribbon

1. In the **Excel Options** dialog, select **Customize Ribbon**.
2. In the tab list on the right side of the dialog, select the name of the group you want to move.
3. Do either of the following:
   - Select the **Move Up** button (the upward-pointing triangle on the far right) to move the group higher in the list and to the left on the ribbon tab.
   - Select the **Move Down** button (the downward-pointing triangle on the far right) to move the group lower in the list and to the right on the ribbon tab.
4. Select **OK**.

To create a custom ribbon tab

- On the **Customize Ribbon** page of the **Excel Options** dialog, select **New Tab**.

To create a custom group on a ribbon tab

1. On the **Customize Ribbon** page of the **Excel Options** dialog, select the ribbon tab on which you want to create the custom group.

2. Select **New Group**.

To add a command to the ribbon

1. On the **Customize Ribbon** page of the **Excel Options** dialog, select the ribbon tab or group to which you want to add a command.

2. If necessary, select the **Customize the Ribbon** arrow and select **Main Tabs** or **Tool Tabs**.

> **TIP** Tool tabs are contextual tabs that appear when you work with workbook elements such as shapes, images, or PivotTables.

3. In the **Choose commands from** list in the upper-left corner of the page, select the category of commands from which you want to choose, or select **All Commands**.

4. For each command you want to add to the ribbon, do either of the following:

   - In the left pane, select the command. Then, in the center, select **Add**.

   - In the left pane, double-click the command.

5. Select **OK**.

To rename a ribbon element

1. On the **Customize Ribbon** page of the **Excel Options** dialog, select the ribbon tab or group you want to rename, and then select **Rename**.

2. In the **Rename** dialog, enter a new name for the ribbon element, and then select **OK**.

To remove an element from the ribbon

1. Display the **Customize Ribbon** page of the **Excel Options** dialog:

2. For each command you want to remove from the ribbon, do either of the following:

   • In the right pane, select the command. Then, in the center, select **Remove**.

   • In the right pane, double-click the command.

3. Select **OK**.

 SEE ALSO For information about exporting and importing ribbon customizations, see the following section, "Manage the Quick Access Toolbar."

To reset the ribbon to its original configuration

1. On the **Customize Ribbon** page of the **Excel Options** dialog, select **Reset**, and then select **Reset all customizations**.

2. In the dialog that appears, select **Yes**.

To hide or unhide the formula bar

■ On the **View** tab, in the **Show** group, select or clear the **Formula Bar** checkbox.

To hide or unhide the row and column headings

■ In the **Show** group, select or clear the **Headings** checkbox.

To hide or unhide gridlines

■ In the **Show** group, select or clear the **Gridlines** checkbox.

Manage the Quick Access Toolbar

As you continue to work with Excel for Microsoft 365, you might discover that you use certain commands much more frequently than others. If your workbooks draw data from external sources, for example, you might find yourself using certain ribbon buttons more often than the app's designers might have expected.

You can make any button accessible with one click by adding the button to the Quick Access Toolbar. In previous versions of Excel, the Quick Access Toolbar was located by default above the left end of the ribbon, and you could move it below the ribbon to bring the commands closer to the worksheet content. Excel for Microsoft 365 now defaults to hiding the Quick Access Toolbar until you want to use it. You'll find the command to do so, and the tools you need to add and manage Quick Access Toolbar buttons, in the Excel Options dialog.

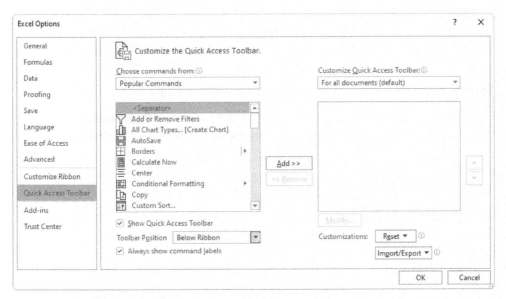

Control the display of commands on the Quick Access Toolbar

You can add buttons to the Quick Access Toolbar, change their positions, and remove them when you no longer need them. Later, if you want to return the Quick Access Toolbar to its original state, you can reset it.

You can also choose whether your Quick Access Toolbar changes affect all your workbooks or only the active workbook. If you'd like to export your Quick Access Toolbar customizations to a file that can be used to apply those changes to another Excel for Microsoft 365 installation, you can do so quickly.

To display the Quick Access Toolbar adjacent to the ribbon

- On the **Ribbon Display Options** menu, select **Show tabs only**.

Or

1. Open the **Excel Options** dialog.

2. In the left pane, select **Quick Access Toolbar**.

3. In the lower-left corner of the **Customize the Quick Access Toolbar** page, select the **Show Quick Access Toolbar** checkbox.

4. In the **Toolbar Position** list, select **Above Ribbon** or **Below Ribbon**.

5. Select **OK**.

> ⊘ **TIP** When the Quick Access Toolbar is visible, you can quickly display the Quick Access
> Toolbar page of the Excel Options dialog by selecting the Customize Quick Access Toolbar
> button located at the right end of the Quick Access Toolbar and then selecting More Commands.

To remove the Quick Access Toolbar from the ribbon area

■ At the right end of the Quick Access Toolbar, select the **Customize Quick Access Toolbar** button, and then select **Hide Quick Access Toolbar**.

The Customize Quick Access Toolbar menu

■ Right-click any area of the ribbon, and then select **Hide Quick Access Toolbar**.

■ On the **Quick Access Toolbar** page of the **Excel Options** dialog, clear the **Show Quick Access Toolbar** checkbox, and then select **OK**.

To change the location of the Quick Access Toolbar

■ At the right end of the Quick Access Toolbar, select the **Customize Quick Access Toolbar** button, and then select **Show Above the Ribbon** or **Show Below the Ribbon**.

■ On the **Quick Access Toolbar** page of the **Excel Options** dialog, In the **Toolbar Position** list, select **Above Ribbon** or **Below Ribbon**, and then select **OK**.

To add a command to the Quick Access Toolbar

■ At the right end of the Quick Access Toolbar, select the **Customize Quick Access Toolbar** button, and then select the command you want to add.

■ On the ribbon, right-click any command, and then select **Add to Quick Access Toolbar**.

Or

1. Display the **Quick Access Toolbar** page of the **Excel Options** dialog.

2. In the **Choose commands from** list in the upper-left corner of the page, select the category of commands from which you want to choose, or select **All Commands**.

3. Do either of the following for each command you want to add to the Quick Access Toolbar:

   • In the left pane, select the command. Then, in the center, select **Add** to show the command in the right pane.

   • In the left pane, double-click the command.

4. Select **OK** to add the selected commands to the Quick Access Toolbar.

 TIP If you're uncertain which of similarly named commands to add to the ribbon, add them all, try them out, and then remove the ones you don't want.

To add a group of commands to the Quick Access Toolbar

■ On the ribbon, right-click in the blank space to either side of the group name, and then select **Add to Quick Access Toolbar**.

To hide command labels on the Quick Access Toolbar

1. Display the **Quick Access Toolbar** page of the **Excel Options** dialog.

2. Clear the **Always show command labels** checkbox, and then select **OK**.

To change the order of buttons on the Quick Access Toolbar

1. Display the **Quick Access Toolbar** page of the **Excel Options** dialog.

2. In the right pane, which contains the buttons on the **Quick Access Toolbar**, select the button you want to move.

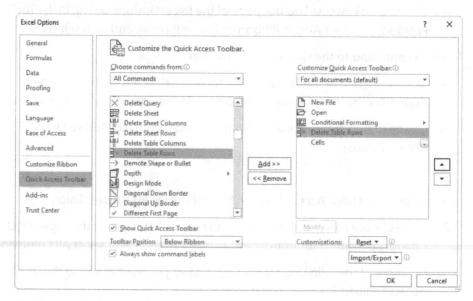

Reorder the Quick Access Toolbar buttons

3. Do either of the following:

    *   Select the **Move Up** button (the upward-pointing triangle on the far right) to move the button higher in the list and to the left on the **Quick Access Toolbar**.

    *   Select the **Move Down** button (the downward-pointing triangle on the far right) to move the button lower in the list and to the right on the **Quick Access Toolbar**.

4. Select **OK**.

To remove a command from the Quick Access Toolbar

1. Display the **Quick Access Toolbar** page of the **Excel Options** dialog.

2. Do either of the following for each command you want to remove:

   - In the right pane, select the command. Then, in the center, select **Remove**.

   - In the right pane, double-click the command.

3. Select **OK**.

To export the Quick Access Toolbar and ribbon configurations to a file

1. Display the **Quick Access Toolbar** page of the **Excel Options** dialog.

2. Select **Import/Export**, and then select **Export all customizations**.

3. In the **File Save** dialog, in the **File name** box, enter a name for the customization file, and then select **Save**.

To import the Quick Access Toolbar and ribbon configurations from a file

1. Display the **Quick Access Toolbar** page of the **Excel Options** dialog.

2. Select **Import/Export**, and then select **Import customization file**.

3. In the **File Open** dialog, browse to and select the .exportedUI file from which you want to import the settings. Then select **Open**.

4. In the **Microsoft Office** message box prompting you to confirm that you want to import the ribbon and Quick Access Toolbar customizations, select **Yes**.

To reset the Quick Access Toolbar to its original configuration

1. Display the **Quick Access Toolbar** page of the **Excel Options** dialog.

2. Select **Reset**, and then select **Reset only Quick Access Toolbar**.

3. In the **Microsoft Office** message box prompting you to confirm the reset, select **Yes**.

Customize the status bar

The status bar at the bottom of the Excel program window can display a variety of information about the workbook and its content, currently selected cells, background processes, and even keyboard settings. It can also display commands that you can use to interact with the Excel program window, including macro-recording commands and commands for changing the worksheet view and magnification.

The status bar spans the entire width of the Excel window

You can specify the information and commands that you do and don't want to appear on the status bar. The status bar will display different types of information only when appropriate but will always display the commands.

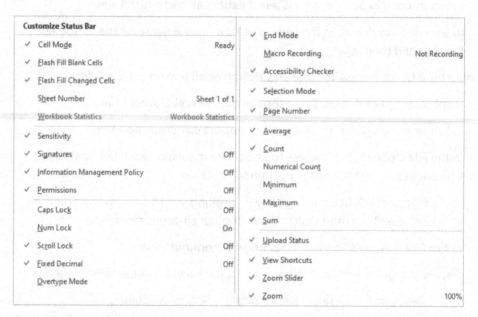

Control the display of commands on the status bar

 SEE ALSO For information about the calculations displayed on the status bar, see "Manipulate worksheet data" in Chapter 5, "Manage worksheet data."

To change what the status bar displays

1. Right-click a blank area of the status bar.

2. On the **Customize Status** bar menu, a check mark to the left of a menu item indicates that it is turned on. Select any menu item to toggle it on or off.

Change the magnification level of a worksheet

One way to make Excel easier to work with is to change the app's zoom level. Just as you can zoom in with a camera to increase the size of an object in the camera's viewfinder, you can use the zoom setting in Excel for Microsoft 365 to change the size of objects in the app window. You can change the zoom level from the ribbon or by using the Zoom control on the status bar in the lower-right corner of the Excel window. The minimum zoom level in Excel for Microsoft 365 is 10 percent; the maximum is 400 percent.

Change worksheet magnification by using the Zoom slider or command

To zoom in on a worksheet

- On the right end of the **Zoom** slider, select the **Zoom In** button (+).

- Drag the **Zoom** slider to the right.

To zoom out on a worksheet

- On the left end of the **Zoom** slider, select the **Zoom Out** button (-).

- Drag the **Zoom** slider to the left.

To set the zoom level to 100 percent

- On the **View** tab, in the **Zoom** group, select the **100%** button.

To set a specific zoom level

1. At the right end of the status bar or in the **Zoom** group, select the **Zoom** button.

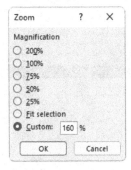

Set a magnification level by using the Zoom dialog

2. In the **Zoom** dialog, choose one of the preset values, or enter a value in the **Custom** box.

3. Select **OK**.

To zoom in on specific worksheet highlights

1. Select the cells you want to zoom in on.

2. In the **Zoom** group, select the **Zoom to Selection** button.

Arrange multiple workbook windows

As you work with Excel, you might need more than one workbook open at a time. For example, you might open a workbook that contains customer contact information and copy it into another workbook to be used as the source data for a mass mailing you create in Word for Microsoft 365. When you have multiple workbooks open simultaneously, you can switch between them or arrange them on the desktop so that most of the active workbook is shown prominently but the others are easily accessible.

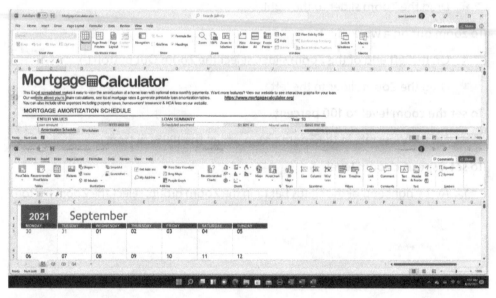

Two workbooks arranged horizontally

Many Excel for Microsoft 365 workbooks contain formulas on one worksheet that derive their value from data on another worksheet, which means you need to switch between two worksheets every time you want to see how modifying your data changes the formula's result. To facilitate this, you can display two copies of the same workbook simultaneously in separate windows, with the worksheet that contains the data in one window and the worksheet with the formula in the other window. Changes made in either window are immediately reflected in both windows. Excel indicates the different windows by appending the window numbers to the file name in the title bars.

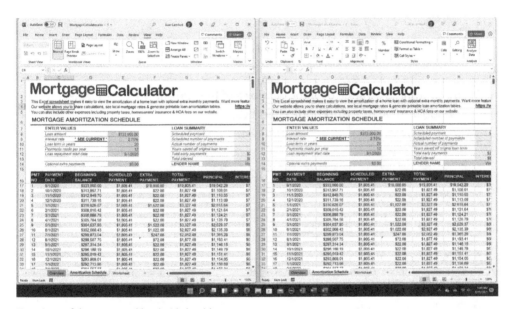

Two views of the same workbook side by side

To switch to another open workbook

1. On the **View** tab, in the **Window** group, select **Switch Windows**.

2. In the **Switch Windows** list, select the workbook you want to display.

To open another window into the current workbook

- On the **View** tab, in the **Window** group, select **New Window**.

To change how Excel displays multiple open workbooks

1. In the **Window** group, select **Arrange All**.

2. In the **Arrange Windows** dialog, select the window arrangement you want.

The window-arrangement options

3. If you want to arrange only the windows of the current workbook, select the **Windows of active workbook** checkbox.

4. Select **OK**.

Skills review

In this chapter, you learned how to:

- Create workbooks
- Modify workbooks
- Modify worksheets
- Merge and unmerge cells
- Customize the Excel app window

Practice tasks

Before you can complete these tasks, you must copy the book's practice files to your computer. The practice files for these tasks are in the **Excel365SBS\Ch01** folder. You can save the results of the tasks in the same folder.

The introduction includes a complete list of practice files and download instructions.

Create workbooks

Open the **CreateWorkbooks** workbook in Excel, and then perform the following tasks:

1. Close the **CreateWorkbooks** file, and then create a new, blank workbook.

2. Save the new workbook as Exceptions2022.

3. Add the following tags to the file's properties: exceptions, regional, and percentage.

4. Add a tag to the **Category** property called performance.

5. Create a custom property called Performance, leave the value of the **Type** field as **Text**, and assign the new property the value Exceptions.

6. Save your work.

Modify workbooks

Open the **ModifyWorkbooks** workbook in Excel, and then perform the following tasks:

1. Create a new worksheet named 365.

2. Rename the **Sheet1** worksheet to 2021 and change its tab color to green.

3. Delete the **ScratchPad** worksheet.

4. Copy the **365** worksheet to a new workbook, and then save the new workbook under the name Archive2021.

5. In the **ModifyWorkbooks** workbook, hide the **2021** worksheet.

Modify worksheets

Open the **ModifyWorksheets** workbook in Excel, and then perform the following tasks:

1. On the **May 12** worksheet, insert a new column **A** and a new row **1**.

2. After you insert the new row **1**, select the **Insert Options** button, and then select **Clear Formatting**.

3. Hide column **E**.

4. On the **May 13** worksheet, delete cell **B6**, shifting the remaining cells up.

5. Select cell **C6**, and then insert a cell, shifting the other cells down. Enter the value 4499 in the new cell **C6**.

6. Select cells **E13:F13** and move them to cells **B13:C13**.

Merge and unmerge cells

Open the **MergeCells** workbook in Excel, and then perform the following tasks:

1. Merge cells **B2:D2**.

2. Merge and center cells **B3:F3**.

3. Merge the cell range **B4:E7** by using **Merge Across**.

4. Unmerge cell **B2**.

Customize the Excel app window

Open the **CustomizeRibbonTabs** workbook in Excel, and then perform the following tasks:

1. Add the **Spelling** button to the **Quick Access Toolbar**.

2. Move the **Review** ribbon tab so it is positioned between the **Insert** and **Page Layout** tabs.

3. Create a new ribbon tab named **My Commands**.

4. Rename the **New Group (Custom)** group to **Formatting**.

5. In the list on the left side of the **Excel Options** dialog, display the main tabs.

6. From the buttons on the **Home** tab, add the **Styles** group to the **My Commands** ribbon tab you created earlier.

7. Again using the buttons available on the **Home** tab, add the **Number** group to the **Formatting** group on your custom ribbon tab.

8. Save your ribbon changes and select the **My Commands** tab on the ribbon.

Work with data and Excel tables

2

With Excel, you can visualize and present information effectively by using charts, graphics, and formatting, but the data is the most important part of any workbook. By learning to enter data efficiently, you will make fewer data-entry errors and give yourself more time to analyze your data so you can make decisions about your organization's performance and direction.

Excel provides a wide variety of tools you can use to enter and manage worksheet data effectively. For example, you can organize your data into Excel tables so that you can store and analyze your data quickly and efficiently. You can also quickly enter a data series, repeat one or more values, and control how Excel formats cells, columns, and rows that you move from one part of a worksheet to another, all with minimal effort. Finally, with Excel, you can check the spelling of worksheet text, use the thesaurus to look up alternative words, and translate words to foreign languages.

This chapter guides you through procedures related to entering and revising Excel data, using the Flash Fill feature, selecting and moving data within a workbook, finding and replacing existing data, using proofing and reference tools, and managing data in Excel tables.

In this chapter

- Enter and revise data
- Manage data by using Flash Fill
- Move data within a workbook
- Find and replace data
- Correct and fine-tune data
- Define Excel tables

Enter and revise data

After you create a workbook, you can begin entering data. The simplest way to enter data is to select a cell and type a value. This method works very well when you're entering a few pieces of data, but it is less than ideal when you're entering long sequences or series of values.

	A	B	C	D
1				
2		**Customer**	**Month**	**Total**
3		Contoso Suites	January	$ 182,423
4		Contoso Suites	February	$ 173,486
5		Contoso Suites	March	$ 88,027
6		Fabrikam, Inc.	January	$ 139,434
7		Fabrikam, Inc.	February	$ 29,461
8		Fabrikam, Inc.	March	$ 91,295
9		Lucerne Publishing	January	$ 136,922
10		Lucerne Publishing	February	$ 151,370
11		Lucerne Publishing	March	$ 160,250
12		Wide World Importers	January	$ 109,903
13		Wide World Importers	February	$ 102,243
14		Wide World Importers	March	$ 105,077

Store important business data in your worksheets

 TIP To cancel data entry and return a cell to its previous state, press Esc.

For example, suppose you are creating a worksheet to track each customer's monthly program savings. You could repeatedly enter the sequence *January, February, March,* and so on by copying and pasting the first occurrence of the sequence, but there's an easier way to do it: by using AutoFill. With AutoFill, you enter the first element in a recognized series, and then drag the fill handle in the lower-right corner of the cell until the series extends far enough to accommodate your data. By using a similar tool, Fill Series, you can enter two values in a series and use the fill handle to extend the series in your worksheet.

2

You do have some control over how Excel extends the values in a series when you drag the fill handle. If you drag the fill handle up or to the left, Excel extends the series to include previous values. For example, if you enter *January* in a cell and then drag that cell's fill handle up or to the left, Excel places *December* in the first cell, *November* in the second cell, and so on.

Another way to control how Excel extends a data series is by holding down the Ctrl key while you drag the fill handle. If you select a cell that contains the value *January* and then drag the fill handle down, Excel extends the series by placing *February* in the next cell, *March* in the cell after that, and so on. If you hold down the Ctrl key while you drag the fill handle, however, Excel repeats the value *January* in each cell you add to the series.

 TIP Experiment with how the fill handle extends your series and how pressing the Ctrl key changes that behavior. Using the fill handle can save you a lot of time entering data.

Other data-entry techniques you'll learn about in this section include the following:

- **AutoComplete** This detects when a value you're entering is similar to previously entered values.

- **Pick from Drop-Down List** You can use this to choose a value from among the existing values in a column.

- **Ctrl+Enter** Use this to enter a value in multiple cells simultaneously.

 TIP If an AutoComplete suggestion doesn't appear as you begin entering a cell value, the option might be turned off. To turn on AutoComplete, display the Advanced page of the Excel Options dialog. In the Editing Options section, select the Enable AutoComplete For Cell Values checkbox, and then select OK.

The following table summarizes these data-entry techniques.

Method	Action
AutoFill	Enter the first value in a recognized series and drag the fill handle to extend the series.
Fill Series	Enter the first two values in a series and drag the fill handle to extend the series.
AutoComplete	Enter the first few letters in a cell. If a similar value exists in the same column, Excel suggests the existing value.
Pick from Drop-Down List	Right-click a cell, and then on the context menu, select Pick From Drop-Down List. A list of existing values in the cell's column is displayed. Select the value you want to enter into the cell.
Ctrl+Enter	When you want several cells to all contain the same data, select the range, enter the data in the active cell, and then press Ctrl+Enter.

> **TIP** To display a context menu, right-click or long-press (tap and hold) the element.

Another handy feature in Excel is the AutoFill Options button that appears next to data you add to a worksheet by using the fill handle.

Use AutoFill options to control how the fill handle affects your data

2

Selecting the AutoFill Options button displays a menu of actions Excel can take regarding the cells affected by your fill operation. The options on the menu are summarized in the following table.

Option	Action
Copy Cells	Copies the contents of the selected cells to the cells indicated by the fill operation.
Fill Series	Fills the cells indicated by the fill operation with the next items in the series.
Fill Formatting Only	Copies the format of the selected cells to the cells indicated by the fill operation, but does not place any values in the target cells.
Fill Without Formatting	Fills the cells indicated by the fill operation with the next items in the series but ignores any formatting applied to the source cells.
Fill Days, Weekdays, and so on	The appearance of this option changes according to the series you extend. For example, if you extend the values *Wed*, *Thu*, and *Fri*, Excel presents two options: Fill Days and Fill Weekdays. You can then select which one you intended. If you do not use a recognized sequence, this option does not appear.
Flash Fill	Enters values based on patterns established in other cells in the column.

 SEE ALSO For more information about Flash Fill, see the following section, "Manage data by using Flash Fill."

To enter values into a cell

1. Select the cell into which you want to enter the value.

2. Type the value, and then do either of the following:

   - Press **Enter** to enter the value and move one cell down.

   - Press **Tab** to enter the value and move one cell to the right.

To extend a series of values by using the fill handle

1. Select the cells that contain the series values.

2. Drag the fill handle to cover the cells where you want the new values to appear.

To enter a value into multiple cells at the same time

1. Select the cells into which you want to enter the value.

2. Enter the value.

3. Press **Ctrl+Enter**.

To enter cell data by using AutoComplete

1. Start entering a value into a cell.

2. Use the arrow keys or the mouse to highlight a suggested AutoComplete value.

3. Press **Tab**.

To enter cell data by picking from a list

1. Right-click the cell below a list of data.

2. Select **Pick from Drop-Down List**.

3. Select the value you want to enter.

To control AutoFill options

1. Create an AutoFill sequence.

2. Select the **AutoFill Options** button.

3. Select the option you want to apply.

Manage data by using Flash Fill

When you manage data in Excel, you will often find that you want to combine values from several cells into a single value. For example, one common data configuration is to have a customer's last name, first name, and middle initial in separate cells.

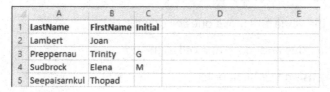

	A	B	C	D	E
1	LastName	FirstName	Initial		
2	Lambert	Joan			
3	Preppernau	Trinity	G		
4	Sudbrock	Elena	M		
5	Seepaisarnkul	Thopad			

A basic data collection

2

You could combine this data into a separate cell to show each customer's full name, either manually or by creating a formula. Alternatively, you can begin entering the full names and then let Flash Fill finish the job.

	A	B	C	D	E
1	LastName	FirstName	Initial	FullName	
2	Lambert	Joan		Joan Lambert	
3	Preppernau	Trinity	G	Trinity Preppernau	
4	Sudbrock	Elena	M	Elena Sudbrock	
5	Seepaisarnkul	Thopad		Thopad Seepaisarnkul	
6					

Flash Fill suggests values if it detects a pattern in your data entry

Note that in this example, Flash Fill did not include middle initials in the FullName column. This was because the first rows did not contain a middle initial. If you select the FullName cell next to a row that contains a value in the Initial column and edit the name as you would like it to appear, Flash Fill recognizes the new pattern for this subset of the data and offers to fill in the values. Press Enter to accept the values Flash Fill suggests.

	A	B	C	D	E
1	LastName	FirstName	Initial	FullName	
2	Lambert	Joan		Joan Lambert	
3	Preppernau	Trinity	G	Trinity G. Preppernau	
4	Sudbrock	Elena	M	Elena M. Sudbrock	
5	Seepaisarnkul	Thopad		Thopad Seepaisarnkul	

Edit a Flash Fill value to add data to the pattern

To enter data by using Flash Fill

1. In a cell on the same row as data you're working with, enter the value based on data in that row, and then press **Enter**.

2. In the cell directly below the first cell into which you entered data, start entering a new value based on data in that row.

3. Press **Enter** to accept the suggested value.

To correct a Flash Fill entry

1. Create a series of Flash Fill values in a worksheet.

2. Edit a cell that contains an incorrect Flash Fill value so that it contains the correct value.

3. Press **Enter**.

Move data within a workbook

You can move and copy data in many ways. First, though, you must select the data. The most direct method of selecting data is to select the cell that contains it. The cell you select will be outlined in black, and its contents, if any, will appear in the formula bar. When a cell is outlined, it is the active cell. You can cut, copy, delete, or change the format of the contents of a selected cell.

You're not limited to selecting cells individually. You can also select cells that are a part of a range. Alternatively, you can select an entire column or row. For example, you might need to move a column of price data one column to the right to make room for a column of headings that indicate to which category a set of numbers belongs. To move an entire column (or columns) of data at a time, you first select the column's header, located at the top of the worksheet. Selecting a column header highlights every cell in that column so that you can copy or cut the column and paste it else-where in the workbook. Similarly, selecting a row's header highlights every cell in that row so that you can copy or cut the row and paste it elsewhere in the workbook.

> **IMPORTANT** When you select a group of cells, the first cell you select is designated as the active cell.

When you copy a cell, cell range, row, or column, Excel copies the cells' contents and formatting. The Live Preview feature of Excel (and other Office apps) shows you what the data will look like without forcing you to commit to the paste operation.

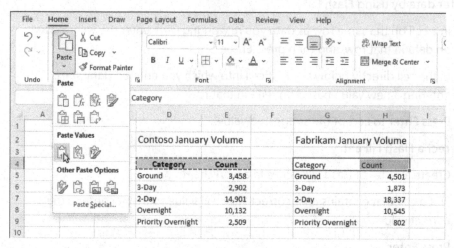

Display live previews of data-pasting options

2

If you point to one icon in the Paste gallery and then point to another icon without selecting either, Excel updates the preview to reflect the new option. Depending on the cells' formatting, two or more of the paste options might lead to the same result.

 TIP You can turn the Live Preview feature on and off in the User Interface Options section of the General page of the Excel Options dialog.

After you select an icon to complete the paste operation, Excel displays the Paste Options button next to the pasted cells. Selecting the Paste Options button displays the Paste Options palette. Note that pointing to the options in the palette doesn't generate a live preview.

 TIP If the Paste Options button doesn't appear, you can turn the feature on from the Advanced page of the Excel Options dialog. In the Cut, Copy, And Paste area, select the Show Paste Options Button When Content Is Pasted checkbox.

After cutting or copying data to the Clipboard, you can access additional paste options from the Paste gallery and from the Paste Special dialog.

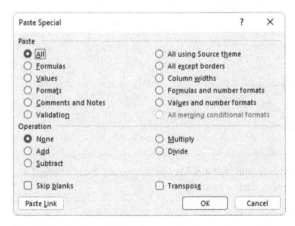

Use the Paste Special dialog for uncommon paste operations

In the Paste Special dialog, you can specify which aspect of the Clipboard contents you want to paste, restricting the pasted data to values, formats, comments, or one of several other options. You can also perform mathematical operations involving the cut or copied data and the existing data in the cells you paste the content into, and you can transpose data—that is, change rows to columns and columns to rows—when you paste it.

To select a cell or cell range

- Select the first cell you want to select, and then drag to highlight the other cells you want to select.

To select disconnected groups of cells

1. Select the first cell you want to select.

2. Hold down the **Ctrl** key and select additional cells you want to include in the selection.

To move a cell range

1. Select a cell range.

2. Point to the edge of the selection.

3. When the cursor changes to a four-way arrow, drag the range to its new location.

	A	B	C	D	E
1					
2		**Customer**	**Month**	**Total**	
3		Contoso Suites	January	$ 182,423	
4		Contoso Suites	February	$ 173,486	
5		Fabrikam, Inc.	January	$ 139,434	
6		Fabrikam, Inc.	February	$ 29,461	
7		Fabrikam, Inc.	March	$ 91,295	
8		Contoso Suites	March	$ 88,027	
9					
10					
11					
12		B9:D11			
13					

Excel indicates the drop location of the range

> ✓ **TIP** If you move the cell range to cover cells that already contain values, Excel displays a message box asking if you want to replace the existing data.

To select one or more rows

- At the left edge of the worksheet, select the row's header.

- Select a row header and drag to select other row headers.

- Select a row header, press and hold the **Ctrl** key, and then select the headers of other rows you want to copy. It is not necessary for the rows to be adjacent to each other.

To select one or more columns

- At the top edge of the worksheet, select the column's header.

- Select a column header and drag to select other column headers.

- Select a column header, press and hold the **Ctrl** key, and then select the column headers of other columns you want to copy. It is not necessary for the columns to be adjacent to each other.

To copy a cell range to the Clipboard

1. Select the cell range you want to copy.

2. Do either of the following:

   - On the **Home** tab of the ribbon, in the **Clipboard** group, select **Copy**.

   - Press **Ctrl+C**.

To cut a cell range to the Clipboard

1. Select the cell range you want to cut.

2. Do either of the following:

   - In the **Clipboard** group, select **Cut**.

   - Press **Ctrl+X**.

To paste a cell range from the Clipboard

1. Copy or cut a cell range.

2. Select the cell in the upper-left corner of the range where you want the pasted range to appear.

3. Do either of the following:

   - In the **Clipboard** group, select **Paste**.

   - Press **Ctrl+V**.

To paste a cell range by using paste options

1. Copy a cell range.

2. Select the cell in the upper-left corner of the range where you want the pasted range to appear.

3. In the **Clipboard** group, select the **Paste** arrow (not the button).

4. Select the icon representing the paste operation you want to use.

To display a preview of a cell range you want to paste

1. Copy or cut a cell range.

2. Select the cell in the upper-left corner of the range where you want the pasted range to appear.

3. Select the **Paste** arrow (not the button).

4. Point to the icon representing the paste operation for which you want to see a preview.

To paste a cell range by using the Paste Special dialog controls

1. Copy a cell range.

2. Select the cell in the upper-left corner of the range where you want the pasted range to appear.

3. Select the **Paste** arrow (not the button), and then select **Paste Special** (scroll down if necessary).

4. Select the options you want for the paste operation, and then select **OK**.

Quickly access data-formatting commands

When you select data within a workbook, the Quick Analysis button appears in the lower-right corner of the selection. Selecting the button displays the Quick Analysis toolbar, which presents common formatting, charting, and summary tools in one convenient location, when and where you will use them. It's like the Mini Toolbar in Word.

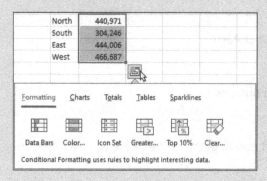

Apply formatting or create objects based on the selected data

2

You can access the following functionality from the Quick Analysis toolbar:

- **Conditional formatting** Display data bars, color scales, or icon sets; highlight data that meets specific criteria; or clear conditional formatting.

- **Charts** Create a chart of any type from the selected data.

- **Totals** Append the sum, average, count, or total (as a number or percentage) to either rows or columns.

- **Tables** Format the selected data as a table or create a PivotTable (on a separate worksheet) based on the selected data.

- **Sparklines** Represent the selected data in line, column, or win/loss charts to the right of the selected data.

To display the Quick Analysis toolbar, select at least two cells that contain content, and then select the **Quick Analysis** button that appears in the lower-right corner of the selection (or press **Ctrl+Q**.)

TIP The Quick Analysis tool is not available when only empty cells are selected.

To hide the Quick Analysis button or toolbar, select any cell, apply any command, or press **Esc**.

You use the tools on the Quick Analysis toolbar in the same way that you do from the primary location of these tools, each of which is covered in depth later in this book.

Find and replace data

Excel worksheets can hold more than 1 million rows of data. With a large data collection, it's unlikely that you would have the time to move through a worksheet one row at a time to locate the data you want to find.

You can locate specific data in an Excel worksheet by using the Find and Replace dialog. It contains two tabs—one named Find, the other named Replace—that you can use to search for cells that contain specific values. Using the controls on the Find tab, you can identify cells that contain the data you specify; using the controls on the Replace tab, you can substitute one value for another.

When you need more control over the data that you find and replace—for example, if you want to find cells in which the entire cell value matches the value you're searching for—you can expand the Find and Replace dialog to display more options.

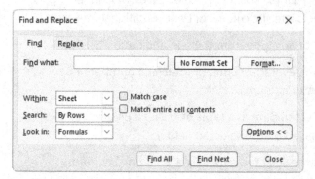

Expand the Find and Replace dialog for more options

 TIP By default, Excel looks in formulas, not cell values. To change that option, open the Look In drop-down list and select Values.

The following table summarizes the elements of the Find and Replace dialog.

Element	Function
Find What box	Contains the value you want to find or replace
Find All button	Locates and selects every cell that contains the value in the Find What field
Find Next button	Locates and selects the next cell that contains the value in the Find What field
Replace With box	Contains the value to overwrite the value in the Find What box
Replace All button	Replaces every instance of the value in the Find What box with the value in the Replace With box
Replace button	Replaces the highlighted occurrence of the value in the Find What box and highlights the next cell that contains that value
Options button	Expands the Find and Replace dialog to display additional capabilities
Format button	Displays the Find Format dialog, which you can use to specify the format of values to be found or values to be replaced

2

Element	Function
Within box	Used to select whether to search the active worksheet or the entire workbook
Search box	Used to select whether to search by rows or by columns
Look In box	Used to select whether to search cell formulas, values, or comments
Match Case checkbox	When selected, requires that all matches have the same capitalization as the text in the Find What box (for example, *cat* doesn't match *Cat*)
Match Entire Cell Contents checkbox	Requires that the cell contain exactly the same value as in the Find What box (for example, *Cat* doesn't match *Catherine*)
Close button	Closes the Find and Replace dialog

To edit a cell's contents

- Select the cell, enter a new value, and then press **Enter**.
- Select the cell, edit the value on the formula bar, and then press **Enter**.
- Double-click the cell, edit the value in the body of the cell, and then press **Enter**.

To edit part of a cell's contents

1. Select the cell.
2. Edit the part of the cell's value that you want to change on the formula bar.
3. Press **Enter**.

Or

1. Double-click the cell.
2. Edit the part of the cell's value that you want to change in the body of the cell.
3. Press **Enter**.

To display the Find & Select menu

- On the **Home** tab, in the **Editing** group, select **Find & Select**.

To find a value in a worksheet

1. Do either of the following to display the **Find** tab of the **Find and Replace** dialog:

   - On the **Find & Select** menu, select **Find**.

   - Press **Ctrl+F**.

2. In the **Find what** box, enter the value you want to find.

3. Do either of the following:

   - To select the next instance of the value, select **Find Next**.

   - To display a list of all instances of the value, select **Find All**.

To replace a value with another value

1. Do either of the following to display the **Replace** tab of the **Find and Replace** dialog:

   - On the **Find & Select** menu, select **Replace**.

   - Press **Ctrl+H**.

2. In the **Find what** box, enter the value you want to change.

3. In the **Replace with** box, enter the value you want to replace the value from the **Find what** box.

4. Do either of the following:

   - Select the **Replace** button to replace the next occurrence of the value.

   - Select the **Replace All** button to replace all occurrences of the value.

To require the find or replace operation to match an entire cell's contents

1. On the **Find & Select** menu, select either **Find** or **Replace**.

2. Set your **Find what** and, if applicable, **Replace with** values.

3. Select **Options**.

4. Select the **Match entire cell contents** checkbox.

5. Complete the find or replace operation.

To require the find or replace operation to match cell contents, including uppercase and lowercase letters

1. On the **Find & Select** menu, select either **Find** or **Replace**.

2. Set your **Find what** and, if applicable, **Replace with** values.

3. Select **Options**.

4. Select the **Match case** checkbox.

5. Complete the find or replace operation.

To find or replace formats

1. On the **Find & Select** menu, select either **Find** or **Replace**.

2. Select **Options**.

3. Select the **Find what** row's **Format** button, set a format by using the **Find Format** dialog, and then select **OK**.

4. If you want to perform a Replace operation, select the **Replace with** row's **Format** button, set a format by using the **Find Format** dialog, and then select **OK**.

5. Complete the find or replace operation.

Correct and fine-tune data

After you make a change in a workbook, you can usually undo the change, as long as you haven't closed the workbook. You can even change your mind again if you decide you want to restore your change after undoing it.

You can ensure that the text in a workbook is spelled correctly by using the Excel spelling checker. When the spelling checker encounters a word it doesn't recognize, it highlights the word and offers suggestions representing its best guess of the correct word. You can then edit the word directly, pick the proper word from the list of suggestions, or have the spelling checker ignore the misspelling. You can also use the spelling checker to add new words to a custom dictionary so that Excel will recognize them later, saving you time by not requiring you to identify the words as correct every time they occur in your worksheets.

If you're not sure of your word choice, or if you use a word that is almost but not quite right for your intended meaning, you can check for alternative words by using the thesaurus included with Excel.

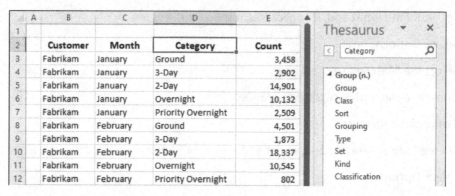

Get suggestions for alternative words

Excel for Microsoft 365 includes a new capability called Smart Lookup, which lets you use the Bing search engine to find information related to a highlighted word. When you use Smart Lookup, Excel displays the Insights task pane, which has two tabs: Explore and Define. The Explore tab displays search results from Wikipedia and other web resources. The Define tab displays definitions provided by Oxford Dictionaries from Oxford University Press.

Finally, if you want to translate a word from one language to another, you can do so by selecting the cell that contains the value you want to translate and selecting the Translate button on the Review tab. The Translator task pane opens and displays tools you can use to select the original and destination languages.

> ⚠️ **IMPORTANT** If you are asked whether you want to use Intelligent Services, select Turn On. Intelligent Services are the backbone of Microsoft's Smart Lookup and Translator tools. The Smart Lookup and Translator tools require an internet connection.

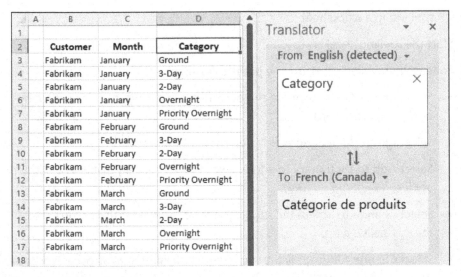

	A	B	C	D
1				
2		**Customer**	**Month**	**Category**
3		Fabrikam	January	Ground
4		Fabrikam	January	3-Day
5		Fabrikam	January	2-Day
6		Fabrikam	January	Overnight
7		Fabrikam	January	Priority Overnight
8		Fabrikam	February	Ground
9		Fabrikam	February	3-Day
10		Fabrikam	February	2-Day
11		Fabrikam	February	Overnight
12		Fabrikam	February	Priority Overnight
13		Fabrikam	March	Ground
14		Fabrikam	March	3-Day
15		Fabrikam	March	2-Day
16		Fabrikam	March	Overnight
17		Fabrikam	March	Priority Overnight
18				

Translator

From English (detected) ▾

Category ✕

⇅

To French (Canada) ▾

Catégorie de produits

Translate words to other languages

⚠ **IMPORTANT** Excel translates a sentence by using word substitutions, which means that the translation routine doesn't always pick the best word for a specific context. In other words, the translated sentence might not capture your exact meaning.

To undo an action

- On the Quick Access Toolbar, click the **Undo** button.

- Press **Ctrl+Z**.

To restore an action

- On the Quick Access Toolbar, click the **Redo** button.

- Press **Ctrl+Y**.

To start the spelling checker

- On the **Review** tab, in the **Proofing** group, select **Spelling**.

- Press **F7**.

To check spelling in a worksheet

1. Start the spelling checker.

2. For each misspelled word, do one of the following:

    - Select **Ignore Once** to ignore this occurrence of the word and move to the next misspelled word.

    - Select **Ignore All** to ignore all occurrences of the word.

    - Select **Add to Dictionary** to add the word to your locally installed dictionary file.

    - Select **Change** to accept the suggested replacement for this occurrence of the misspelled word.

    - Select **Change All** to apply the suggested replacement to all occurrences of the word in the worksheet.

    - Select a different word from the **Suggestions** list to replace the misspelled word, and then select **Change** or **Change All**.

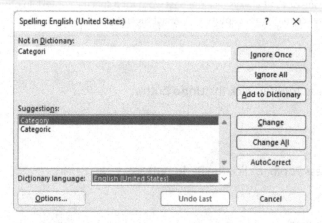

Excel checks spelling against the selected dictionary language

> ✓ **TIP** Excel starts checking spelling with the active cell. If that cell isn't A1, Excel checks spelling to the end of the worksheet and then asks if you want to continue from the beginning of the worksheet.

To add a word to the main dictionary

1. Start the spelling checker.

2. When the word you want to add appears in the **Not in Dictionary** box, select **Add to Dictionary.**

3. Finish checking spelling and then select **Close.**

To change the dictionary used to check spelling

1. Start the spelling checker.

2. Select the arrow next to the **Dictionary language** box, and then select the dictionary you want to use.

To look up word alternatives in a thesaurus

1. Select the cell that contains the word for which you want to find alternatives.

2. On the **Review** tab, in the **Proofing** group, select **Thesaurus.**

3. Use the tools in the **Thesaurus** task pane to find alternative words.

4. On the title bar of the **Thesaurus** task pane, select the **Close** button to close the task pane.

To research a word by using Smart Lookup

1. Select the cell that contains the word you want to research.

2. On the **Review** tab, in the **Insights** group, select the **Smart Lookup** button. The Search pane that opens displays definitions and results from searches of the web, media, help file, OneNote notebooks, and other files.

To translate text from one language to another

1. Select the cell that contains the word or phrase you want to translate.

2. On the **Review** tab, in the **Language** group, select **Translate.**

3. In the **Translator** pane, if necessary, choose the original language in the **From** list.

4. Choose the target language from the **To** list and review the results.

5. Select the **Close** button to close the Translator pane.

Define Excel tables

With Excel, you've always been able to manage lists of data effectively so that you can sort your worksheet data based on the values in one or more columns, limit the data displayed by using criteria (for example, show only package delivery routes with fewer than 100 stops), and create formulas that summarize the values in visible (that is, unfiltered) cells. Excel for Microsoft 365 provides those capabilities, and more, through Excel tables.

Route	Sorting Time (Minutes)	Deliveries	Return Time
101	102	552	5:03 PM
102	162	480	4:15 PM
103	165	324	4:18 PM
104	91	492	3:56 PM
105	103	486	4:02 PM
106	127	277	5:30 PM
107	112	560	6:45 PM
108	137	413	4:31 PM
109	102	254	4:18 PM
110	147	595	5:49 PM
111	163	459	3:30 PM
112	109	338	4:14 PM
113	91	313	5:38 PM
114	107	458	4:19 PM
115	93	316	4:24 PM

Manage data more easily in Excel tables

 TIP Sorting, filtering, and summarizing data are all covered elsewhere in this book.

You can create an Excel table from an existing data range, provided that the range contains no blank rows or columns and there is no extra data immediately next to or below the range.

 TIP To create an Excel table by using a keyboard shortcut, press Ctrl+L, specify the range that contains the data, and then select OK.

Entering values into a cell below or to the right of an Excel table adds a row or column to the table. After you enter the value and move out of the cell, the AutoCorrect Options button appears. If you didn't mean to include the data in the Excel table, you can select Undo Table AutoExpansion to exclude the cells from the Excel table. If you never want Excel to include adjacent data in an Excel table again, select Stop Automatically Expanding Tables.

> ✓ **TIP** To stop Table AutoExpansion before it starts, display the Proofing page of the Excel Options dialog, and then select the AutoCorrect Options button to open the AutoCorrect dialog. Select the AutoFormat As You Type tab, clear the Include New Rows and Columns in Table checkbox, and then select OK twice.

You can resize an Excel table manually by using your mouse. If your Excel table's headers contain a recognizable series of values (such as *Region1*, *Region2*, and *Region3*) and you drag the resize handle to create a fourth column, Excel creates the column with a label that is the next value in the series—in this example, *Region4*.

Excel tables often contain data you can summarize by calculating a sum or average, or by finding the maximum or minimum value in a column. To summarize one or more columns of data, you can add a Total row to the table.

	A	B	C	D	E
1					
2		Route ▾	Sorting Time (Minutes) ▾	Deliveries ▾	Return Time ▾
3		101	102	552	5:03 PM
4		102	162	480	4:15 PM
5		103	165	324	4:18 PM
6		104	91	492	3:56 PM
7		105	103	486	4:02 PM
8		106	127	277	5:30 PM
9		107	112	560	6:45 PM
10		108	137	413	4:31 PM
11		109	102	254	4:18 PM
12		110	147	595	5:49 PM
13		111	163	459	3:30 PM
14		112	109	338	4:14 PM
15		113	91	313	5:38 PM
16		114	107	458	4:19 PM
17		115	93	316	4:24 PM
18		Total	▾	6317 ▾	
19			None		
20			Average		
21			Count		
22			Count Numbers		
23			Max		
24			Min		
25			Sum		
			StdDev		
			Var		
			More Functions...		

An Excel table with a Total row

When you add the Total row, Excel creates a formula that summarizes the values in the rightmost Excel table column. You can select a summary function for each column of the table by selecting in the Total row and selecting from the list of available options.

Much as it does when you create a new worksheet, Excel gives your Excel tables generic names such as *Table1* and *Table2*. You can change an Excel table's name to something easier to recognize in your formulas. Changing an Excel table name might not seem important, but it helps make formulas that summarize Excel table data much easier to understand. You should make a habit of renaming your Excel tables so you can recognize the data they contain.

If for any reason you want to convert your Excel table back to a normal range of cells, you can do so quickly.

To create an Excel table

1. Select a cell in the list of data you want to make into an Excel table.

2. On the **Home** tab, in the **Styles** group, select **Format as Table**.

3. In the gallery that appears, select the style you want to apply to the table.

4. In the **Create Table** dialog, verify that the cell range is correct.

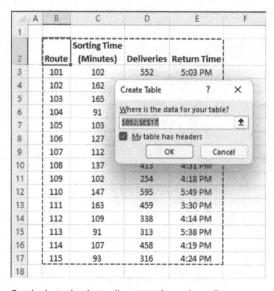

Excel selects the data adjacent to the active cell

5. If necessary, select or clear the **My table has headers** checkbox, and then select **OK**.

To create an Excel table with default formatting

1. Select a cell in the range that you want to make into an Excel table.

2. Do one of the following:

   - On the **Insert** tab, in the **Tables** group, select **Table**.

   - Press **Ctrl+L**.

   - Press **Ctrl+T**.

3. In the **Create Table** dialog, verify that the cell range is correct.

4. Select **OK**.

To add a column or row to an Excel table

1. Select a cell in the row below or the column to the right of the Excel table.

2. Enter the desired data and press **Enter**.

To expand or contract an Excel table

1. Select any cell in the Excel table.

2. Point to the lower-right corner of the Excel table.

3. When the mouse pointer changes to a diagonal arrow, drag the Excel table's outline to redefine the table.

To add a Total row to an Excel table

1. Select any cell in the Excel table.

2. On the **Table Design** tool tab, in the **Table Style Options** group, select the **Total Row** checkbox.

To change the calculation used in a Total row cell

1. Select any **Total** row cell that contains a calculation.

2. Select the cell's arrow.

3. Select a summary function.

   Or

   Select **More Functions**, use the **Insert Function** dialog to create the formula, and then select **OK**.

SEE ALSO For more information about using the Insert Function dialog and about referring to tables in formulas, see "Create formulas to calculate values" in Chapter 3, "Perform calculations on data."

To rename an Excel table

1. Select any cell in the Excel table.

2. On the **Table Design** tool tab, in the **Properties** group, enter a new name for the Excel table in the **Table Name** box.

3. Press **Enter**.

To convert an Excel table to a cell range

1. Select any cell in the Excel table.

2. On the **Table Design** tool tab, in the **Tools** group, select **Convert to Range**.

3. In the confirmation dialog that appears, select **Yes**.

Skills review

In this chapter, you learned how to:

- Enter and revise data
- Manage data by using Flash Fill
- Move data within a workbook
- Find and replace data
- Correct and fine-tune data
- Define Excel tables

2

Practice tasks

Before you can complete these tasks, you must copy the book's practice files to your computer. The practice files for these tasks are in the **Excel365SBS\Ch02** folder. You can save the results of the tasks in the same folder.

Enter and revise data

Open the **EnterData** workbook in Excel, and then perform the following tasks:

1. Use the fill handle to copy the value from cell **B3**, *Fabrikam*, to cells **B4:B7**.

2. Extend the series of months starting in cell **C3** to cell **C7**, and then use the **Auto Fill Options** button to copy the cell's value instead of extending the series.

3. In cell **B8**, enter the letters *Fa* and accept the AutoComplete value *Fabrikam*.

4. In cell **C8**, enter *February*.

5. Enter the value *Ground* in cell **D8** by using **Pick from Drop-Down List**.

6. Edit the value in cell **E5** to $6,591.30.

Manage data by using Flash Fill

Open the **CompleteFlashFill** workbook in Excel, and then perform the following tasks:

1. On the **Names** worksheet, in cell **D2**, type *Mark Hassall* and press **Enter**.

2. In cell **D3**, enter *J* and, when Excel displays a series of names in column **D**, press **Enter** to accept the Flash Fill suggestions.

3. Edit the value in cell **D3** to include the middle initial found in cell **C3**, and then press **Enter**.

4. Select the **Addresses** sheet tab.

5. Select cells **F2:F5** and then apply the **Text** number format.

6. In cell **F2**, type *03214* and press **Enter**.

7. In cell **F3**, type *0* and then press **Enter** to accept the Flash Fill suggestions.

8. Edit the value in cell **F4** to read *98012*.

Move data within a workbook

Open the **MoveData** workbook in Excel, and then perform the following tasks:

1. On the **Count** worksheet, copy the values in cells **B2:D2**.

2. Display the **Sales** worksheet, preview what the data would look like if pasted as values only, and paste the contents you just copied into cells **B2:D2**.

3. On the **Sales** worksheet, cut column **I** and paste it into the space currently occupied by column **E**.

Find and replace data

Open the **FindValues** workbook in Excel, and then perform the following tasks:

1. On the **Time Summary** worksheet, find the cell that contains the value *114*.

2. On the **Time Summary** worksheet, find all cells with contents formatted as italic type.

3. Select the **Customer Summary** sheet tab.

4. Replace all instances of the value *Contoso* with the value Northwind Traders.

Correct and fine-tune data

Open the **ResearchItems** workbook in Excel, and then perform the following tasks:

1. Check spelling in the file and accept the suggested changes for *shipped* and *within*.

2. Ignore the suggestion for *TwoDay*.

3. Add the word *ThreeDay* to the main dictionary.

4. Use the thesaurus to find alternate words for the word *Overnight* in cell **B6**, and then translate the same word to French.

5. Select cell **B2** and use Smart Lookup to find more information about the word *level*.

Define Excel tables

Open the **CreateExcelTables** workbook in Excel, and then perform the following tasks:

1. Create an Excel table from the list of data on the **Sort Times** worksheet.

2. Add a row of data to the Excel table for driver D116 and assign a value of 100 sorting minutes.

3. Add a Total row to the Excel table, and then change the summary function to **Average**.

4. Rename the Excel table to SortTimes.

Perform calculations on data

3

Excel workbooks provide an easy interface for storing and organizing data, but Excel can do so much more than that. Using the built-in functions, you can easily perform a variety of calculations—from simple tasks such as calculating totals to complex financial calculations. Excel can report information such as the current date and time, the maximum value or number of blank cells in a data set, and the cells that meet specific conditions, and it can use this information when performing calculations. To simplify the process of referencing cells or data ranges in your calculations, you can name them. Excel provides guidance for creating formulas to perform calculations and for identifying and fixing any errors in the calculations.

This chapter guides you through procedures related to naming data ranges, creating formulas to calculate values, summarizing data in one or more cells, copying and moving formulas, creating array formulas, troubleshooting issues with formula calculations, and configuring automatic and iterative calculation options.

In this chapter

- Name data ranges
- Create formulas to calculate values
- Summarize data that meets specific conditions
- Copy and move formulas
- Create array formulas
- Find and correct errors in calculations
- Configure automatic and iterative calculation options

Name data ranges

When you work with large amounts of data, it's often useful to identify groups of cells that contain related data. For example, you might have a worksheet for a delivery service in which:

■ Each column of data summarizes the number of packages handled during one hour of the day.

■ Each row of data represents a region that handled packages.

	A	B	C	D	E	F	G	H	I
1									
2			5:00 PM	6:00 PM	7:00 PM	8:00 PM	9:00 PM	10:00 PM	11:00 PM
3		Northeast	53,587	41,438	36,599	43,023	37,664	44,030	36,930
4		Atlantic	8,896	14,467	9,209	10,767	11,277	10,786	14,838
5		Southeast	7,207	13,475	13,589	14,702	7,769	10,979	10,919
6		North Central	9,829	9,959	10,367	8,962	14,847	12,085	8,015
7		Midwest	7,397	7,811	10,292	7,776	14,805	8,777	14,480
8		Southwest	7,735	11,352	7,222	11,412	14,948	10,686	14,741
9		Mountain West	9,721	8,404	11,944	8,162	14,531	11,348	8,559
10		Northwest	9,240	10,995	7,836	9,702	9,265	14,240	9,798
11		Central	11,810	13,625	8,921	13,593	11,042	10,223	13,338

Worksheets often contain logical groups of data

Instead of specifying a cell or range of cells individually every time you want to reference the data they contain, you can name the cell or cells—in other words, create a *named range*. For example, you could group the packages handled in the Northeast region during all time periods into a range named *Northeast*. Whenever you want to use the contents of that range in a calculation, you can reference Northeast instead of $C$3:$I$3. That way, you don't need to remember the cell range or even the worksheet it's on.

	A	B	C	D	E	F	G	H	I
1									
2			5:00 PM	6:00 PM	7:00 PM	8:00 PM	9:00 PM	10:00 PM	11:00 PM
3		Northeast	53,587	41,438	36,599	43,023	37,664	44,030	36,930
4		Atlantic	8,896	14,467	9,209	10,767	11,277	10,786	14,838
5		Southeast	7,207	13,475	13,589	14,702	7,769	10,979	10,919

Select a group of cells to create a named range

> ✓ **TIP** Range names can be simple or complex. In a workbook that contains different kinds of data, a more descriptive name such as *NortheastVolume* can help you remember the data the range includes.

If you have a range of data with consistent row or column headings, you can create a series of ranges at one time instead of having to create each individually.

By default, when you create a named range, its scope is the entire workbook. This means that you can reference the name in a formula on any worksheet in the workbook. If a workbook contains a series of worksheets with the same content—for example, sales data worksheets for each month of a year—you might want to set the scope of ranges on those worksheets to the worksheet instead of to the workbook.

After you create a named range, you can edit the name, the cells the range includes, or the scope in which the range exists, or delete a range you no longer need, in the Name Manager.

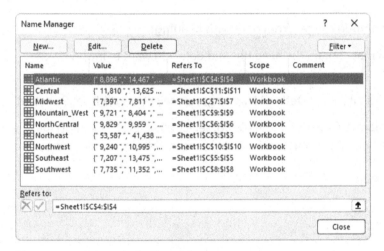

Manage named ranges in the Name Manager

> **TIP** If your workbook contains a lot of named ranges, tables, or other objects, you can filter the Name Manager list to locate objects more easily.

To create a named range

1. Select the cells you want to include in the named range.

2. In the **Name Box**, next to the formula bar, enter a name for your named range.

Or

1. Select the cells you want to include in the named range.

2. On the **Formulas** tab, in the **Defined Names** group, select **Define Name**.

3. In the **New Name** dialog, do the following:

   a. In the **Name** box, enter a name for the range. The name must begin with a letter or underscore and may not contain spaces.

   b. If you want to restrict the range to use on a specific worksheet, select that worksheet in the **Scope** list.

   c. If you want to provide additional information to help workbook users identify the range, enter a description of up to 255 characters in the **Comment** box.

   d. Verify that the **Refers to** box includes the cells you want to include in the range.

   e. Select **OK**.

To create a series of named ranges from data with headings

1. Select the cells that contain the headings and data you want to include in the named ranges.

2. On the **Formulas** tab, in the **Defined Names** group, select **Create from Selection**.

3. In the **Create Names from Selection** dialog, select the checkbox next to the location of the heading text from which you want to create the range names.

Name ranges by any outer row or column in the selection

4. Select **OK**.

To open the Name Manager

- On the **Formulas** tab, in the **Defined Names** group, select **Name Manager**.

To change the name of a named range

1. Open the **Name Manager**.

2. Select the range you want to rename, and then select **Edit**.

3. In the **Edit Name** dialog, in the **Name** box, change the range name, and then select **OK**.

To change the cells in a named range

1. Open the **Name Manager**.

2. Select the range you want to edit, and then do either of the following:

   - In the **Refers to** box, change the cell range.

   - Select **Edit**. In the **Edit Name** dialog, in the **Refers to** box, change the cell range, and then select **OK**.

To change the scope of a named range

1. Select the range you want to change the scope of and note the range name shown in the **Name Box**.

2. On the **Formulas** tab, in the **Defined Names** group, select **Define Name**.

3. In the **New Name** dialog, do the following:

   a. In the **Name** box, enter the existing range name that you noted in step 1.

   b. In the **Scope** list, select the new scope.

   c. If you want to provide additional information to help workbook users identify the range, enter a description of up to 255 characters in the **Comment** box.

   d. Verify that the **Refers to** box includes the cells you want to include in the range.

   e. Select **OK**.

To delete a named range

1. Open the **Name Manager**.

2. Select the range you want to delete, and then select **Delete**.

3. In the Microsoft Excel dialog prompting you to confirm the deletion, select **OK**.

Create formulas to calculate values

After you enter data on a worksheet and, optionally, define ranges to simplify data references, you can create formulas to performs calculations on your data. For example, you can calculate the total cost of a customer's shipments, figure the average number of packages for all Wednesdays in the month of January, or find the highest and lowest daily package volumes for a week, month, or year.

You can enter a formula directly into a cell or into the formula bar located between the ribbon and the worksheet area.

Every formula begins with an equal sign (=), which tells Excel to interpret the expression after the equal sign as a calculation instead of as text. The formula that you enter after the equal sign can include simple references and mathematical operators, or it can begin with an Excel function. For example, you can find the sum of the numbers in cells C2 and C3 by using the formula =C2+C3. You can edit formulas by selecting the cell and then editing the formula in the cell or in the formula bar.

Operators and precedence

When you create an Excel formula, you use the built-in functions and arithmetic operators that define operations such as addition and multiplication. The following table displays the order in which Excel evaluates mathematical operations.

Precedence	Operator	Description
1	-	Negation
2	%	Percentage
3	^	Exponentiation
4	* and /	Multiplication and division
5	+ and –	Addition and subtraction
6	&	Concatenation

If two operators at the same level, such as + and −, occur in the same equation, Excel evaluates them from left to right.

For example, Excel evaluates the operations in the formula = *4 + 8 * 3 − 6* in this order:

1. 8 * 3 = 24

2. 4 + 24, with a result of 28

3. 28 − 6, with a final result of 22

You can control the order in which Excel evaluates operations by using parentheses. Excel always evaluates operations in parentheses first.

For example, if the previous equation were rewritten as = *(4 + 8) * 3 − 6*, Excel would evaluate the operations in this order:

1. (4 + 8), with a result of 12

2. 12 * 3, with a result of 36

3. 36 − 6, with a final result of 30

In a formula that has multiple levels of parentheses, Excel evaluates the expressions within the innermost set of parentheses first and works its way out. As with operations on the same level, expressions at the same parenthetical level are evaluated from left to right.

For example, Excel evaluates the formula = *4 + (3 + 8 * (2 + 5)) − 7* in this order:

1. (2 + 5), with a result of 7

2. 7 * 8, with a result of 56

3. 56 + 3, with a result of 59

4. 4 + 59, with a result of 63

5. 63 − 7, with a final result of 56

You can perform mathematical operations on numbers by using the mathematical operators for addition (+), subtraction (–), multiplication (*), division (/), negation (-), and exponentiation (^). You can perform other operations on a range of numbers by using the following Excel functions:

- **SUM** Returns the sum of the numbers.

- **AVERAGE** Returns the average of the numbers.

- **COUNT** Returns the number of entries in the cell range.

- **MAX** Returns the largest number.

- **MIN** Returns the smallest number.

These functions are available from the AutoSum list, which is in the Editing group on the Home tab of the ribbon and in the Function Library group on the Formulas tab. The Function Library is also where you'll find the rest of the Excel functions, organized into categories.

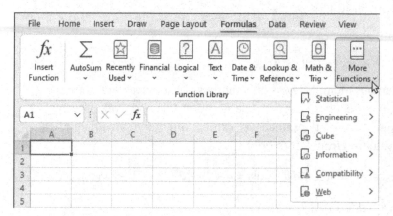

Excel includes a wide variety of functions

The Formula AutoComplete feature simplifies the process of referencing functions, named ranges, and tables in formulas. It provides a template for you to follow and suggests entries for each function argument. Here's how it works:

1. As you begin to enter a function name after the equal sign, Excel displays a list of functions matching the characters you've entered. You can select a function from the list and then press Tab to enter the function name and the opening parenthesis in the cell or formula bar.

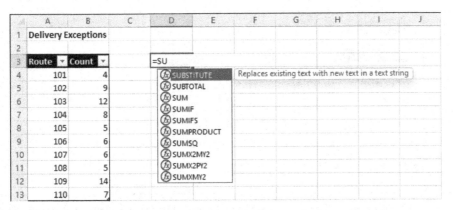

Select a function from the list

2. After the opening parenthesis, Excel displays the arguments that the selected function accepts. Bold indicates required arguments and square brackets enclose optional arguments. You can simply follow the prompts to enter or select the necessary information, and then enter a closing parenthesis to finish the formula.

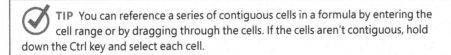

Excel prompts you for required and optional information

3. To reference a named range, table, or table element, start entering the name (or an opening square bracket to indicate a table element) and Excel displays a list of options to choose from.

> **TIP** You can reference a series of contiguous cells in a formula by entering the cell range or by dragging through the cells. If the cells aren't contiguous, hold down the Ctrl key and select each cell.

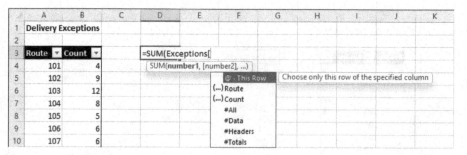

Excel displays the available table elements

 SEE ALSO For information about using keyboard shortcuts to select cell ranges, see the appendix, "Keyboard shortcuts."

If you're creating a more complex formula and want extra guidance, you can assemble the formula in the Insert Function dialog. All the Excel functions are available from within the dialog.

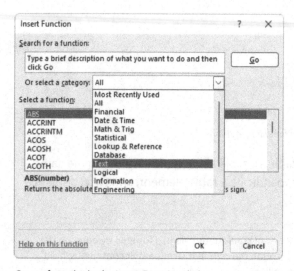

Create formulas in the Insert Function dialog

If you're uncertain which function to use, you can search for one by entering a simple description of what you'd like to accomplish. Selecting any function displays the function's arguments and description.

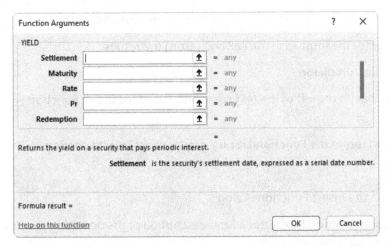

Activate any field to display a description of the argument

After you select a function, Excel displays an interface in which you can enter all the function arguments. The complexity of the interface depends on the function.

Whether you enter a formula directly or assemble it in the Insert Function dialog, you can reference data in cells (A3) or cell ranges (A3:J12), in named ranges (Northeast), or in table columns (TableName[ColumnName]). For example, if the Northeast range refers to cells C3:I3, you can calculate the average of cells C3:I3 by using the formula =AVERAGE(Northeast).

To create a formula manually

1. Select the cell in which you want to create the formula.

2. In the cell or in the formula bar, enter an equal sign (=).

3. If the formula will call a function, enter the function name and an opening parenthesis to begin the formula and display the required and optional arguments.

4. Enter the remainder of the formula:

    • Reference cells by entering the cell reference or selecting the cell.

    • Reference cell ranges by entering the cell range or dragging across the range.

    • Reference named ranges and tables by entering the range or table name.

    • Reference table elements by entering [after the table name, selecting the element from the list, and then entering].

5. If the formula includes a function, enter the closing parenthesis to end it.

6. Press **Enter** to enter the formula in the cell and return the results.

To open the Insert Function dialog

- On the formula bar, to the left of the text entry box, select the **Insert Function** button (*fx*).

- On the **Formulas** tab, in the **Function Library** group, select **Insert Function**.

- Press **Shift+F3**.

To locate a function in the Insert Function dialog

- In the **Search for a function** box, enter a brief description of the operation you want to perform, and then select **Go**.

Or

1. In the **Or select a category** list, select the function category.

2. Scroll down the **Select a function** list to the function.

To create a formula in the Insert Function dialog

1. Open the **Insert Function** dialog.

2. Select the function you want to use in the formula, and then select **OK**.

3. In the **Function Arguments** dialog, enter the function's arguments, and then select **OK**.

To reference a named range in a formula

- Enter the range name in place of the cell range.

To reference an Excel table column in a formula

- Enter the table name followed by an opening bracket ([), the column name, and a closing bracket (]).

Summarize data that meets specific conditions

Another use for formulas is to display messages when certain conditions are met. This kind of formula is called a *conditional formula*. One way to create a conditional formula in Excel is to use the IF function. Selecting the Insert Function button next to the formula bar and then choosing the IF function displays the Function Arguments dialog with the fields required to create an IF formula.

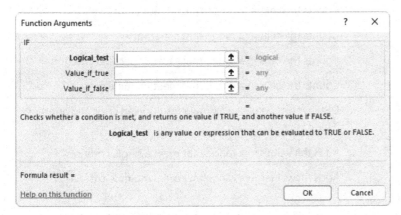

The Function Arguments dialog for an IF formula

When you work with an IF function, the Function Arguments dialog displays three input boxes:

- **Logical_test** The condition you want to check.

- **Value_if_true** The value to display if the condition is met. This could be a cell reference, or a number or text enclosed in quotes.

- **Value_if_false** The value to display if the condition is not met.

The following table displays other conditional functions you can use to summarize data.

Function	Description
AVERAGEIF	Finds the average of values within a cell range that meet a specified criterion
AVERAGEIFS	Finds the average of values within a cell range that meet multiple criteria
COUNT	Counts the cells in a range that contain numerical values
COUNTA	Counts the cells in a range that are not empty
COUNTBLANK	Counts the cells in a range that are empty
COUNTIF	Counts the cells in a range that meet a specified criterion
COUNTIFS	Counts the cells in a range that meet multiple criteria
IFERROR	Displays one value if a formula results in an error and another if it doesn't
SUMIF	Adds the values in a range that meet a single criterion
SUMIFS	Adds the values in a range that meet multiple criteria

To create a formula that uses the AVERAGEIF function, you define the range to be examined for the criterion, the criterion, and, if required, the range from which to draw the values. As an example, consider a worksheet that lists each customer's ID number, name, state, and total monthly shipping bill. If you want to find the average order of customers from the state of Washington (abbreviated in the worksheet as WA), you can create the formula =AVERAGEIF(C3:C6, "WA", D3:D6).

	A	B	C	D
1	CustomerID	CustomerName	State	Total
2	CN100	Contoso	WA	$118,476.00
3	CN101	Fabrikam	WA	$125,511.00
4	CN102	Northwind Traders	OR	$103,228.00
5	CN103	Adventure Works	WA	$ 86,552.00

Sample data that illustrates the preceding example

The AVERAGEIFS, SUMIFS, and COUNTIFS functions extend the capabilities of the AVERAGEIF, SUMIF, and COUNTIF functions to allow for multiple criteria. For example, if you want to find the sum of all orders of at least $100,000 placed by companies in Washington, you can create the formula =SUMIFS(D2:D5, C2:C5, "=WA", D2:D5, ">=100000").

The AVERAGEIFS and SUMIFS functions start with a data range that contains values that the formula summarizes. You then list the data ranges and the criteria to apply to that range. In generic terms, the syntax is =AVERAGEIFS(data_range, criteria_range1, criteria1[,criteria_range2, criteria2...]). The part of the syntax in brackets (which aren't used when you create the formula) is optional, so an AVERAGEIFS or SUMIFS formula that contains a single criterion will work. The COUNTIFS function, which doesn't perform any calculations, doesn't need a data range; you just provide the criteria ranges and criteria. For example, you could find the number of customers from Washington who were billed at least $100,000 by using the formula =COUNTIFS(C2:C5, "=WA", D2:D5, ">=100000").

You can use the IFERROR function to display a custom error message instead of relying on the default Excel error messages to explain what happened. For example, you could create this type of formula to employ the VLOOKUP function to look up a customer's name in the second column of a table named Customers based on the customer identification number entered into cell G8. That formula might look like this: =IFERROR(VLOOKUP(G8,Customers,2,FALSE),"Customer not found"). If the function finds a match for the customer ID in cell G8, it displays the customer's name; if not, it displays the text "Customer not found."

> **TIP** The last two arguments in the VLOOKUP function tell the formula to look in the Customers table's second column and to require an exact match. For more information about the VLOOKUP function, see "Look up data from other locations" in Chapter 7, "Combine data from multiple sources."

To summarize data by using the IF function

- Use the syntax =IF(*logical_test, value_if_true, value_if_false*) where:
  - *logical_test* is the logical test to be performed.
  - *value_if_true* is the value the formula returns if the test is true.
  - *value_if_false* is the value the formula returns if the test is false.

To count cells that contain numbers in a range

- Use the syntax =COUNT(*range*), where *range* is the cell range in which you want to count cells.

To count cells that are non-blank

- Use the syntax =COUNTA(*range*), where *range* is the cell range in which you want to count cells.

To count cells that contain a blank value

- Use the syntax =COUNTBLANK(*range*), where *range* is the cell range in which you want to count cells.

To count cells that meet one condition

- Use the syntax =COUNTIF(*range*, *criteria*) where:

  - *range* is the cell range that might contain the criteria value.

  - *criteria* is the logical test used to determine whether to count the cell.

To count cells that meet multiple conditions

- Use the syntax =COUNTIFS(*criteria_range1*, *criteria1*, *criteria_range2*, *criteria2*,...) where for each *criteria_range* and *criteria* pair:

  - *criteria_range* is the cell range that might contain the criteria value.

  - *criteria* is the logical test used to determine whether to count the cell.

To find the sum of data that meets one condition

- Use the syntax =SUMIF(*range*, *criteria*, *sum_range*) where:

  - *range* is the cell range that might contain the criteria value.

  - *criteria* is the logical test used to determine whether to include the cell.

  - *sum_range* is the range that contains the values to be included if the range cell in the same row meets the criterion.

To find the sum of data that meets multiple conditions

- Use the syntax =SUMIFS(*sum_range*, *criteria_range1*, *criteria1*, *criteria_range2*, *criteria2*,...) where:

  - *sum_range* is the range that contains the values to be included if all *criteria_range* cells in the same row meet all criteria.

  - *criteria_range* is the cell range that might contain the criteria value.

  - *criteria* is the logical test used to determine whether to include the cell.

To find the average of data that meets one condition

■ Use the syntax =AVERAGEIF(*range*, *criteria*, *average_range*) where:

- *range* is the cell range that might contain the *criteria* value.

- *criteria* is the logical test used to determine whether to include the cell.

- *average_range* is the range that contains the values to be included if the *range* cell in the same row meets the criterion.

To find the average of data that meets multiple conditions

■ Use the syntax =AVERAGEIFS(*average_range*, *criteria_range1*, *criteria1*, *criteria_range2*, *criteria2*,...) where:

- *average_range* is the range that contains the values to be included if all *criteria_range* cells in the same row meet all criteria.

- *criteria_range* is the cell range that might contain the *criteria* value.

- *criteria* is the logical test used to determine whether to include the cell.

To display a custom message if a cell contains an error

■ Use the syntax =IFERROR(*value*, *value_if_error*) where:

- *value* is a cell reference or formula.

- *value_if_error* is the value to be displayed if the *value* argument returns an error.

Copy and move formulas

After you create a formula, you can copy it and paste it into another cell. When you do, Excel changes the formula to work in the new cells. For instance, suppose you have a worksheet in which cell C7 contains the formula =SUM(C2:C6). If you copy cell C7 and paste the copied formula into cell D7, Excel enters =SUM(D2:D6). Excel knows to change the cells used in the formula because the formula uses a *relative reference*—a reference that can change if the formula is copied to another cell. Relative references are written with just the cell row and column—for example, C14.

Relative references are useful when you summarize rows of data and want to use the same formula for each row. As an example, suppose you have a worksheet with two columns of data, labeled Sale Price and Rate, and you want to calculate a sales representative's commission by multiplying the two values in a row. To calculate the commission for the first sale, you would enter the formula =A2*B2 in cell C2.

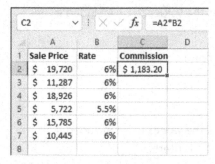

	A	B	C	D
			fx	=A2*B2
	A	B	C	D
1	Sale Price	Rate	Commission	
2	$ 19,720	6%	$ 1,183.20	
3	$ 11,287	6%		
4	$ 18,926	6%		
5	$ 5,722	5.5%		
6	$ 15,785	6%		
7	$ 10,445	6%		
8				

Use formulas to calculate values such as commissions

Selecting cell C2 and dragging the fill handle down through cell C7 copies the formula from cell C2 into each of the other cells. Because you created the formula by using relative references, Excel updates each cell's formula to reflect its position relative to the starting cell (in this case, cell C2). The formula in cell C7, for example, is =A7*B7.

C7			fx	=A7*B7
	A	B	C	D
1	Sale Price	Rate	Commission	
2	$ 19,720	6%	$ 1,183.20	
3	$ 11,287	6%	$ 677.22	
4	$ 18,926	6%	$ 1,135.56	
5	$ 5,722	5.5%	$ 314.71	
6	$ 15,785	6%	$ 947.10	
7	$ 10,445	6%	$ 626.70	
8				

Copying formulas to other cells to summarize additional data

When you enter a formula in a cell of an Excel table column, Excel automatically copies the formula to the rest of the column and updates any relative references in the formula.

If you want a cell reference to remain constant when you copy a formula to another cell, use an *absolute reference* by inserting a dollar sign ($) before the column letter and row number or a *mixed reference* by inserting a dollar sign before either the column letter or row number.

> ✓ **TIP** In addition to using an absolute reference, another way to ensure that your cell references don't change when you copy a formula to another cell is to select the cell that contains the formula, copy the formula's text in the formula bar, press the Esc key to exit cut-and-copy mode, select the cell where you want to paste the formula, and press Ctrl+V. Excel doesn't change the cell references when you copy your formula to another cell in this manner.

One quick way to change a cell reference from relative to absolute is to select the cell reference in the formula bar and then press F4. Pressing F4 cycles a cell reference through the four possible types of references:

- Relative columns and rows (for example, C4)

- Absolute columns and rows (for example, $C$4)

- Relative columns and absolute rows (for example, C$4)

- Absolute columns and relative rows (for example, $C4)

To copy a formula without changing its cell references

1. Select the cell that contains the formula you want to copy.

2. In the formula bar, select the formula text.

3. Press **Ctrl+C**.

4. Select the cell in which you want to paste the formula.

5. Press **Ctrl+V**.

6. Press **Enter**.

To move a formula without changing its cell references

1. Select the cell that contains the formula you want to copy.

2. Point to the edge of the selected cell until the pointer changes to a black four-headed arrow.

3. Drag the outline to the cell where you want to move the formula.

To copy a formula and change its cell references

1. Select the cell that contains the formula you want to copy.

2. Press **Ctrl+C**.

3. Select the cell in which you want to paste the formula.

4. Press **Ctrl+V**.

To create relative and absolute cell references

1. Enter a cell reference into a formula.

2. Do either of the following:

   • Enter a $ in front of a row or column reference you want to make absolute.

   • Select within the cell reference, and then press **F4** to advance through the four possible combinations of relative and absolute row and column references.

Create array formulas

Most Excel formulas calculate values to be displayed in a single cell. For example, you could add the formulas =B1*B4, =B1*B5, and =B1*B6 to consecutive worksheet cells to calculate shipping insurance costs based on the value of a package's contents.

	A	B	C	D
1	Insurance Rate:	2.25%		
2				
3	PackageID	Value	Premium	
4	PK101352	$ 591.00		
5	PK101353	$1,713.00		
6	PK101354	$3,039.00		
7				

A worksheet with data to be summarized by an array formula

Instead of entering the same formula in multiple cells one cell at a time, you can enter a formula in every cell in the target range at the same time by creating an *array formula*. To calculate package insurance rates by multiplying the values in the cell range B4:B6 by the insurance rate in cell B1, you select the target cells (C4:C6) and enter the formula =B1*B4:B6. Note that you must select a range of the same shape as the values you're using in the calculation. (For example, if the value range is three columns wide by one row high, the target range must also be three columns wide by one row high.) If you enter the array formula into a range of the wrong shape, Excel displays duplicate results, incomplete results, or error messages, depending on how the target range differs from the value range.

When you press Ctrl+Shift+Enter, Excel creates an array formula in the selected cells. The formula appears within a pair of braces to indicate that it is an array formula.

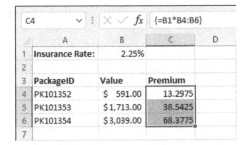

An array formula calculates multiple results

 IMPORTANT You can't add braces to a formula to make it an array formula. You must press Ctrl+Shift+Enter to create it.

To create an array formula

1. Select the cells in which you want to display the formula results.

2. In the formula bar, enter the array formula.

3. Press **Ctrl+Shift+Enter**.

To edit an array formula

1. Select every cell that contains the array formula.

2. In the formula bar, edit the array formula.

3. Press **Ctrl+Shift+Enter** to re-enter the formula as an array formula.

Find and correct errors in calculations

Including calculations in a worksheet gives you valuable answers to questions about your data. As is always true, however, it's possible for errors to creep into your formulas. With Excel, you can find the source of errors in your formulas by identifying the cells used in a specific calculation and describing any errors that have occurred. The process of examining a worksheet for errors is referred to as *auditing*.

Excel identifies errors in several ways. The first way is to display an error code in the cell that contains the formula generating the error.

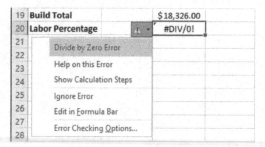

A warning triangle and pound sign indicate an error

When the active cell generates an error, Excel displays an Error button next to it. Pointing to the button displays information about the error, and selecting the button displays a menu of options for handling the error.

The following table explains the most common error codes.

Error code	Description
#####	The column isn't wide enough to display the value.
#VALUE!	The formula has the wrong type of argument, such as text in a cell where a numerical value is required.
#NAME?	The formula contains text that Excel doesn't recognize, such as an unknown named range.
#REF!	The formula refers to a cell that doesn't exist, which can happen whenever cells are deleted.
#DIV/0!	The formula attempts to divide by zero.

Another technique you can use to find the source of formula errors is to ensure that the appropriate cells are providing values for the formula. You can identify the source of an error by having Excel trace a cell's *precedents*, which are the cells with values used in the active cell's formula. You can also audit your worksheet by identifying cells with formulas that use a value from a particular cell. Cells that use another cell's value in their calculations are known as *dependents*, meaning that they depend on the value in the other cell to derive their own value. They are identified in Excel by tracer arrows. If the cells identified by the tracer arrows aren't the correct cells, you can hide the arrows and correct the formula.

9	Loading Dock		
10	Concrete	$ 2,169.00	
11	Labor	$ 4,500.00	
12	Posts	$ 300.00	
13	Excavation	$ 2,500.00	
14	Drain	$ 1,800.00	
15	Rails	$ 495.00	
16	Stairs	$ 1,295.00	
17	*Subtotal*		$13,059.00
18			
19	**Build Total**		$ 31,385.00
20	**Labor Percentage**		34%

Tracing a cell's dependents

If you prefer to have the elements of a formula error presented as text in a dialog, you can use the Error Checking tool to locate errors one after the other. You can choose to ignore the selected error or move to the next or the previous error.

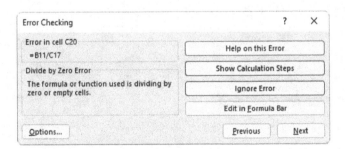

Identify and manage errors from the Error Checking window

> ✓ **TIP** You can have the Error Checking tool ignore formulas that don't use every cell in a region (such as a row or column). To do so, on the Formulas tab of the Excel Options dialog, clear the Formulas Which Omit Cells In A Region checkbox. Excel will no longer mark these cells as an error.

When you just want to display the results of each step of a formula and don't need the full power of the Error Checking tool, you can use the Evaluate Formula dialog to move through each element of the formula. The Evaluate Formula dialog is particularly useful for examining formulas that don't produce an error but aren't generating the result you expect.

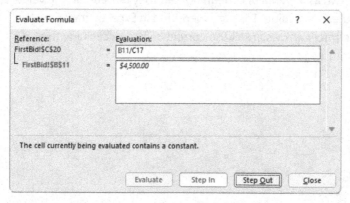

Step through formulas in the Evaluate Formula window

Finally, you can monitor the value in a cell regardless of where you are in your workbook by opening a Watch Window that displays the value in the cell. For example, if one of your formulas uses values from cells in other worksheets or even other workbooks, you can set a watch on the cell that contains the formula, and then change the values in the other cells. As you change the precedent values, the formula result changes in the Watch Window. When you're done watching the formula, you can delete the watch and close the Watch Window.

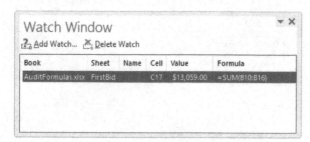

Monitor formula results in the Watch Window

To display information about a formula error

1. Select the cell that contains the error.

2. Point to the error indicator next to the cell to display information about the error.

3. Select the error indicator to display options for correcting or learning more about the error.

To identify the cells that a formula references

1. Select the cell that contains the formula.

2. On the **Formulas** tab, in the **Formula Auditing** group, select **Trace Precedents**.

To identify formulas that reference a specific cell

1. Select the cell.

2. In the **Formula Auditing** group, select **Trace Dependents**.

To remove tracer arrows

- In the **Formula Auditing** group, do one of the following:

  - To remove all the arrows, select the **Remove Arrows** button (not its arrow).

  - To remove only precedent or dependent arrows, select the **Remove Arrows** arrow, and then select **Remove Precedent Arrows** or **Remove Dependent Arrows**.

To evaluate a formula one calculation at a time

1. Select the cell that contains the formula you want to evaluate.

2. In the **Formula Auditing** group, select **Evaluate Formula**.

3. In the **Evaluate Formula** dialog, select **Evaluate**. Excel replaces the underlined calculation with its result.

4. Do either of the following:

   - Select **Step In** to move forward by one calculation.

   - Select **Step Out** to move backward by one calculation.

5. When you finish, select **Close**.

To change error display options

1. Display the **Formulas** page of the **Excel Options** dialog.

2. In the **Error Checking** section, select or clear the **Enable background error checking** checkbox.

3. Select the **Indicate errors using this color** button and select a color.

4. Select **Reset Ignored Errors** to return Excel to its default error indicators.

5. In the **Error checking rules** section, select or clear the checkboxes next to errors you want to indicate or ignore, respectively.

To watch the values in a cell range

1. Select the cell range you want to watch.

2. In the **Formula Auditing** group, select the **Watch Window** button.

3. In the **Watch Window** dialog, select **Add Watch**.

4. In the **Add Watch** dialog, confirm the cell range, and then select **Add**.

To delete a watch

1. Select the **Watch Window** button.

2. In the **Watch Window** dialog, select the watch you want to delete.

3. Select **Delete Watch**.

Configure automatic and iterative calculation options

Excel formulas use values in other cells to calculate their results. If you create a formula that refers to the cell that contains the formula, the result is a circular reference.

Under most circumstances, Excel treats a circular reference as a mistake for two reasons. First, most Excel formulas don't refer to their own cell, so a circular reference is unusual enough to be identified as an error. The second, more serious consideration is that a formula with a circular reference can slow down your workbook. Because Excel repeats, or iterates, the calculation, you must set limits on how many times the app repeats the operation.

You can control how often Excel recalculates formulas. Three calculation options are available from the Formulas tab and from the Formulas page of the Excel Options dialog.

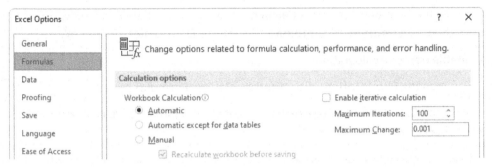

You can modify the iterative calculation options Excel uses

The calculation options work as follows:

- **Automatic** recalculates a worksheet whenever a value that affects a formula changes. This is the default setting.

- **Automatic Except for Data Tables** recalculates a worksheet whenever a value changes but doesn't recalculate data tables.

- **Manual** recalculates formulas only when you tell Excel to do so.

You can also use options in the Calculation Options section to allow or disallow iterative calculations (repeating calculations of formulas that contain circular references). The default values (a maximum of 100 iterations and a maximum change per iteration of 0.001) are appropriate for all but the most unusual circumstances.

To manually recalculate the active workbook

- On the **Formulas** tab, in the **Calculation** group, select **Calculate Now**.

- Press **F9**.

To manually recalculate the active worksheet

- In the **Calculation** group, select the **Calculate Sheet** button.

To set worksheet calculation options

- Display the worksheet whose calculation options you want to set.

- On the **Formulas** tab, in the **Calculation** group, select **Calculation Options**, and then select **Automatic**, **Automatic Except for Data Tables**, or **Manual**.

To enable iterative calculations

1. Open the **Excel Options** dialog and display the **Formulas** page.

2. In the **Calculation options** section, select the **Enable iterative calculation** checkbox.

3. In the **Maximum Iterations** box, enter the maximum iterations allowed for a calculation.

4. In the **Maximum Change** box, enter the maximum change allowed for each iteration.

5. Select **OK**.

Skills review

In this chapter, you learned how to:

- Name data ranges
- Create formulas to calculate values
- Summarize data that meets specific conditions
- Copy and move formulas
- Create array formulas
- Find and correct errors in calculations
- Configure automatic and iterative calculation options

3

Practice tasks

Before you can complete these tasks, you must copy the book's practice files to your computer. The practice files for these tasks are in the **Excel365SBS\Ch03** folder. You can save the results of the tasks in the same folder.

Name data ranges

Open the **NameRanges** workbook in Excel, and then perform the following tasks:

1. Create a named range named Monday for the V_101 through V_109 values (found in cells **C4:C12**) for that weekday.

2. Edit the **Monday** named range to include the V_110 value for that column.

3. Select cells **B4:H13** and create a batch of named ranges for V_101 through V_110, using the row headings as the range names.

4. Delete the **Monday** named range.

Create formulas to calculate values

Open the **BuildFormulas** workbook in Excel, and then perform the following tasks:

1. On the **Summary** worksheet, in cell **F9**, create a formula that displays the value from cell **C4**.

2. Edit the formula in cell **F9** so it uses the SUM function to find the total of values in cells **C3:C8**.

3. In cell **F10**, create a formula that finds the total expenses for desktop software and server software.

4. Edit the formula in **F10** so the cell references are absolute references.

5. On the **JuneLabor** worksheet, in cell **F13**, create a SUM formula that finds the total of values in the **JuneSummary** table's **Labor Expense** column.

Summarize data that meets specific conditions

Open the **CreateConditionalFormulas** workbook in Excel, and then perform the following tasks:

1. In cell **G3**, create an IF formula that tests whether the value in **F3** is greater than or equal to 35,000. If it is, display Request discount; if not, display No discount available.

2. Copy the formula from cell **G3** to the range **G4:G14**.

3. In cell **I3**, create a formula that finds the average cost of all expenses in cells **F3:F14** where the **Type** column contains the value *Box*.

4. In cell **I6**, create a formula that finds the sum of all expenses in cells **F3:F14** where the **Type** column contains the value *Envelope,* and the **Destination** column contains the value *International.*

Create array formulas

Open the **CreateArrayFormulas** workbook in Excel, and then perform the following tasks:

1. On the **Fuel** worksheet, in cells **C11:F11**, enter the array formula =C3*C9:F9.

2. Edit the array formula you just created to read =C3*C10:F10.

3. On the **Volume** worksheet, in cells **D4:D7**, create the array formula =B4:B7*C4:C7.

Find and correct errors in calculations

Open the **AuditFormulas** workbook in Excel, and then perform the following tasks:

1. Set a watch on the value in cell **C19**.

2. Display the precedents for the formula in cell **C7**.

3. Hide the tracer arrows.

4. Use the **Error Checking** dialog to identify the error in cell **C20**.

5. Show the tracer arrows for the error.

6. Hide the arrows, and then change the formula in cell **C20** to =C12/D20.

7. Use the **Evaluate Formula** dialog to step through the formula in cell **C20**.

8. Delete the watch you created in step 1.

Configure automatic and iterative calculation options

Open the **SetIterativeOptions** workbook in Excel, and then perform the following tasks:

1. On the **Formulas** tab, in the **Calculation** group, select the **Calculation Options** button, and then select **Manual**.

2. In cell **B6**, enter the formula =B7*B9, and then press **Enter**.

3. Note that this result is incorrect because the Gross Savings value minus the Savings Incentive value should equal the Net Savings value, which it does not.

4. Press **F9** to recalculate the workbook and read the message box indicating that you have created a circular reference.

5. Select **OK**.

6. Use options in the **Excel Options** dialog to enable iterative calculation.

7. Close the **Excel Options** dialog and recalculate the worksheet.

8. Change the workbook's calculation options back to **Automatic**.

Change workbook appearance

4

Efficiently entering data into a workbook saves you time, but you must also ensure that your data is easy to read and understand. Excel gives you a wide variety of ways to achieve this. For example, you can change the font, character size, or color used to present a cell's contents. Changing how data appears on a worksheet helps set the contents of a cell apart from the contents of surrounding cells. To save time, you can define custom formats and then apply them quickly to the cells you want to emphasize.

You might also want to specially format a cell's contents to reflect the value in that cell. For example, you could create a worksheet that displays the percentage of improperly delivered packages from each regional distribution center. If that percentage exceeds a threshold, Excel could display a red traffic light icon, indicating that the center's performance requires attention.

This chapter guides you through procedures related to changing the appearance of data by applying manual formatting, styles, and themes; formatting numbers; applying conditional formats; and adding images to worksheets.

In this chapter

- Format cells
- Define and manage cell styles
- Apply and modify workbook themes
- Apply and modify table styles
- Make numbers easier to read
- Change the appearance of data based on its value
- Add images to worksheets

Format cells

Excel worksheets can hold and process lots of data, but when you manage numerous worksheets, it can be hard to remember from a worksheet's title exactly what data is kept in that worksheet. Data labels give you and your colleagues information about data in a worksheet, but it's important to format the labels so that they stand out visually. To make your data labels or any other data stand out, you can change the format of the cells that hold your data.

	A	B	C	D
1	Call Volume			
2	Northeast	13,769		
3	Atlantic	19,511		
4	Southeast	11,111		
5	North Central	24,972		
6	Midwest	11,809		
7	Southwest	20,339		
8	Mountain West	20,127		
9	Northwest	12,137		
10	Central	20,047		

Use formatting to set labels apart from worksheet data

 TIP Deleting the content of a cell doesn't affect the formatting that has been applied to the cell.

Many of the formatting-related buttons on the ribbon have arrows at their right edges. Selecting the arrow displays a list of options for that button, such as the fonts available on your system or the colors you can assign to a cell.

 TIP Selecting the body of the Border, Fill Color, or Font Color button applies the most recently applied formatting to the currently selected cells.

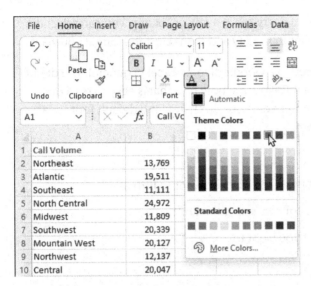

Change the font color to help distinguish labels and values

You can also make a cell stand apart from its neighbors by adding a border around the cell or changing the color or shading of the cell's interior.

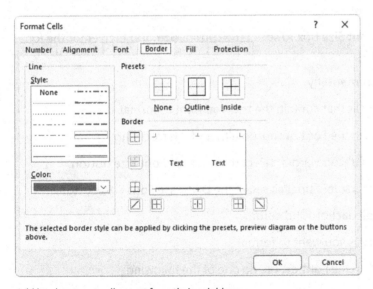

Add borders to set cells apart from their neighbors

> **TIP** You can display the most commonly used formatting controls by right-clicking a selected range. When you do, a mini toolbar containing a subset of the Home tab formatting tools appears above the shortcut menu.

If you want to change the attributes of every cell in a row or column, you can select the header of the row or column you want to modify and then select the format you want.

You can change the default font used in a workbook or in Excel in general. The default font when you install Excel is 11-point Calibri, a simple font that is easy to read on a computer screen and on the printed page. You can change the default font for a single workbook or for the Excel app.

To change text font

1. Select the cell or cells that contain the text you want to format.

2. On the **Home** tab, in the **Font** group, select the **Font** arrow.

3. In the font list, select the font you want to apply.

To change to a specific text size

1. Select the cell or cells that contain the text you want to format.

2. On the **Home** tab, in the **Font** group, do either of the following:

   - Select the **Font Size** arrow, and then in the list, select the size (in points) that you want to apply.

   - Select in the **Font Size** box to select the current size, and then enter the font size you want.

To change text size incrementally

1. Select the cell or cells that contain the text you want to format.

2. On the **Home** tab, in the **Font** group, do either of the following:

   - To make the characters larger, select the **Increase Font Size** button.

   - To make the characters smaller, select the **Decrease Font Size** button.

To apply or change a cell background color

1. Select the cell or cells you want to format.

2. On the **Home** tab, in the **Font** group, do one of the following:

   - Select the **Fill Color** button to apply the most recently used fill color, which is shown on the button.

   - Select the **Fill Color** arrow (not the button), and then in the **Theme Colors** or **Standard Colors** palette, select the color you want to apply.

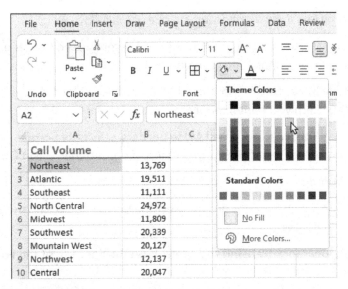

Change the fill color of a cell to make it stand out

- Select the **Fill Color** arrow, select **More Colors**, select the color you want from the **Colors** dialog, and then select **OK**.

To remove a cell background color

1. Select the cell or cells you want to format.

2. On the **Home** tab, in the **Font** group, select the **Fill Color** arrow (not the button), and then select **No Fill**.

To change the text color

1. Select the cell or cells that contain the text you want to format.

2. On the **Home** tab, in the **Font** group, do one of the following:

   - Select the **Font Color** button to apply the most recently used font color, which is shown on the button.

   - Select the **Font Color** arrow (not the button), and then in the **Theme Colors** or **Standard Colors** palette, select the color you want to apply.

   - Select the **Font Color** arrow, select **More Colors**, select the color you want from the **Colors** dialog, and then select **OK**.

To apply a cell border

1. Select the cell or cells you want to format.

2. On the **Home** tab, in the **Font** group, do one of the following:

   - Select the **Border** button to apply the most recently used border pattern, which is shown on the button and named in the tooltip.

   - Select the **Border** arrow (not the button), and then in the list, select the border pattern you want to apply.

   - Select the **Border** arrow, select **More Borders**, select the borders you want from the **Border** tab of the **Format Cells** dialog, and then select **OK**.

To remove a cell border

   - On the **Home** tab, in the **Font** group, select the **Border** arrow, and then in the list, select **No Border**.

To change font appearance by using the controls on the Font tab of the Format Cells dialog

1. On the **Home** tab, select the **Font** dialog launcher.

2. Make the formatting changes you want, and then select **OK**.

To copy formatting between cells

1. Select the cell that has the formatting you want to copy.

2. Select the **Format Painter** button to temporarily turn it on.

3. Select the cell range to which you want to apply the formatting.

Or

1. Select the cell that has the formatting you want to copy.

2. Double-click the **Format Painter** button to turn it on until you turn it off. An outline indicates that the button is active.

3. Select each cell range to which you want to apply the formatting.

4. To turn off the Format Painter, press the **Esc** key or select the **Format Painter** button.

To delete cell formatting

1. Select the cell or cells from which you want to remove formatting.

2. In the **Editing** group, select the **Clear** button, and then select **Clear Formats**.

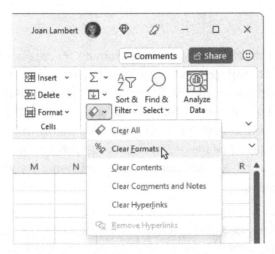

Quickly clear the formatting, content, comments, notes, and hyperlinks from a cell

To open the Excel Options dialog

1. Display the Backstage view.

2. Do either of the following:

   - At the bottom of the left pane, select **Options**.

   - If the window isn't tall enough to display all the content of the left pane, select **More** and then select **Options**.

To change the default Normal font of a workbook

1. Display the **General** page of the **Excel Options** dialog.

2. In the **Use this as the default font** list, select the font you want to use.

3. In the **Font size** list, select the font size you want.

4. Select **OK** to close the **Excel Options** dialog.

5. Exit and restart Excel to complete the default font change.

To change the default Body and Heading fonts of a workbook

- On the **Page Layout** tab, in the **Themes** group, select **Fonts**, and then select the font set you want.

 SEE ALSO For more information about themes and font sets, including custom font sets, see "Apply and modify workbook themes" later in this chapter.

Define and manage cell styles

As you work with Excel, you will probably develop preferred formats for data labels, titles, and other worksheet elements. Instead of adding a format's characteristics one element at a time to the target cells, you can format the cell in one action by using a cell style. Excel comes with many built-in styles, which you can apply by using the Cell Styles gallery. You can also create your own styles by using the Style dialog, which will appear in a separate group at the top of the gallery when you open it. If you want to preview how the contents of your cell (or cells) will look when you apply the style, point to the style to get a live preview.

> **TIP** The Cell Styles gallery on the ribbon displays only a few of the available styles. To display the entire gallery of styles, select the More button (labeled with a small black triangle) in the lower-right corner of the gallery on the ribbon.

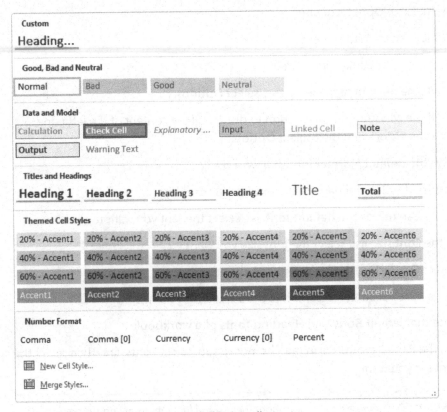

Apply, modify, and create styles from the Cell Styles gallery

It's likely that any cell styles you create will be useful for more than one workbook. If you want to include cell styles from another workbook in your current workbook, you can merge the two workbooks' style collections.

To apply a cell style to worksheet cells

1. Select the cells to which you want to apply the style.

2. On the **Home** tab, in the **Styles** group, select the **Cell Styles** button.

3. In the gallery that appears, select the style you want to apply.

To create a new cell style

1. Select the **Cell Styles** button, and then at the bottom of the menu, select **New Cell Style**.

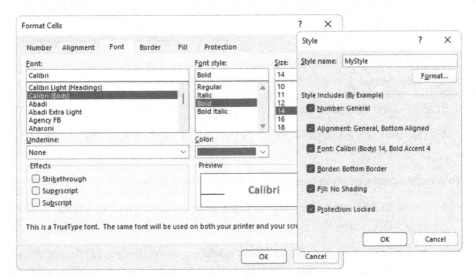

Define any cell element as part of a custom style

2. In the **Style** dialog, enter a name for the new style.

3. Select the checkboxes next to any elements you want to include in the style definition.

4. Select the **Format** button.

5. Use the controls in the **Format Cells** dialog to define your style, and then select **OK**.

To create a cell style based on existing cell formatting

1. Select a cell that contains the formatting on which you want to base your new cell style.

2. On the **Cell Styles** menu, select **New Cell Style**.

   Excel displays the **Style** dialog with the active cell's characteristics filled in.

3. Enter a name for the new style, and then select **OK**.

To modify an existing cell style

1. In the **Cell Styles** gallery, right-click the style you want to modify, and then, from the context menu, select **Modify**.

    TIP To display a context menu, right-click or long-press (tap and hold) the element.

2. In the **Style** dialog, make the necessary changes to your style name and style elements.

3. Select the **Format** button.

4. Use the controls in the **Format Cells** dialog to define your style, and then select **OK**.

To create a new cell style based on an existing cell style

1. In the **Cell Styles** gallery, right-click the style you want to duplicate, and then select **Duplicate**.

2. In the **Style** dialog, enter a distinct name for the duplicate version of the style, and select the elements of the existing style that you want to include in the duplicated one.

3. Select the **Format** button, and then configure the settings in the **Format Cells** dialog to make any other changes to the duplicate style.

4. Select **OK** in each dialog to create the style.

To merge cell styles from another open workbook

1. At the bottom of the **Cell Styles** menu, select **Merge Styles**.

2. In the **Merge Styles** dialog, select the workbook from which you want to import cell styles, and then select **OK**.

To delete a custom cell style

- In the **Cell Styles** gallery, right-click the style you want to delete, and then select **Delete**.

Apply and modify workbook themes

Excel for Microsoft 365 includes powerful design tools that you can use to quickly create workbooks and worksheets that look attractive and professional. These tools include workbook themes and table styles.

A theme is a way to specify the default colors, fonts, and graphic effects that Excel applies to workbook content. Excel, Word, and PowerPoint share a theme gallery that includes many preconfigured options.

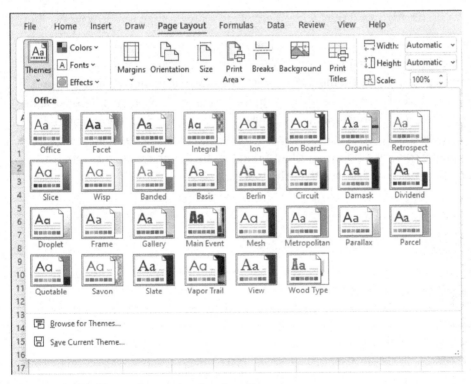

Change a workbook's overall appearance by using a theme

If the combination of colors, fonts, and effects assigned to a theme doesn't meet your needs, you can change to another preconfigured color, font, or effect set. You can also create your own custom color palette or font set—for example, one that uses your company's corporate colors and fonts. If you like a specific combination of theme elements, you can save it as a new theme.

A theme or theme element that you create in Excel, Word, or PowerPoint is available to you in all three programs on the computer on which you create it. You can copy custom Office themes and theme elements to other computers and distribute them to other people. (This is a common task to perform in Word or PowerPoint but rarely necessary in an Excel workbook.)

> **SEE ALSO** For information about creating custom color palettes and font sets, see *Microsoft Word Step by Step (Office 2021 and Microsoft 365)*, by Joan Lambert (Microsoft Press, 2022).

When you create or change the color of any workbook element, the color options include two palettes: Standard Colors, which remain constant regardless of the workbook's theme, and Theme Colors, which are available within the active theme. If you format workbook elements by using theme colors, applying a different theme changes the colors of those elements. Similarly, when you copy a theme-colored object between workbooks, it picks up the theme colors of the destination workbook. Using theme colors is a good way of ensuring that the graphic elements within a workbook remain consistent with each other.

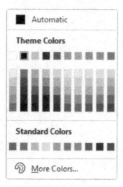

Select theme-specific or standard colors

To apply a theme to a workbook

- On the **Page Layout** tab, in the **Themes** group, select the **Themes** button, and then in the gallery, select the theme you want to apply.

To change the colors, fonts, or effects of the current workbook to another built-in set

1. On the **Page Layout** tab, in the **Themes** group, select the **Colors**, **Fonts**, or **Effects** button.

2. In the gallery of options, select the set of colors, fonts, or effects that you want to apply.

To create a new theme based on an existing theme

1. Change the colors, fonts, or effects of the workbook.

2. On the **Page Layout** tab, in the **Themes** group, select the **Themes** button, and then select **Save Current Theme**.

3. Enter a name for the new theme, and then select **Save**.

To delete a custom theme

1. Select the **Themes** button, and then select **Save Current Theme**.

2. In the **Save Current Theme** dialog, right-click the theme you want to delete, and then select **Delete**.

3. In the dialog, select **Yes**.

Apply and modify table styles

Just as you can apply themes to entire workbooks and create custom themes, you can apply table styles to Excel tables and create custom table styles. Excel has 60 built-in table styles—light, medium, and dark options corresponding to the current theme colors.

Apply a default Excel table style

Each table style includes formatting for a variety of optional elements, including a header row, first column, last column, and row or column banding. Excel applies the optional formatting to the table only if you select that option in the Table Style Options group on the Table Design tool tab.

Creating a custom table style is a bit more challenging than creating a custom theme, but it is an option if one of the many predefined table styles doesn't meet your needs. After you give the style a descriptive name, you can set the appearance for each Excel table element and decide whether to make the new style the default for the current document.

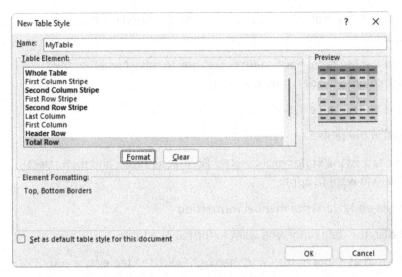

Bold formatting identifies the table elements you've defined

To format a cell range as a table and apply the default table style

1. Select any cell in the data range that you want to format as a table.

2. On the **Insert** tab, in the **Tables** group, select **Table**.

3. In the **Create Table** dialog, verify that Excel has correctly identified the data range.

Verify that Excel has identified your table data correctly

4. Select or clear the **My table has headers** checkbox to reflect whether the cell range has column headers, and then select **OK**.

To format a cell range as a table and apply an existing table style

1. Select any cell in the data range that you want to format as a table.

2. On the **Home** tab, in the **Styles** group, select **Format as Table**, and then select the table style you want to apply.

3. In the **Format as Table** dialog, verify that Excel has identified the data range correctly.

4. Select or clear the **My table has headers** checkbox to reflect whether the cell range has column headers, and then select **OK**.

To change the table style of an existing table

1. Select any cell in the table.

2. On the **Home** tab, in the **Styles** group, select **Format as Table**, and then select the table style you want to apply.

To apply a table style and overwrite manual formatting

1. Select any cell in the data range you want to format as a table.

2. Select the **Format as Table** button, and then right-click the table style you want to apply.

3. On the shortcut menu that appears, select **Apply and Clear Formatting**, and then select **OK**.

To create a custom table style

1. On the **Home** tab, in the **Styles** group, select **Format as Table**, and then select **New Table Style**.

2. In the **New Table Style** dialog, enter a name for the new style.

3. For each table element that you want to format, follow these steps:

    a. In the **Table Element** list, select the element name.

    b. Select the **Format** button to open the **Format Cells** dialog, displaying only the **Font**, **Border**, and **Fill** tabs.

    c. Specify the font, border, and/or fill attributes of the table element, and then select **OK**.

4. Select **OK** to create the table style, which is now available from the **Custom** section at the top of the **Format As Table** gallery.

To modify a custom table style

1. On the **Home** tab, in the **Styles** group, select **Format as Table**.

2. In the **Custom** section of the **Format as Table** gallery, right-click the table style you want to modify, and then select **Modify**.

    IMPORTANT You can't modify the built-in Excel table styles, only the ones you create.

3. In the **Modify Table Style** dialog, edit the table elements you want to modify, and then select **OK**.

To delete a custom table style

1. On the **Home** tab, in the **Styles** group, select **Format as Table**.

2. In the **Custom** section of the **Format as Table** gallery, right-click the table style you want to delete, and then select **Delete**.

    IMPORTANT You can't delete the built-in Excel table styles, only the ones you create.

3. In the message box that appears, select **OK**.

Make numbers easier to read

Changing the format of the cells in your worksheet can make your data much easier to read, both by setting data labels apart from the actual data and by adding borders to define the boundaries between labels and data even more clearly.

You can also make idiosyncratic data types such as dates, phone numbers, or currency values easier to read by presenting them in a standardized way, regardless of how they were entered into Excel. As an example, consider US phone numbers. These numbers are 10 digits long and have a three-digit area code, a three-digit exchange, and a four-digit line number, written in the form *(###) ###-####*. Although it's certainly possible to enter a phone number with the expected formatting in a cell—that is, with the area code surrounded by parentheses and the exchange and digit values separated by a hyphen—it's much more straightforward to simply enter a sequence of 10 digits and have Excel add those formatting elements. To do so, you indicate to Excel that the contents of the cell will be a phone number. You can watch this format in operation if you compare the contents of the active cell and the contents of the formula box for a cell with the Phone Number formatting.

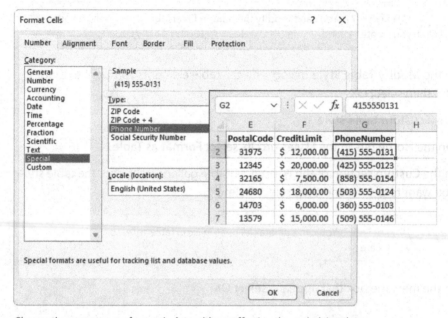

Change the appearance of numeric data without affecting the underlying data

> ⚠ **IMPORTANT** If you enter a nine-digit number in a field that expects a phone number, you won't get an error message; Excel will format the number with a two-digit instead of three-digit area code. For example, the number 425550012 would be displayed as (42) 555-0012. An 11-digit number would be displayed with a four-digit area code. If the area code doesn't look right, you might have entered the wrong number of digits.

Just as you can instruct Excel to expect a phone number in a cell, you can also inform Excel that a cell will contain a date or a currency amount. You can pick from a wide variety of date, currency, and other formats to best reflect your worksheet's contents, your company standards, and how you and your colleagues expect the data to appear.

> **TIP** You can make the most common format changes by displaying the Home tab and then, in the Number group, either selecting a button representing a built-in format or selecting a format from the Number Format list.

4

You can also create a custom numeric format to add a word or phrase to a number in a cell. For example, you can add the phrase *per month* to a cell with a formula that calculates average monthly sales for a year, to ensure that you and your colleagues will recognize the figure as a monthly average. If one of the built-in formats is close to the custom format you'd like to create, you can base your custom format on the one already included in Excel.

> ⚠ **IMPORTANT** You must enclose any text to be displayed as part of the format in quotation marks so that Excel recognizes the text as a string to be displayed in the cell.

To apply a special number format

1. Select the cells to which you want to apply the format.

2. On the **Home** tab, in the **Number** group, select the **Number Format** arrow (not the button), and then on the menu, select **More Number Formats**.

3. In the **Format Cells** dialog, in the **Category** list, select **Special**.

4. In the **Type** list, select the format you want to apply, and then select **OK**.

To create a custom number format

1. On the **Number Format** menu, select **More Number Formats**.

2. In the **Format Cells** dialog, in the **Category** list, select **Custom**.

3. Select the format you want to use as the base for your new format.

4. Edit the format in the **Type** box, and then select **OK**.

To add text to a number format

1. On the **Number Format** menu, select **More Number Formats**.

2. In the **Format Cells** dialog, in the **Category** list, select **Custom**.

3. Select the format you want to use as the base for your new format.

4. In the **Type** box, after the format, enter the text you want to add, in quotation marks—for example, "boxes".

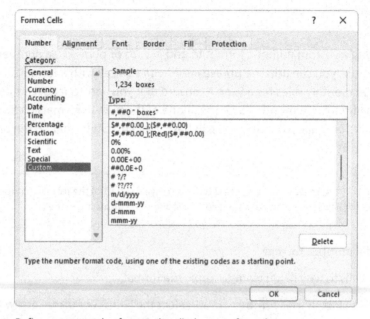

Define custom number formats that display text after values

5. In the **Format Cells** dialog, select **OK**.

Change the appearance of data based on its value

The data you record in a worksheet enables you to make important decisions about your operations. The more data you have, the better informed your decisions can be... but the more difficult it becomes to evaluate the data without some type of visual representation. One of the easiest ways to highlight specific data is by applying a conditional formatting rule.

⊿	A	B	C	D
1	Call Volume			
2	Northeast	13,769	13,769	▷ 13,769
3	Atlantic	19,511	19,511	▷ 19,511
4	Southeast	11,111	11,111	▷ 11,111
5	North Central	24,972	24,972	▷ 24,972
6	Midwest	11,809	11,809	▷ 11,809
7	Southwest	20,339	20,339	▷ 20,339
8	Mountain West	20,127	20,127	▷ 20,127
9	Northwest	12,137	12,137	▷ 12,137
10	Central	20,047	20,047	▷ 20,047

Data bars, color scales, and icon sets indicate relative values in a data range

Conditional formatting rules evaluate the data in a cell to determine whether it meets certain conditions, and then apply formatting to the cell or its contents based on rules that you select or create. Excel has many built-in conditional formatting rules, and if those don't meet your needs, you can define your own. The built-in rules make it easy to identify cells within a selected range that contain values above or below the average values of the related cells, values near the top or bottom of the value range, or values that are duplicated elsewhere in the range

The built-in conditional formatting rules are available from the Home tab

Each built-in conditional formatting rule has a default setting but is easy to modify. For example, when you apply the Top 10 Items rule, Excel prompts you to specify the number of items to format and the formatting to apply. Conditional formatting can modify the number format; font face, style, size, color, and effect; and cell border and fill.

The built-in conditional formatting rules format the cells they evaluate. You can also create conditional formatting rules that format other cells. For example, you can modify the appearance of a row of content based on one of its entries.

	A	B	C	D	E	F
1	Chapter	Title	Pages	Graphics	Due	Status
2	1	Set up a workbook	40	36	1-Aug	Complete
3	2	Work with data and Excel tables	31	16	3-Aug	Complete
4	3	Perform calculations on data	31	22	5-Aug	Complete
5	4	Change workbook appearance	35	24	7-Aug	In Progress
6	5	Manage worksheet data	24	14	9-Aug	Complete
7	6	Reorder and summarize data	18	14	11-Aug	Complete
8	7	Combine data from multiple sources	18	11	13-Aug	Complete
9	8	Analyze alternative data sets	14	14	15-Aug	Complete
10	9	Create charts and graphics	41	40	17-Aug	Due Today
11	10	Use PivotTables and Pivot Charts	35	33	19-Aug	On Time
12	11	Print worksheets and charts	23	16	21-Aug	On Time
13	12	Automate repetitive tasks by using macros	22	14	23-Aug	On Time
14	13	Work with other Microsoft Office apps	15	10	25-Aug	Complete
15	14	Collaborate with colleagues	24	16	27-Aug	On Time
16	15	Perform business intelligence analysis	24	14	29-Aug	On Time
17	16	Create forecasts and visualizations	22	11	31-Aug	On Time

Formatting multiple cells based on the content of one

If the built-in conditional formatting rules don't quite meet your needs, you can create your own. Excel provides templates to follow for this process. You simply select the kind of condition to create and work with the fields and controls to define your rule. If you want to do something more complicated than the template setups, you can write your own formula using the same conditional functions that you use in other Excel formulas.

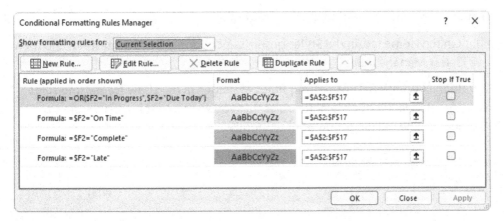

Custom conditional formatting rules

You can apply multiple conditional formats to the same cell range. Excel evaluates the conditions in the order that they appear in the Conditional Formatting Rules Manager. Within that interface, you can reorder the rules and, if appropriate, have Excel skip later rules if a specific condition is true.

To apply a built-in conditional formatting rule

1. Select the cell range to which you want to apply the conditional format.

2. On the **Home** tab, in the **Styles** group, select **Conditional Formatting**, point to the format group, and then select the format you want to apply.

3. In the dialog that appears, specify the condition(s) for the rule.

4. Select from the available formats or select **Custom Format** to open the **Format Cells** dialog, in which you can craft your own combination of font and cell effects.

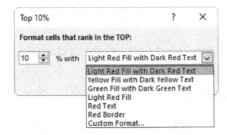

The default format colors are not theme-specific

5. Select **OK** in the open dialog to create and apply the rule.

To modify an active conditional formatting rule

1. On the **Home** tab, in the **Styles** group, select **Conditional Formatting**, and then select **Manage Rules**.

2. In the **Conditional Formatting Rules Manager**, in the **Show formatting rules for** list, select the scope of the rules that you want to display, being sure to include the cell range you want to modify.

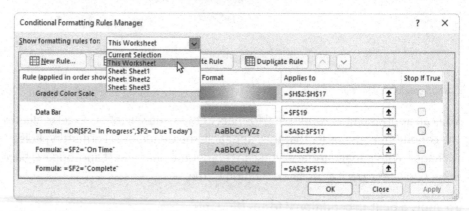

You can edit the conditional formatting rules for only one worksheet at a time

3. If you want to change the cell range to which the rule is applied, edit it in the **Applies to** box for the rule.

4. If you want to change the condition or formatting:

   a. Double-click the rule.

   b. In the **Edit Formatting Rule** dialog, modify the conditions or formatting associated with the rule.

   c. Select **OK** to update the rule.

5. Select **Apply** to test the changes, and then select **OK** or **Close** to close the **Conditional Formatting Rules Manager**.

To create a custom conditional formatting rule

1. Select the cell range to which you want to apply the new rule.

2. On the **Home** tab, in the **Styles** group, select **Conditional Formatting**, and then select **New Rule**.

3. In the **New Formatting Rule** dialog, in the **Select a Rule Type** list, select one of the rule templates.

4. In the **Edit the Rule Description** area, specify the condition and formatting required for the rule.

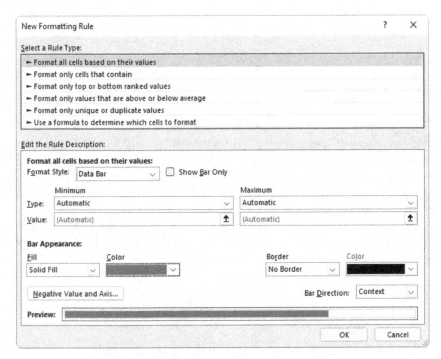

One of the more complex formatting rules

5. Select **OK** to create the rule and apply it to the selected cells.

To create a rule based on a formula

1. Select the cell range to which you want to apply the new rule.

2. On the **Home** tab, in the **Styles** group, select **Conditional Formatting**, and then select **New Rule**.

3. In the **New Formatting Rule** dialog, in the **Select a Rule Type** list, select **Use a formula to determine which cells to format**.

4. In the **Edit the Rule Description** area, use the standard Excel functions to define the formula that identifies the cells to format.

5. Select **Format** to open the **Format Cells** dialog.

6. Select the font and cell formatting that you want to apply to cells that meet the conditions defined by the formula, and then select **OK**.

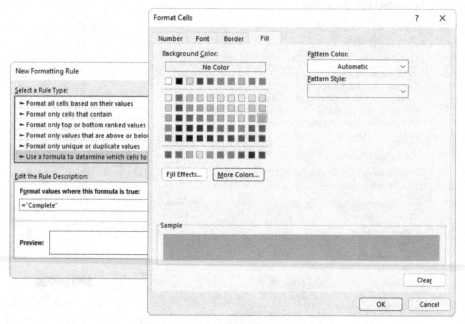

Formulas can be simple or complex

7. Select **OK** to create the rule and apply it to the selected cells.

To manage conditional formatting rules

1. On the **Home** tab, in the **Styles** group, select **Conditional Formatting**, and then select **Manage Rules**.

2. In the **Conditional Formatting Rules Manager**, in the **Show formatting rules for** list, select the scope of the rules that you want to display.

3. Do any of the following:

   - To change the order in which Excel applies conditional formatting rules, select each rule that you want to move, and then select the **Move Up** button (^) or the **Move Down** button (v).

- To stop applying conditional formatting rules when a condition is met, select the **Stop If True** checkbox to the right of the rule where you want Excel to stop.

- To delete a conditional formatting rule, select the rule you want to delete, and then select **Delete Rule**.

4. Select **Apply** to test the changes, and then **OK** or **Close** to close the **Conditional Formatting Rules Manager**.

To delete all conditional formats from a worksheet

- On the **Home** tab, in the **Styles** group, select **Conditional Formatting**, select **Clear Rules**, and then select **Clear Rules from Entire Sheet**.

Add images to worksheets

Most Excel workbook content will be data. However, when appropriate, you can add a logo or other imagery to a worksheet and take advantage of the excellent image resources offered by Excel for Microsoft 365. You can add an image such as a logo from your hard drive or other connected resource or use one of the professional stock images or icons available, at no cost, from the Microsoft image library.

	A	B	C
1		Call Volume	
2		Northeast	13,769
3		Atlantic	19,511
4		Southeast	11,111
5		North Central	24,972
6		Midwest	11,809
7		Southwest	20,339
8		Mountain West	20,127
9		Northwest	12,137
10		Central	20,047

Insert images to enhance your message

When you insert an image onto a worksheet, it effectively floats on top of the content. You can't anchor it to a worksheet element as you can in Word; instead, you adjust the worksheet content around the image. It's far more common to use images on PowerPoint slides and in Word documents, but the same options are available in Excel as in the rest of the Microsoft 365 suite of applications.

For business purposes, Excel users might find the icons available in Excel for Microsoft 365 to be useful. The icon library is large and frequently updated. Inserted icons are black with transparent backgrounds, but you can easily recolor them by using the tools on the Graphics Format tool tab.

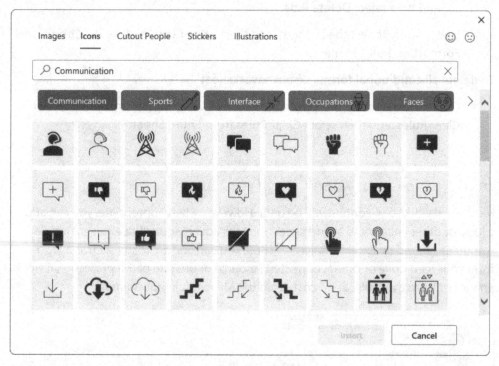

An ever-expanding icon library is available to Microsoft 365 users

To add an image stored on your computer to a worksheet

1. On the **Insert** tab, in the **Illustrations** group, select **Pictures**, and then select **This Device**.

2. In the **Insert Picture** dialog, navigate to the folder that contains the image you want to add to your worksheet.

3. Select the image, and then select **Insert**.

To add professional stock images and iconography to a worksheet

1. On the **Insert** tab, in the **Illustrations** group, select **Pictures**, and then select **Stock Images**.

2. On the **Images**, **Icons**, **Cutout People**, **Stickers**, or **Illustrations** tab, locate the image(s) you want to insert.

3. Select each image. A green check mark indicates that the image is selected. You can select images on multiple tabs and subtabs of the dialog.

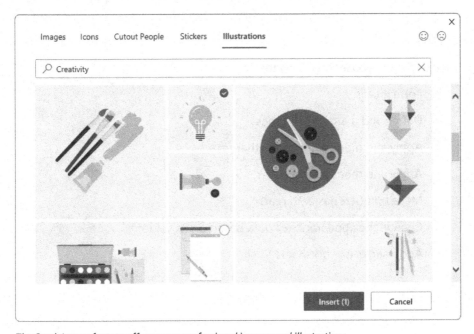

The Stock Image feature offers many professional images and illustrations

4. Select **Insert** to insert the image(s) onto the worksheet.

To resize an image

1. Select the image.

2. Do either of the following:

   - Drag one of the size handles on the image's border.

   - On the **Picture Format** or **Graphics Format** tool tab, in the **Size** group, enter new values for the image's vertical and horizontal size in the **Height** and **Width** boxes.

To edit an image

1. Select the image.

2. On the **Picture Format** or **Graphics Format** tool tab, use the controls in the **Size** group to change the image's appearance.

To delete an image

- Select the image, and then press the **Delete** key.

Skills review

In this chapter, you learned how to:

- Format cells

- Define and manage cell styles

- Apply and modify workbook themes

- Apply and modify table styles

- Make numbers easier to read

- Change the appearance of data based on its value

- Add images to worksheets

Practice tasks

Before you can complete these tasks, you must copy the book's practice files to your computer. The practice files for these tasks are in the **Excel365SBS\Ch04** folder. You can save the results of the tasks in the same folder.

Format cells

Open the **FormatCells** workbook in Excel, and then perform the following tasks:

1. Change the formatting of cell B4 so the text it contains appears in 14-point, bold type.

2. Center the text within cell B4.

3. Change the background fill color of cell B4.

4. Draw a border around the cell range B4:C13.

Define and manage cell styles

Open the **DefineStyles** workbook in Excel, and then perform the following tasks:

1. Apply the **Accent1** cell style to cells B4 and C3.

2. Apply the **40% - Accent1** style to cells B5:B13 and C4:N4.

3. Create a new cell style based on the 40% - Accent1 style. Change the font to **Bold** and save the custom cell style with the name MyStyle.

4. Apply the **MyStyle** style to cells B5:B13 and C4:N4.

Apply and modify workbook themes

Open the **ModifyThemes** workbook in Excel, and then perform the following tasks:

1. Review the workbook theme options. Then change the theme applied to the workbook to one that you like.

2. Change the colors used in the workbook to a different built-in color palette. Note the effect of the change on the workbook content.

3. Change the fonts used in the workbook to a different built-in font set. Note the effect of the change on the workbook content.

4. Save the modified theme settings as a new theme named MyTheme.

Apply and modify table styles

Open the **ModifyTableStyles** workbook in Excel, and then perform the following tasks:

1. Create an Excel table from the list of data in the cell range A1:B10.

2. Define a new Excel table style and apply it to the same data.

Make numbers easier to read

Open the **FormatNumbers** workbook in Excel, and then perform the following tasks:

1. Apply a phone number format to the value in cell G2.

2. Apply a currency or accounting format to the value in cell H2.

3. For cell H3, create a custom number format that displays the value in that cell as *$255,000 plus benefits*.

Change the appearance of data based on its value

Open the **CreateConditionalFormats** workbook in Excel, and then perform the following tasks:

1. Apply a conditional format to cell C15 that displays the cell's contents with a red background if the value in the cell is less than 90 percent.

2. Apply a data bar conditional format to cells C4:C12.

3. Apply a color scale conditional format to cells F4:F12.

4. Apply an icon set conditional format to cells I4:I12.

5. Delete the conditional format from the cell range C4:C12.

6. Edit the data bar conditional format so the bars are a different color.

Add images to worksheets

Open the **AddImages** workbook in Excel, and then perform the following tasks:

1. Insert the **Phone** image from the **Excel365SBS\Ch04** practice file folder.

2. Resize the image so it will fit between the Call Volume label in cell B4 and the top of the worksheet.

3. Move the image to the upper-left corner of the worksheet, resizing it if necessary so it doesn't block any of the worksheet text.

Part 2

Analyze and present data

Manage worksheet data

You can manage vast amounts of data in an Excel workbook, but it's difficult to make business decisions based on that data unless you can focus on the specific information required for each decision.

By working with filtered data, you can more easily discover information such as the percentage of monthly revenue earned in the 10 best days of the month, the average revenue earned on a specific weekday, or the slowest business day of each month.

Just as you can limit the data that a worksheet displays, you can also create validation rules that limit the data entered in them. When you set rules for data entry, you can prevent many common data-entry errors, such as entering values that are too small or too large or attempting to enter a word in a cell that requires a number.

This chapter guides you through procedures related to filtering and summarizing data and creating validation rules that restrict data entry.

In this chapter

- Filter data ranges and tables
- Summarize filtered data
- Enforce data entry criteria

Filter data ranges and tables

An Excel worksheet can hold as much as 1,048,576 rows and 16,384 columns of data. You aren't likely to store that amount of data in a worksheet, but even so, there will be times when you want to display or work with only some of the worksheet data. For example, you might want to see your company's sales revenue for a specific week of the year, only values greater than 10,000, only sales by a specific person, or a combination of these criteria. You can choose to display and work with only the data you want, without disturbing the rest of the data, by creating filters: rules that specify the rows of a table or data range to display. Filtering is turned on by default for Excel tables, but you can also turn it on for data ranges.

> ⚠️ **IMPORTANT** When you turn on filtering, Excel treats the cells in the active cell's column as a range. To ensure that the filtering works properly, you should always have a heading at the top of the column you want to filter. If you don't, Excel still treats the first value in the list as the heading and doesn't include it in the list of values by which you can filter the data.

When you turn on filtering, a filter arrow appears to the right of each column label in the list of data. Selecting the filter arrow displays a menu of filtering options and a list of the unique values in the column. Each value has a checkbox next to it, which you can use to create a selection filter.

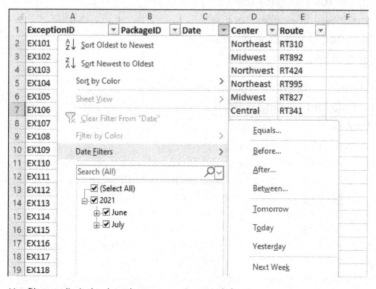

Use filters to limit the data that appears in a worksheet

If the selection filters are too specific for your needs, you can create a custom text, number, or date filter. The specific filtering options vary based on the column data.

When you select a custom filtering option, Excel displays a dialog in which you can define the filter's criteria. For example, you could create a filter that displays only records that were created on or after a specific date. When a column is filtered, the filter arrow changes to a Filter icon, which looks like a small arrow next to a funnel. When you no longer need the filter, you can clear it, or turn off filtering, which hides the filter arrows.

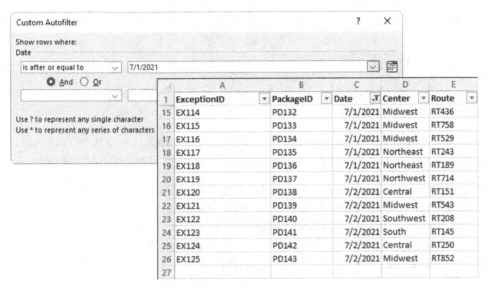

A funnel symbol on a Filter button indicates a filtered column

If you want to display the highest or lowest values in a column of numbers, you can create a Top 10 filter. You can choose whether to show values from the top or bottom of the list and define the number or percentage of items you want to display.

If you know some of the data you're looking for, you can quickly create a search filter in which you enter a search string that Excel uses to identify the items to display. This is particularly useful when you're looking for multiple types of entries.

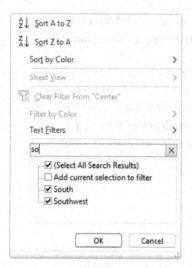

Applying a search filter limits the items that appear in the selection list

To narrow down the displayed data even further, you can apply filters to multiple columns at one time. You can clear individual filters or clear all filters at the same time.

Summarizing numerical values can provide valuable information to help you run your business. It can also be helpful to know how many different values appear within a column. For example, you might want to display all the countries and regions in which your company has customers. If you want to display a list of the unique values in a column, you can do so by creating an advanced filter.

Use the Advanced Filter dialog to find unique records in a list

All you need to do is identify the rows that contain the values you want to filter and indicate that you want to display unique records so that you get only the information you want.

To turn filtering on or off

1. Select any cell in the data range or table.

2. Do either of the following:

   - On the **Home** tab, in the **Editing** group, select **Sort & Filter**, and then select **Filter**.

   - Press **Ctrl+Shift+L**.

To create a selection filter

1. Turn on filtering.

2. Select the filter arrow for the column by which you want to filter the data range or table.

3. Do either of the following:

   - Clear the checkboxes next to the items you want to hide.

   - Clear the **Select All** checkbox and then select the checkboxes next to the items you want to display.

4. Select **OK** to apply the filter.

To create a filter rule

1. With filtering turned on, select the filter arrow for the column by which you want to filter the data range or table.

2. Select *Type* **Filters** to display the available filters for the column's data type.

3. Select the filter you want to create.

4. Enter the arguments required to define the rule, and then select **OK** to apply the filter.

To display the highest or lowest numeric values in a column

1. With filtering turned on, select the filter arrow for a column that contains numeric values, select **Number Filters**, and then select **Top 10**.

2. In the **Top 10 AutoFilter** dialog, do the following:

   a. In the first **Show** list, select **Top** or **Bottom**.

   b. In the second list, enter or select the number or percentage of items you want to display.

   c. In the third list, select **Items** to display the selected number of items or **Percent** to display the selected percentage of items.

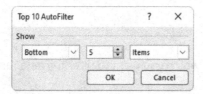

Applying a search filter limits the items that appear in the selection list

3. Select **OK** to apply the filter.

To create a search filter

1. With filtering turned on, select the filter arrow for the column by which you want to filter the data range or table.

2. In the **Search** box, enter the character string that should appear in the values you want to display in the filter list.

> **TIP** The search string can include asterisks to indicate "any character."

3. Select **OK** to apply the filter.

To reapply a filter

- Select the **Filter** button of the filtered column, and then press **Enter** or select **OK**.

To clear a filter

- Select the **Filter** button of the filtered column, and then select **Clear Filter** from "*Field*."

To find unique values within a data range

1. Select any cell in the range for which you want to find unique values.

2. On the **Data** tab, in the **Sort & Filter** group, select **Advanced**.

3. In the **Advanced Filter** dialog, do either of the following:

    *   To display the unique values within the cell range, select **Filter the list, in place**.

    *   To make a separate list of the unique values, select **Copy to another location**.

4. Verify that the correct data range appears in the **List range** box.

> **TIP** If you want to display the unique values from only one column, the List Range box should reference only that column.

5. If you chose the Copy To Another Location option, enter the location where you want to insert the separate list in the **Copy to** box.

6. Select the **Unique records only** checkbox, and then select **OK**.

Summarize filtered data

Excel includes a wide range of tools you can use to summarize worksheet data. This section describes how to summarize filtered data by using the Auto Calculate feature and the SUBTOTAL and AGGREGATE functions.

It's important to be able to analyze the data that's most relevant to your current needs, but there are some limitations when working with filtered data. One important limitation is that formulas that use the SUM or AVERAGE function make calculations based on all the data in a range rather than only the data displayed by the filter.

Excel provides two ways to summarize only the visible cells in a filtered data list. The simplest method is to use the AutoCalculate function, which displays calculation results in the Excel status bar. The more difficult method is to create a formula that uses the SUBTOTAL or AGGREGATE function.

The default AutoCalculate options include SUM, AVERAGE, and COUNT, but you can change the displayed calculations to suit your needs.

	A	B	C	D	E	F	G	H	I	J
1										
2			5:00 PM	6:00 PM	7:00 PM	8:00 PM	9:00 PM	10:00 PM	11:00 PM	
3		Northeast	53,587	41,438	36,599	43,023	37,664	44,030	36,930	
4		Atlantic	8,896	14,467	9,209	10,767	11,277	10,786	14,838	
5		Southeast	7,207	13,475	13,589	14,702	7,769	10,979	10,919	
6		North Central	9,829	9,959	10,367	8,962	14,847	12,085	8,015	
7		Midwest	7,397	7,811	10,292	7,776	14,805	8,777	14,480	
8		Southwest	7,735	11,352	7,222	11,412	14,948	10,686	14,741	
9		Mountain West	9,721	8,404	11,944	8,162	14,531	11,348	8,559	
10		Northwest	9,240	10,995	7,836	9,702	9,265	14,240	9,798	
11		Central	11,810	13,625	8,921	13,593	11,042	10,223	13,338	
12										

< > ... HourlySales +

Ready   Average: 14,317   Count: 63   Sum: 901,946

The status bar displays summary values when you select more than one cell that contains numeric data

AutoCalculate is great for finding a quick total or average for filtered cells, but it doesn't enter the result into the worksheet for you. Formulas such as =SUM(C3:C26) always consider every cell in the range, regardless of whether a row is hidden. To calculate the sum of only the visible values, use either the SUBTOTAL function or the AGGREGATE function. The SUBTOTAL function lets you choose whether to summarize every value in a range or only those values in visible rows. When creating a formula that uses the SUBTOTAL function, you must enter the number of the operation you want to perform.

> ⚠ **IMPORTANT** Be sure to place your SUBTOTAL formula in a row that is even with or above the headers in the range you're filtering. If you don't, your filter might hide the formula's result!

The following table lists the summary operations available for the SUBTOTAL formula. Excel displays the available summary operations as part of the Formula AutoComplete functionality, so you don't need to remember the operation numbers or look them up in the Help system.

All values	Visible values	Function	Description
1	101	AVERAGE	Returns the average of the values in the range
2	102	COUNT	Counts the cells in the range that contain a number
3	103	COUNTA	Counts the nonblank cells in the range
4	104	MAX	Returns the largest (maximum) value in the range
5	105	MIN	Returns the smallest (minimum) value in the range
6	106	PRODUCT	Returns the result of multiplying all numbers in the range
7	107	STDEV.S	Calculates the standard deviation of values in the range by examining a sample of the values
8	108	STDEV.P	Calculates the standard deviation of the values in the range by using all the values
9	109	SUM	Returns the result of adding together all numbers in the range
10	110	VAR.S	Calculates the variance of values in the range by examining a sample of the values
11	111	VAR.P	Calculates the variance of the values in the range by using all the values

As the preceding table shows, the SUBTOTAL function has two sets of operations. The first set (operations 1–11) represents operations that include hidden values in their summary, and the second set (operations 101–111) represents operations that summarize only values visible in the worksheet. Operations 1–11 summarize all cells in a range, regardless of whether the range contains any manually hidden rows. By contrast, operations 101–111 ignore any values in manually hidden rows. What the SUBTOTAL function doesn't do, however, is change its result to reflect rows hidden by using a filter.

> ⚠ IMPORTANT Excel treats the first cell in the data range as a header cell, so it doesn't consider the cell as it builds the list of unique values. Be sure to include the header cell in your data range!

The AGGREGATE function extends the capabilities of the SUBTOTAL function. With it, you can select from a broader range of functions and use another argument to determine which, if any, values to ignore in the calculation. AGGREGATE has two possible syntaxes, depending on the summary operation you select. The first syntax is =AGGREGATE(*function_num*, *options*, *ref1*...), which is similar to the syntax of the SUBTOTAL function. The other possible syntax, =AGGREGATE(*function_num*, *options*, *array*, [*k*]), is used to create AGGREGATE functions that use the LARGE, SMALL, PERCENTILE.INC, QUARTILE.INC, PERCENTILE.EXC, and QUARTILE.EXC operations.

The following table describes the functions available for use in the AGGREGATE function and notes their function numbers.

Number	Function	Description
1	AVERAGE	Returns the average of the values in the range.
2	COUNT	Returns the number of cells in the range that contain numbers.
3	COUNTA	Returns the number of cells in the range that aren't empty.
4	MAX	Returns the largest (maximum) value in the range.
5	MIN	Returns the smallest (minimum) value in the range.
6	PRODUCT	Returns the result of multiplying all numbers in the range.
7	STDEV.S	Calculates the standard deviation of values in the range by examining a sample of the values.
8	STDEV.P	Calculates the standard deviation of the values in the range by using all the values.
9	SUM	Returns the result of adding together all numbers in the range.
10	VAR.S	Calculates the variance of values in the range by examining a sample of the values.
11	VAR.P	Calculates the variance of the values in the range by using all the values.
12	MEDIAN	Returns the value in the middle of a group of values.
13	MODE.SNGL	Returns the most frequently occurring number in the range.

Number	Function	Description
14	LARGE	Returns the kth largest value in a data set. k is specified by using the last function argument. If k is left blank, Excel returns the largest value.
15	SMALL	Returns the kth smallest value in a data set. k is specified by using the last function argument. If k is left blank, Excel returns the smallest value.
16	PERCENTILE.INC	Returns the kth percentile of values in a range, where k is a value from 0 to 1 (inclusive).
17	QUARTILE.INC	Returns the quartile value of a range, based on a percentage from 0 to 1 (inclusive).
18	PERCENTILE.EXC	Returns the kth percentile of values in a range, where k is a value from 0 to 1 (exclusive).
19	QUARTILE.EXC	Returns the quartile value of a range, based on a percentage from 0 to 1 (exclusive).

5

You use the second argument, *options*, to select which items the AGGREGATE function should ignore. These items can include hidden rows, errors, and SUBTOTAL and AGGREGATE functions. The following table summarizes the values available for the *options* argument and the effect they have on the function's results.

Option	Description
0	Ignore nested SUBTOTAL and AGGREGATE functions.
1	Ignore hidden rows and nested SUBTOTAL and AGGREGATE functions.
2	Ignore error values and nested SUBTOTAL and AGGREGATE functions.
3	Ignore hidden rows, error values, and nested SUBTOTAL and AGGREGATE functions.
4	Ignore nothing.
5	Ignore hidden rows.
6	Ignore error values.
7	Ignore hidden rows and error values.

To summarize values by using AutoCalculate

- Select the cells you want to summarize to display the calculations on the status bar.

To change the AutoCalculate summaries displayed on the status bar

1. Right-click a blank area of the status bar to display the Customize Status Bar context menu. The calculation options are near the bottom of the menu.

 TIP To display a context menu, right-click or long-press (tap and hold) the element.

 TIP If you're running Excel on a computer with a low screen resolution, it might be necessary to scroll the menu to see all the options.

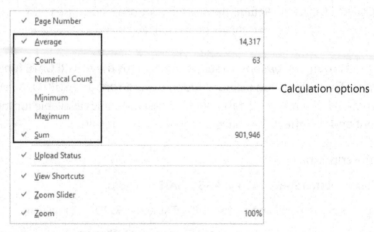

Calculation options

A check mark preceding a calculation indicates that it appears on the status bar

2. Select any calculation option to turn it on or off.

To create a SUBTOTAL formula

- Use the syntax =SUBTOTAL(*function_num, ref1, ref2, ...*) where:

  - *function_num* is the reference number of the function you want to use.

  - *ref1, ref2,* and subsequent *ref* arguments refer to cell ranges.

To create an AGGREGATE formula

- Use the syntax =AGGREGATE(*function_num, options, ref1...*) where:

  - *function_num* is the reference number of the function you want to use.

  - *ref1, ref2,* and subsequent *ref* arguments refer to cell ranges.

5

Randomly select list rows

Excel has a function that can randomly choose rows (records) from a data range or table instead of filtering by specific criteria. This is useful for choosing which customers will receive a special offer, deciding which days of the month to audit, or picking prize winners at an employee party.

To choose rows randomly, you use the RAND function—which generates a random decimal value between 0 and 1—and compare the value it returns with a test value included in a formula.

To use RAND to select a row, create an IF formula that tests the random values. If you want to check 30 percent of the rows, a formula such as =IF(cell_address<0.3, "TRUE", "FALSE") would display TRUE in the formula cells for any value of 0.3 or less and FALSE otherwise.

Because the RAND function is a *volatile function* that recalculates its results every time you update the worksheet, when you're ready to freeze the selection, you should copy the cells that use the RAND function and then paste the formula values (instead of the formula) back into the cells.

TIP The RANDBETWEEN function generates a random whole number within a defined range. For example, the formula =RANDBETWEEN(1,100) generates a random integer value in the range from 1 to 100 (inclusive). This function is very useful for creating sample data collections.

- Use the syntax =AGGREGATE(*function_num*, *options*, *array*, [*k*]) where:

  - *function_num* is the reference number of the function you want to use.

  - *options* is the reference number of the options you want to use.

  - *array* is the cell range that provides data for the formula.

  - The optional *k* argument, used with LARGE, SMALL, PERCENTILE.INC, QUARTILE.INC, PERCENTILE.EXC, or QUARTILE.EXC, indicates which value, percentile, or quartile to return.

Enforce data entry criteria

When multiple people will enter information into a worksheet, you can help ensure the accuracy of the information by creating *validation rules* that govern the information that specific cells can contain. Excel doesn't allow the entry of data that doesn't meet the criteria you define

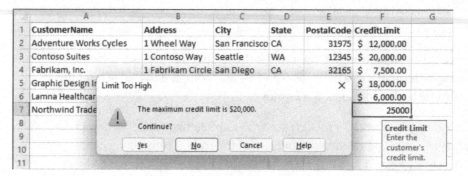

Data-validation rules ensure that users can enter only data that meets your requirements

Data validation includes three components:

- **Validation criteria** The type of data, the range of acceptable values, and whether blank cells are allowed

- **Input message** An optional message that appears when a workbook user selects the cell

- **Error alert** An optional message that appears when a workbook user enters data that doesn't conform to the validation criteria

The following table describes the validation criteria you can configure.

Type	Criteria
Whole number	Between minimum and maximum values
Decimal	Not between minimum and maximum values
Date	Equal to a specific value
Time	Not equal to a specific value
Text length	Greater than a minimum value
	Greater than or equal to a minimum value
	Less than a maximum value
	Less than or equal to a maximum value
List	You specify the list of acceptable text or numeric entries, which can optionally be displayed as an in-cell list.
Custom	You specify a formula.

When you restrict the data that can be entered into a cell, it's nice to include an input message that lets people know what the validation criteria are so they don't become frustrated. The input message appears in a small yellow box adjacent to the cell when it is selected. The message can include a bold title or only the message.

If someone tries to enter invalid data, Excel displays a standard warning message that the value doesn't match the data-validation restrictions for the cell. You can replace the standard message with a custom error alert that displays a Stop, Warning, or Information icon and provides additional information. A Warning alert gives the user the choice to complete the entry. Stop and Information alerts only allow the user to return to the cell.

When you apply validation restrictions to cells that already contain data, Excel doesn't automatically notify you if the existing data conforms to the validation restrictions. You can find out by having Excel circle any cells that contain invalid data. If you want to retain the data that violates the restrictions, you can turn off data validation for those cells.

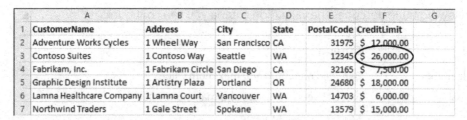

	A	B	C	D	E	F	G
1	CustomerName	Address	City	State	PostalCode	CreditLimit	
2	Adventure Works Cycles	1 Wheel Way	San Francisco	CA	31975	$ 12,000.00	
3	Contoso Suites	1 Contoso Way	Seattle	WA	12345	$ 26,000.00	
4	Fabrikam, Inc.	1 Fabrikam Circle	San Diego	CA	32165	$ 7,500.00	
5	Graphic Design Institute	1 Artistry Plaza	Portland	OR	24680	$ 18,000.00	
6	Lamna Healthcare Company	1 Lamna Court	Vancouver	WA	14703	$ 6,000.00	
7	Northwind Traders	1 Gale Street	Spokane	WA	13579	$ 15,000.00	

Validation circles flag data that violates data-validation rules

To limit data to a range of values or lengths

1. Select the cells to which you want to apply the validation rule.

2. On the **Data** tab, in the **Data Tools** group, select **Data Validation**.

3. In the **Data Validation** dialog, on the **Settings** tab, select the **Allow** arrow, and then select **Whole number**, **Decimal**, **Date**, **Time**, or **Text length**.

4. Define the criteria in the list(s) specific to the rule.

5. If you want to require that users enter a value in the cell, clear the **Ignore blank** checkbox. (This option is selected by default to allow users to navigate away from the cell without entering a value.)

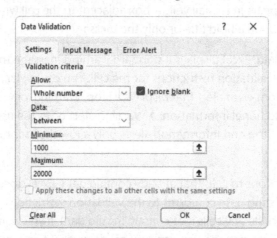

Defining a rule to permit only whole numbers within a specific range

6. If you want to, create an input message and/or error alert.

7. Select **OK** to implement the data-validation rule.

To limit data to a specific list

1. On any worksheet in the workbook, create the list of acceptable entries, with one entry in each cell of a column.

A column heading is optional

2. Select the cells to which you want to apply the validation rule.

3. On the **Data** tab, in the **Data Tools** group, select **Data Validation**.

4. In the **Data Validation** dialog, on the **Settings** tab, select the **Allow** arrow, and then select **List**.

5. In the **Source** box, do either of the following:

    • Enter the cell range (and worksheet, if other than the one you're on).

    • Select the **Collapse** button (the upward-pointing arrow) to hide the rest of the dialog, and then select the list of acceptable entries. (If the list has a heading, don't select the heading.) Excel will enter the cell reference into the box. Then select the **Expand** button (the downward-pointing arrow) to return to the full dialog.

The list can be on any worksheet, even a hidden one

6. If you don't want the list to be available within the cells, clear the **In-cell drop-down** checkbox.

7. If you want to require users to enter a value in the cell, clear the **Ignore blank** checkbox.

8. If you want to, create an input message and/or error alert.

9. Select **OK** to implement the data-validation rule.

To display a message when a user selects the cell

1. In the **Data Validation** dialog, on the **Input Message** tab, ensure that the **Show input message when cell is selected** checkbox is selected.

2. In the **Title** box, enter any text you want to appear in bold at the top of the message.

3. In the **Input message** box, enter the message text.

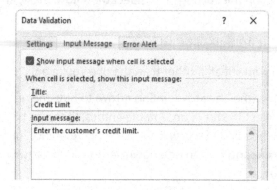

The input message can be up to 255 characters

 TIP The on-screen input message box has a fixed width and dynamic length. Shorter words will fill the message box more neatly.

4. Select **OK** to implement the input message.

To configure an error alert

1. In the **Data Validation** dialog, on the **Error Alert** tab, ensure that the **Show error alert after invalid data is entered** checkbox is selected.

2. In the **Style** list, select one of the following:

   - **Stop** to display a stop icon in the alert box and prevent the data entry.

   - **Warning** to require the user to confirm that they want to enter the data.

   - **Information** to display an information icon in the alert box and prevent the data entry.

3. In the **Title** box, enter the text you want to appear in the alert box title bar.

4. In the **Error message** box, enter the alert text, and then select **OK** to implement the error alert.

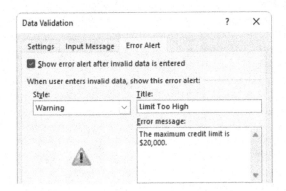

The error alert can be up to 224 characters

To edit a validation rule

1. Select one or more cells that contain the validation rule.

2. On the **Data** tab, in the **Data Tools** group, select **Data Validation**.

3. On the **Settings** tab, do either of the following:

   - To implement the change for all cells in the data-validation range, select the **Apply these changes to all other cells with the same settings** checkbox.

   - To change the data-validation rule in only the selected cells, clear the **Apply these changes to all other cells with the same settings** checkbox.

4. Use the controls in the dialog to edit the rule, input message, and error alert.

5. Select **OK**.

To circle invalid data in a worksheet

- On the **Data** tab, in the **Data Tools** group, select the **Data Validation** arrow, and then select **Circle Invalid Data**.

To remove validation circles

- On the **Data** tab, in the **Data Tools** group, select the **Data Validation** arrow, and then select **Clear Validation Circles**.

Skills review

In this chapter, you learned how to:

- Filter data ranges and tables
- Summarize filtered data
- Enforce data entry criteria

Practice tasks

Before you can complete these tasks, you must copy the book's practice files to your computer. The practice files for these tasks are in the **Excel365SBS\Ch05** folder. You can save the results of the tasks in the same folder.

Filter data ranges and tables

Open the **FilterData** workbook in Excel, and then perform the following tasks:

1. Create a filter that displays only those package exceptions that happened on *RT189*.

2. Clear the previous filter, and then create a filter that shows exceptions for the *Northeast* and *Northwest* centers.

3. With the filter still in place, create a second filter that displays only those exceptions that occurred in the month of April.

4. Clear the filter that shows values related to the *Northeast* and *Northwest* centers.

5. Turn off filtering for the list of data.

Summarize filtered data

Open the **SummarizeValues** workbook in Excel, and then perform the following tasks:

1. Combine the IF and RAND functions into formulas in cells **H3:H27** that display TRUE if the value is less than 0.3 and FALSE otherwise.

2. Use AutoCalculate to find the SUM, AVERAGE, and COUNT of cells **G12:G16**.

3. Remove the COUNT summary from the status bar and add the MINIMUM summary.

4. Create a SUBTOTAL formula that finds the average of the values in cells **G3:G27**.

5. Create an AGGREGATE formula that finds the maximum of values in cells **G3:G27**.

6. Create an advanced filter that finds the unique values in cells **F3:F27**.

Enforce data entry criteria

Open the **ValidateData** workbook in Excel, and then perform the following tasks:

1. Create a data-validation rule in cells **J4:J9** that requires values entered into those cells to be no greater than $25,000.

2. Attempt to type the value 30000 in cell **J7**, observe the message that appears, and then cancel data entry.

3. Edit the rule you created so it includes an input message and an error alert.

4. Display validation circles to highlight data that violates the rule you created, and then hide the circles.

Reorder and summarize data

6

One of the most important uses of business information is to keep a record of when something happens. Whether you ship a package to a client or pay a supplier, tracking when you took those actions, and in what order, helps you analyze your performance. Sorting your information based on the values in one or more columns helps you discover useful trends, such as whether your sales are generally increasing or decreasing, whether you do more business on specific days of the week, or whether you sell products to lots of customers from certain regions of the world.

Excel includes capabilities you might expect to find only in a database program: the ability to organize your data into levels of detail you can show or hide and formulas that let you look up values in a list of data. Organizing data by detail level lets you focus on specific aspects of the data, and looking up values in a worksheet helps you find specific data. If a customer calls to ask about an order, you can use the order number or customer number to discover the information that customer needs.

This chapter guides you through procedures related to sorting your data by using one or more criteria, sorting data against custom lists, outlining data, and calculating subtotals.

In this chapter

- Sort worksheet data
- Sort data by using custom lists
- Outline and subtotal data

Sort worksheet data

Although Excel makes it easy to enter your business data and to manage it after you've saved it in a worksheet, unsorted data will rarely answer every question you want to ask. For example, you might want to discover which of your services generates the most profits or which service costs the most for you to provide. You can discover that information by sorting your data.

When you sort data in a worksheet, you rearrange the rows that contain the data based on the contents of cells in a specific column or set of columns. The first step in sorting a range of data is to identify the column or columns that contain the values by which you want to sort. You can sort by as many of the columns as you want to.

	A	B	C
1	**Customer**	**Service**	**Revenue**
2	Contoso	2-Day	$ 246,811
3	Fabrikam	2-Day	$1,152,558
4	Tailspin Toys	2-Day	$ 851,922
5	Contoso	3-Day	$ 318,710
6	Fabrikam	3-Day	$ 658,371
7	Tailspin Toys	3-Day	$1,026,163
8	Contoso	Ground	$ 941,717
9	Fabrikam	Ground	$ 964,280
10	Tailspin Toys	Ground	$1,147,078
11	Contoso	Overnight	$ 675,122
12	Fabrikam	Overnight	$ 801,656
13	Tailspin Toys	Overnight	$ 35,456
14	Contoso	Priority Overnight	$ 955,755
15	Fabrikam	Priority Overnight	$ 175,699
16	Tailspin Toys	Priority Overnight	$ 161,061

A data range sorted by Service and then Customer

If you want to sort data by only one column that contains words, numbers, or dates, you can quickly do so from the Home tab of the ribbon.

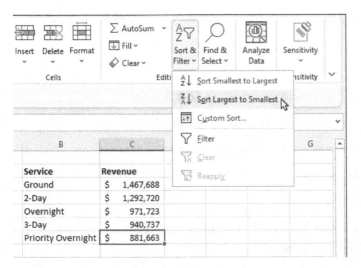

A simple sort from the ribbon

The options on the Sort & Filter menu vary depending on whether you're sorting a column of words, numbers, or dates. Excel sorts words from A to Z or Z to A, numbers from smallest to largest or largest to smallest, and dates from newest to oldest or oldest to newest.

You perform multiple-column sort operations from the Sort dialog, in which you can specify the columns to sort by, the order in which to sort each column, and the order in which to perform the sort operations. When creating similar rules, you can save time by copying one rule and changing only the field name.

If cell values within the data range have font or fill colors applied to them, either manually or though conditional formatting, you can sort the data to place a specific color at the beginning or end of the column.

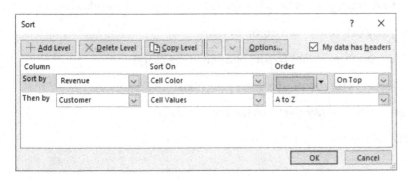

Sort by multiple columns and properties

You can easily change the order in which rules are applied, as well as edit and delete rules, in the Sort dialog.

To display the Sort & Filter menu

- On the **Home** tab, in the **Editing** group, select **Sort & Filter**.

To sort a data range alphanumerically by a single column

1. Select a cell in the column by which you want to sort the data range.

2. Display the **Sort & Filter** menu.

3. Do either of the following:

   - Select **Sort A to Z**, **Sort Smallest to Largest**, or **Sort Oldest to Newest** to sort the data in ascending order.

   - Select **Sort Z to A**, **Sort Largest to Smallest**, or **Sort Newest to Oldest** to sort the data in descending order.

Or

1. Select the data range you want to sort or a cell in the range.

2. Display the **Sort & Filter** menu and then select **Custom Sort**.

3. If appropriate, select the **My data has headers** checkbox.

4. In the **Sort by** list, select the field by which you want to sort.

5. In the **Sort On** list, select **Cell Values**.

6. In the **Order** list, do either of the following:

   - Select **A to Z** or **Smallest to Largest** to sort the data in ascending order.

   - Select **Z to A** or **Largest to Smallest** to sort the data in descending order.

To sort a data range by cell color, font color, or icon

1. Select the data range you want to sort or a cell in the range.

2. Display the **Sort & Filter** menu, and then select **Custom Sort**.

3. If appropriate, select the **My data has headers** checkbox.

4. In the **Sort by** list, select the field by which you want to sort.

5. In the **Sort On** list, select **Cell Color**, **Font Color**, or **Conditional Formatting Icon**.

6. In the **Order** list, select the cell or font color or icon that you want to isolate. Then, in the last list box, do either of the following:

   - Select **On Top** to sort that color or icon to the beginning of the list.

   - Select **On Bottom** to sort that color or icon to the end of the list.

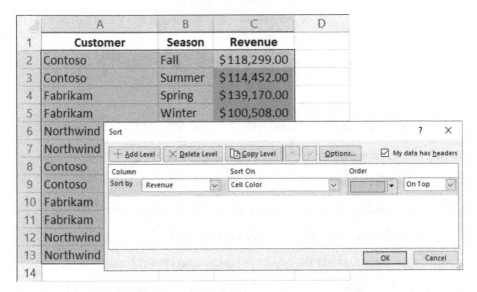

Sort lists of data using cell fill color as a criterion

7. Select **OK** to sort the values.

Or

1. In the data range, right-click the cell that has the color or icon you want to isolate, and then on the context menu, select **Sort**.

 TIP To display a context menu, right-click or long-press (tap and hold) the element.

2. On the **Sort** submenu, select **Put Selected *Attribute* On Top**.

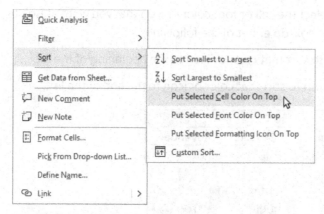

Sort by multiple columns and properties

To sort a data range based on values in multiple columns

1. Select the data range you want to sort or a cell in the range.

2. On the **Home** tab, in the **Editing** group, select **Sort & Filter**.

3. On the **Sort & Filter** menu, select **Custom Sort**.

4. If appropriate, select the **My data has headers** checkbox.

5. In the **Sort by** list, select the first field by which you want to sort.

6. In the **Sort On** list, select the option by which you want to sort the data (**Cell Values**, **Cell Color**, **Font Color**, or **Conditional Formatting Icon**).

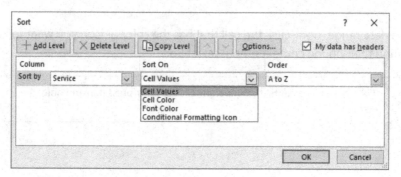

Create sorting rules in the Sort dialog

7. In the **Order** list, select an order for the sort operation.

8. For each additional column by which you want to sort, do the following:

   a. Select **Add Level**.

   b. In the **Then by** list, select the column.

   c. Select values in the **Sort On** and **Order** lists.

9. Select **OK** to sort the values.

	A	B	C
1	**Customer**	**Season**	**Revenue**
2	Contoso	Summer	$114,452.00
3	Contoso	Fall	$118,299.00
4	Contoso	Winter	$183,651.00
5	Contoso	Spring	$201,438.00
6	Fabrikam	Winter	$100,508.00
7	Fabrikam	Spring	$139,170.00
8	Fabrikam	Summer	$183,632.00
9	Fabrikam	Fall	$255,599.00
10	Northwind Traders	Spring	$120,666.00
11	Northwind Traders	Summer	$129,732.00
12	Northwind Traders	Winter	$174,336.00
13	Northwind Traders	Fall	$188,851.00

A data range sorted by Customer and then by Revenue

To copy a sorting level

1. In the **Sort** dialog, select the sorting level you want to copy.

2. Select the **Copy Level** button.

To move a sorting rule up or down in priority

1. In the **Sort** dialog, select the sorting rule you want to move.

2. Do either of the following:

   - Select the **Move Up** (^) button to move the rule earlier in the order.

   - Select the **Move Down** (v) button to move the rule later in the order.

To delete a sorting rule

1. In the **Sort** dialog, select the sorting level you want to delete.

2. Select **Delete Level**.

Sort data by using custom lists

By default, Excel sorts words in alphabetical order and numbers in numeric order. But that pattern doesn't work for some sets of values. For example, if you're sorting a series of months, alphabetical order begins with April and ends with September.

Fortunately, Excel recognizes days of the week and months of the year as special lists that it uses for sorting and when filling series. You can add custom series to Excel for the same purposes, either by entering the list values or copying them from a worksheet.

To define a custom list by entering its values

1. Display the **Advanced** page of the **Excel Options** dialog.

2. Scroll to the **General** section, and then select **Edit Custom Lists**.

3. In the **Custom Lists** dialog, with *NEW LIST* active, activate the **List entries** box.

4. Enter the custom list items in order, pressing **Enter** between items.

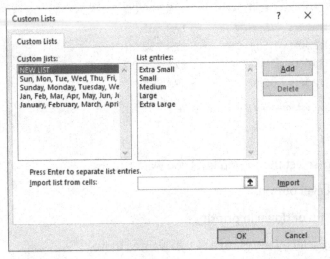

Manage lists in the Custom Lists dialog

5. After you enter all the list items, select **Add** to move them to the Custom Lists pane.

6. Select **OK**, and then select **OK** again to close the **Excel Options** dialog.

To define a custom list by copying values from a worksheet

1. Enter the custom list values in a column, in the correct sort order (first to last, from top to bottom), and then select the cells that contain the list values.

2. Open the **Custom Lists** dialog.

3. Verify that the **Import list from cells** box contains the correct cells, and then select **Import**.

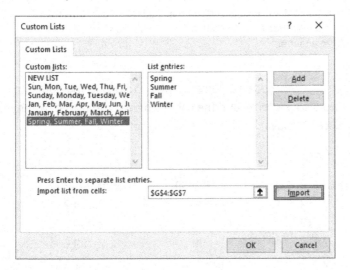

Sort and fill series from any list

4. Select **OK**, and then select **OK** again to close the **Excel Options** dialog.

To sort worksheet data by using a custom list

1. Select a cell in the list of data you want to sort.

2. On the **Home** tab, select the **Sort & Filter** button, and then select **Custom Sort**.

3. If necessary, select the **My data has headers** checkbox.

4. In the **Sort by** list, select the field that contains the data by which you want to sort.

5. If necessary, in the **Sort On** list, select **Values**.

6. In the **Order** list, select **Custom List**.

7. In the **Custom Lists** dialog, select the list you want to use. Then select **OK**.

8. In the **Sort** dialog, select **OK** to close the dialog and sort the data.

Outline and subtotal data

When your data range is sorted into the order you want, you can use the Subtotal feature to have Excel outline the data by specific categories and summarize the categories. The available summary functions are SUM, COUNT, AVERAGE, MAX, MIN, PRODUCT, COUNT NUMBERS, STDDEV, STDDEVP, VAR, and VARP.

> ⚠ **IMPORTANT** You can outline, group, and summarize data ranges by using the SUBTOTAL feature; it does not work on data in Excel tables. To subtotal table data, you must first convert it to a range.

In a subtotal operation, you choose the column by which to group the data, the summary calculation you want to perform, and the values to be summarized. After you define the subtotals, Excel displays them in your worksheet.

	A	B	C	D
1	**Year**	**Quarter**	**Month**	**Package Volume**
2	2019	1	January	5,213,292
3	2019	1	February	2,038,516
4	2019	1	March	2,489,601
5	2019	2	April	9,051,231
6	2019	2	May	5,225,156
7	2019	2	June	3,266,644
8	2019	3	July	2,078,794
9	2019	3	August	1,591,434
10	2019	3	September	8,518,985
11	2019	4	October	1,973,050
12	2019	4	November	7,599,195
13	2019	4	December	9,757,876
14	**2019 Total**			58,803,774
15	2020	1	January	5,304,039
16	2020	1	February	5,465,096

A data range with subtotal outlining applied

Excel also defines groups based on the subtotal calculation. The groups form an out-line of the data based on the criteria you used to create the subtotals. For example, all the rows representing months in the year 2019 could be in one group, rows represent-ing months in 2020 in another, and so on. You can use the controls in the outline area on the left side of the worksheet to hide or display groups of data.

	A	B	C	D
1	**Year**	**Quarter**	**Month**	**Package Volume**
14	**2019 Total**			58,803,774
15	2020	1	January	5,304,039
16	2020	1	February	5,465,096
17	2020	1	March	1,007,799
18	2020	2	April	4,010,287
19	2020	2	May	4,817,070
20	2020	2	June	8,155,717
21	2020	3	July	6,552,370
22	2020	3	August	2,295,635
23	2020	3	September	7,115,883
24	2020	4	October	1,362,767
25	2020	4	November	8,935,488
26	2020	4	December	9,537,077
27	**2020 Total**			64,559,228
28	**Grand Total**			123,363,002

The data range with details for the year 2019 hidden

The numbers above the outline controls are the level buttons. Each represents a level of data organization. Selecting a level button hides all levels of detail below that of the button you selected.

The following table describes the data contained at each level of a worksheet with three levels of organization.

Level	Description
1	Grand total
2	Subtotals for each group
3	Individual rows in the worksheet

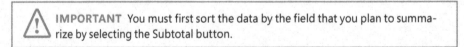

	A	B	C	D
1	Year	Quarter	Month	Package Volume
14	2019 Total			58,803,774
27	2020 Total			64,559,228
28	Grand Total			123,363,002

The data range with details hidden at level 2

You can add custom levels of detail to the outline that Excel creates by grouping specific rows. (For example, you can hide revenues from specific months.) You can also delete groups you don't need and remove the subtotals and outlining entirely.

To organize data into levels

1. Sort the data range, ensuring that the top-level sort is on the column by which you want to group the data.

2. Select the data range you want to sort or a cell in the range.

3. On the **Data** tab, in the **Outline** group, select the **Subtotal** button.

4. In the **Subtotal** dialog, in the **At each change in** list, select the field by which you want to group the data.

> ⚠️ **IMPORTANT** You must first sort the data by the field that you plan to summarize by selecting the Subtotal button.

5. In the **Use function** list, select the summary function you want to use for each subtotal.

6. In the **Add subtotal to** group, select the checkbox next to any field you want to summarize. Then select **OK**.

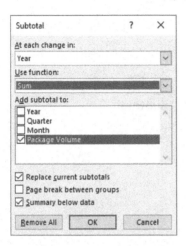

Apply subtotals to data from the Subtotal dialog

To show or hide detail in an outlined range

- To hide or show one group, select its **Hide Detail** (+) or **Show Detail** (–) control.

- To hide or show one level, select the level button.

To create a custom group in an outlined range

1. Select the rows you want to include in the group.

2. On the **Data** tab, in the **Outline** group, select the **Group** button (not the arrow).

	A	B	C	D
1	**Year**	**Quarter**	**Month**	**Package Volume**
2	2019	1	January	5,213,292
3	2019	1	February	2,038,516
4	2019	1	March	2,489,601
5	2019	2	April	9,051,231

A custom group within an outline

To remove a custom group from an outlined range

1. Select the rows you want to remove from the group.

2. On the **Data** tab, in the **Outline** group, select the **Ungroup** button (not the arrow).

To remove subtotals from a data range

1. Select any cell in the range.

2. On the **Data** tab, in the **Outline** group, select **Subtotal**.

3. In the **Subtotal** dialog, select **Remove All**.

Skills review

In this chapter, you learned how to:

- Sort worksheet data

- Sort data by using custom lists

- Outline and subtotal data

Practice tasks

Before you can complete these tasks, you must copy the book's practice files to your computer. The practice files for these tasks are in the **Excel365SBS\Ch06** folder. You can save the results of the tasks in the same folder.

Sort worksheet data

Open the **SortData** workbook in Excel, and then perform the following tasks:

1. Sort the data in the cell range **B3:D14** in ascending order by the values in the Revenue column.

2. Sort the data range in descending order by the values in the Revenue column.

3. Perform a two-level sort of the data range:

    a. In ascending order by Customer.

    b. In ascending order by Season.

    Review the effect of the multiple-column sort. Be sure that you understand the effect of the sort operation order.

4. Reverse the order of the fields in the Sort dialog to sort first by Season and then by Customer.

5. Sort the data range by the Revenue column so that the cells that have a red fill color are at the top of the list.

6. Save and close the file.

Sort data by using custom lists

Open the **CustomSortData** workbook in Excel, and then perform the following tasks:

1. Create a custom list by using the values in cells **G4:G7**.

2. Sort the data in the cell range **B2:D14** by the Season column based on the custom list you just created.

3. Perform a two-level sort of the data range:

   a. By Customer in ascending order.

   b. By Season in the custom list order.

4. Save and close the file.

Outline and subtotal data

Open the **OutlineData** workbook in Excel, and then perform the following tasks:

1. Outline the data list in cells **A1:D25** to find the subtotal for each year.

2. Hide the details of rows for the year 2020.

3. Create a new group consisting of the rows showing data for June and July 2019.

4. Hide the details of the group you just created.

5. Show the details of all months for the year 2020.

6. Remove the subtotal outline from the entire data list.

7. Save and close the file.

Combine data from multiple sources

Excel gives you a wide range of tools with which to format, summarize, and present your data. After you've created a workbook to hold data, you can create as many worksheets as you need to make that data easier to find. If you want every workbook you create to have a similar appearance, you can create a workbook with the characteristics you want and save it as a template for similar workbooks you create in the future.

A consequence of organizing data into different workbooks and worksheets is that you need methods of managing, combining, and summarizing data from more than one Excel file. Of course, you can always copy data from one workbook or worksheet to another, but if a value in the original, or source, workbook or worksheet were to change, that change would not be reflected in the workbook or worksheet into which you copied the data. Rather than manually updating cells in the copy workbook or worksheet, you can create a link between the two. That way, whenever you open the copy workbook or worksheet, Excel will automatically update it to reflect the source workbook or worksheet. On a related note, if multiple worksheets hold related values, you can use links to summarize those values in a single worksheet.

In this chapter

- Look up data from other locations
- Link to data in other locations
- Consolidate multiple sets of data

This chapter guides you through procedures related to looking up data from other location, linking to data in other workbooks, and consolidating multiple sets of data into a single workbook.

Look up data from other locations

Whenever you create a worksheet that holds information about a list of distinct items, such as products offered for sale by a company, you should ensure that at least one column in the list contains a unique value that distinguishes that row (and the item the row represents) from every other row in the list. Assigning each row a column that contains a unique value means that you can associate data in one list with data in another list. For example, if you assign every customer a unique identification number, you can store a customer's contact information in one worksheet and all orders for that customer in another worksheet. You can then include the customer ID in both worksheets to associate the customer's orders and contact information without writing the contact information in a worksheet every time the customer places an order.

In technical terms, the column that contains a unique value for each row is known as the *primary key column*. If you know an item's primary key value, it's no trouble to look through a list of 20 or 30 items to find it. If, however, you have a list of many thousands of items, looking through the list to find one would take quite a bit of time. Instead, you can use the VLOOKUP, HLOOKUP, or XLOOKUP function to find the value you want.

- VLOOKUP locates information in the same *row* as the lookup value. The lookup value and the return value must be in the same data range or table (the table array). The V indicates a vertical data layout, with the lookup values in the left-most column of the table array.

- HLOOKUP locates information in the same *column* as the lookup value. The lookup value and the return value must be in the same table array. The H indicates a horizontal data layout, with the lookup values in the topmost row of the table array.

- XLOOKUP was added to Excel in 2020 and essentially renders VLOOKUP and HLOOKUP unnecessary. It locates information in the same row *or* column as the lookup value, which can be located anywhere in the table array.

You can look up data from the same worksheet, from another worksheet in the same workbook, or from another open workbook, so you don't have to reproduce the same data in multiple locations. VLOOKUP and HLOOKUP are slightly simpler to use than XLOOKUP, but XLOOKUP is far more versatile. This chapter covers the use of all three, so you can use what you're most comfortable with.

Locate information in the same row (VLOOKUP)

The VLOOKUP function finds a value in the leftmost column of a data range or table and returns the value a specific number of cells to the right in the same row. A properly formed VLOOKUP function has four arguments and the following syntax:

=VLOOKUP(*lookup_value, table_array, col_index_num, range_lookup*)

The following table describes the VLOOKUP function arguments.

Argument	Expected value
lookup_value	The value to be found in the first column of the range specified by the *table_array* argument. The *lookup_value* argument can be a cell reference, a value, or a text string.
	If the lookup value is a text string, enclose it in quotation marks (for example, "Word").
	If the lookup value is a text string, it may include the wildcard characters ? (question mark) representing any one character and * (asterisk) representing any sequence of characters. If the lookup value is a text string that contains a question mark or asterisk, insert a tilde (~) before the character.
table_array	The multicolumn range, named range, or named table that contains the lookup value and the return value.
col_index_num	The number of the column in the named range in which the return value will be found, counting the lookup value column as 1.
range_lookup	Optional. A TRUE or FALSE value, indicating whether the function should find an approximate match (TRUE) or an exact match (FALSE) for the lookup value. If this argument is left blank, the default value for it is TRUE. The value you most likely want to use, however, is FALSE, because TRUE can easily return data other than what you're looking for.
	When *range_lookup* is left blank or set to TRUE, the table array must be sorted in ascending order by the first column (the lookup value column).

7

The VLOOKUP results can differ depending on whether the *range_lookup* argument is set to TRUE or FALSE:

- If the *range_lookup* argument is left blank or set to TRUE, and VLOOKUP doesn't find the specified lookup value, the function substitutes the largest value that is less than the lookup value. (If the lookup value is larger than all values in the lookup value column, the function substitutes the largest value.)

- If the *range_lookup* argument is left blank or set to TRUE, VLOOKUP doesn't find the lookup value, and the lookup value is smaller than all values in the lookup value column, the function returns an #N/A error.

- If the *range_lookup* argument is set to FALSE and VLOOKUP doesn't find the specified lookup value, the function returns an #N/A error.

As an example of a VLOOKUP function, consider the data range in the following image, with headers in the first worksheet row (row 1) and the unique lookup values in the first worksheet column (column A).

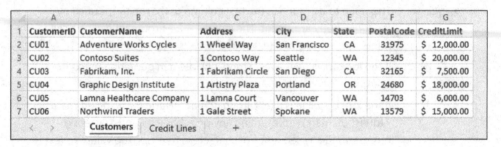

Data structured for use by the VLOOKUP function

From another location, you can quickly use the unique customer ID to retrieve each customer's credit limit for a different use.

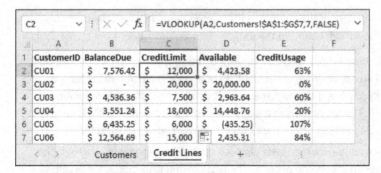

A VLOOKUP formula that pulls information from another worksheet

To look up values by using VLOOKUP

1. Identify the data range that contains the lookup values and return values. Ensure that the lookup values are in the leftmost column, or to the left of the return values.

2. In the cell where you want to display the return value, enter a formula using the syntax =VLOOKUP(*lookup_value, table_array, col_index_num, range_lookup*) where:

   - *lookup_value* is the specific value or text string or the cell reference of the value or text string you want to look up.

   - *table_array* is the data range or table you identified in step 1, beginning with the column that contains the lookup value.

     If the table array is a cell range (such as A1:G7) and you intend to copy or fill the formula to other cells, select the table array and press **F4** to make it an absolute value ($A$1:$G$7).

   - *col_index_number* is the number of the column in which the formula will find the return value. Count beginning with the lookup value column.

   - *range_lookup* is FALSE if the formula must find the exact lookup value and otherwise is TRUE or blank.

 IMPORTANT If the *range_lookup* argument is TRUE or blank, sort the data range you identified in step 1 in ascending order by the lookup values.

 SEE ALSO Refer to the table earlier in this section for additional information about the VLOOKUP function arguments.

Locate information in the same column (HLOOKUP)

The HLOOKUP function finds a value in the first row of a data range or table and returns the value a specific number of cells below in the same column. A properly formed HLOOKUP function has four arguments and the following syntax:

=HLOOKUP(*lookup_value, table_array, row_index_num, range_lookup*)

The following table describes the HLOOKUP function arguments.

Argument	Expected value
lookup_value	The value to be found in the first column of the range specified by the *table_array* argument. The *lookup_value* argument can be a cell reference, a value, or a text string. If the lookup value is a text string, enclose it in quotation marks (for example, "Word"). If the lookup value is a text string, it may include the wildcard characters ? (question mark) representing any one character and * (asterisk) representing any sequence of characters. If the lookup value is a text string that contains a question mark or asterisk, insert a tilde (~) before the character.
table_array	The multicolumn range, named range, or named table that contains the lookup value and the return value.
row_index_num	The number of the row in the named range in which the return value will be found, counting the lookup value row as *1*.
range_lookup	Optional. A TRUE or FALSE value, indicating whether the function should find an approximate match (TRUE) or an exact match (FALSE) for the lookup value. If this argument is left blank, the default value for it is TRUE. The value you most likely want to use, however, is FALSE, because TRUE can easily return data other than what you're looking for. When *range_lookup* is left blank or set to TRUE, the table array must be sorted in ascending order by the first column (the lookup value column).

The HLOOKUP results can differ depending on whether the *range_lookup* argument is set to TRUE or FALSE:

- If the *range_lookup* argument is left blank or set to TRUE, and HLOOKUP doesn't find the specified lookup value, the function substitutes the largest value that is less than the lookup value. (If the lookup value is larger than all values in the lookup value column, the function substitutes the largest value.)

- If the *range_lookup* argument is left blank or set to TRUE, HLOOKUP doesn't find the lookup value, and the lookup value is smaller than all values in the lookup value column, the function returns an #N/A error.

- If the *range_lookup* argument is set to FALSE and HLOOKUP doesn't find the specified lookup value, the function returns an #N/A error.

As an example of an HLOOKUP function, consider the data range in the following image, with headers in the first worksheet column (column A) and the unique lookup values in the first worksheet row (row 1).

	A	B	C	D	E	F	G
1	Order quantity	1	2	3	4	5	6
2	Unit price	$ 19.99	$ 19.49	$ 19.00	$ 18.53	$ 18.06	$ 17.61
3							

Price Sheet | Order Information | +

Data structured for use by the HLOOKUP function

From another location, you can quickly use the unique order quantity to retrieve the unit price for a different use.

B3			f_x	=HLOOKUP(B2,'Price Sheet'!A1:M2,2,FALSE)			
	A	B	C	D	E	F	G
1	Order #	12345					
2	Quantity ordered	4					
3	Unit price	$ 18.53					
4	Subtotal	$ 74.11					
5	Tax	$ 5.37					
6	Total	$ 79.48					
7							

Price Sheet | Order Information | +

An HLOOKUP formula that pulls information from another worksheet

To look up values by using HLOOKUP

1. Identify the data range that contains the lookup values and return values. Ensure that the lookup values are in the top row or above the return values.

2. In the cell where you want to display the return value, enter a formula using the syntax =HLOOKUP(*lookup_value, table_array, row_index_num, range_lookup*) where:

   - *lookup_value* is the specific value or text string or the cell reference of the value or text string you want to look up.

   - *table_array* is the data range or table you identified in step 1, beginning with the row that contains the lookup value.

     If the table array is a cell range (such as A1:G7) and you intend to copy or fill the formula to other cells, select the table array and press **F4** to make it an absolute value ($A$1:$G$7).

7

- *row_index_num* is the number of the row in which the formula will find the return value. Count beginning with the lookup value row.

- *range_lookup* is FALSE if the formula must find the exact lookup value and otherwise is TRUE or blank.

 IMPORTANT If the *range_lookup* argument is TRUE or blank, sort the data range you identified in step 1 in ascending order by the lookup values.

 SEE ALSO Refer to the table earlier in this section for additional information about the HLOOKUP function arguments.

Locate information anywhere (XLOOKUP)

The XLOOKUP function finds a value in a row or column of a data range or table and returns the value from another row or column. The lookup range and return range must be the same size.

A properly formed XLOOKUP function has six arguments and the following syntax:

=XLOOKUP(*lookup_value, lookup_array, return_array, if_not_found, match_mode, search_mode*)

The following table describes the XLOOKUP function arguments.

Argument	Expected value
lookup_value	The value to be found in the first column of the range specified by the *table_array* argument. The *lookup_value* argument can be a cell reference, a value, or a text string.
	If the lookup value is a text string, enclose it in quotation marks (for example, "Word").
	If the lookup value is a text string, it may include the wildcard characters ? (question mark) representing any one character and * (asterisk) representing any sequence of characters. If the lookup value is a text string that contains a question mark or asterisk, insert a tilde (~) before the character.
lookup_array	The cell range that contains the lookup value.

Argument	Expected value
return_array	The cell range that contains the return value.
if_not_found	Optional. This is the text the function returns if the lookup value is not found in the lookup array. Enclose the *if_not_found* value in quotes. If left blank, the default value is #N/A.
match_mode	Optional. Similar to the *range_lookup* argument, XLOOKUP has four match types:
	0 specifies an exact match and returns #N/A if the lookup value is not found. This is the default value.
	−1 substitutes the next smaller value if the lookup value is not found.
	1 substitutes the next larger value if the lookup value is not found.
	2 specifies a wildcard match.
search_mode	Optional. XLOOKUP has four search modes:
	1 searches forward from the first item in the lookup range. This is the default value.
	−1 searches backward from the last item in the lookup range.
	2 performs a binary search and requires that the lookup array is sorted in ascending order.
	−2 performs a binary search and requires that the lookup array is sorted in descending order.

7

As an example of a XLOOKUP function, consider the data range in the following image, with headers in the first worksheet row (row 1).

	A	B	C	D	E
1	ID	Product Code	Product Name	Cost	List Price
2	1	NWTB-1	Northwind Traders Chai	$13.50	$18.00
3	3	NWTCO-3	Northwind Traders Syrup	$7.50	$10.00
4	4	NWTCO-4	Northwind Traders Cajun Seasoning	$16.50	$22.00
5	5	NWTO-5	Northwind Traders Olive Oil	$16.01	$21.35
6	6	NWTJP-6	Northwind Traders Boysenberry Spread	$18.75	$25.00
7	7	NWTDFN-7	Northwind Traders Dried Pears	$22.50	$30.00
8	8	NWTS-8	Northwind Traders Curry Sauce	$30.00	$40.00
9	14	NWTDFN-14	Northwind Traders Walnuts	$17.44	$23.25
10	17	NWTCFV-17	Northwind Traders Fruit Cocktail	$29.25	$39.00

Data structured for use by the XLOOKUP function

From another location, you can quickly use the unique product code to retrieve the retail list price and wholesale cost of an item. This example calculates the per-item profit by subtracting one from the other.

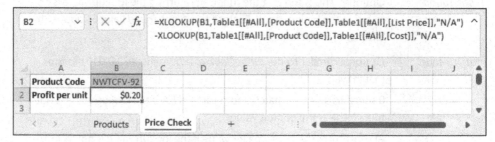

Calculating return based on two XLOOKUP formulas

To look up values by using XLOOKUP

1. Identify the data range that contains the lookup values and return values. Ensure that the lookup values are in the top row, or above the return values.

2. In the cell where you want to display the return value, enter a formula using the syntax =XLOOKUP(*lookup_value, lookup_array, return_array, if_not_found, match_mode, search_mode*) where:

   • *lookup_value* is the specific value or text string or the cell reference of the value or text string you want to look up.

   • *lookup_array* is the data range or table you identified in step 1, beginning with the row that contains the lookup value.

     If the lookup array is a cell range (such as A1:G7) and you intend to copy or fill the formula to other cells, select the table array and press **F4** to make it an absolute value ($A$1:$G$7).

   • *return_array* is the number of the row in which the formula will find the return value. Count beginning with the lookup value row.

   • *if_not_found, match_mode*, and *search_mode* are optional values.

 SEE ALSO Refer to the table earlier in this section for additional information about the XLOOKUP function arguments.

Link to data in other locations

Copying and pasting data from one workbook or worksheet to another is a quick and easy way to gather related data in one place, but there is a substantial limitation: If data in the source workbook or worksheet changes, the change is not reflected in the copy workbook or worksheet. In other words, copying and pasting a cell's contents doesn't create a relationship between the original cell and the target cell.

You can ensure that the data in the target cell reflects any changes in the original cell by creating a link between the two cells. Instead of entering a value into the target cell by typing or pasting, you create a formula that identifies the source from which Excel derives the target cell's value and updates the value when it changes in the source cell.

You can link to a cell in another workbook or worksheet by starting to create your formula, displaying the worksheet that contains the value you want to use, and then selecting the cell or cell range you want to include in the calculation. When you press Enter and switch back to the workbook with the target cell, the value in the formula bar shows that Excel has filled in the formula with a reference to the cell you selected.

A cell reference to another workbook

The reference ='[FleetOperatingCosts.xlsx]Truck Fuel'!$C$15 provides three pieces of information:

- The name of the workbook (FleetOperatingCosts.xlsx), enclosed in brackets
- The name of the worksheet (Truck Fuel)
- The worksheet cell (C15)

The single quotes around the workbook name and worksheet name allow for the space in the Truck Fuel worksheet's name. This type of reference is known as a 3-D reference, reflecting the three dimensions (workbook, worksheet, and cell range) that you need to point to a group of cells in another workbook.

> ✅ **TIP** References to cells in the same workbook don't include the bracketed workbook name. Likewise, references to cells on the same worksheet don't include the worksheet name.

You can also link to cells in an Excel table. Such links include the workbook name, worksheet name, the name of the Excel table, and the row and column references of the cell to which you've linked. Creating a link to the *Cost* column's cell in a table's *Totals* row, for example, results in a reference such as ='FleetOperatingCosts.xlsx'!Truck Maintenance[[#Totals],[Cost]].

A2	⌄ :	× ✓ *fx*	=FleetOperatingCosts.xlsx!TruckMaintenance[[#Totals],[Cost]]					
	A	B	C	D	E	F	G	H
1	Truck Maintenance Costs							
2	$ 1,060,566.00							
3								

Link to an Excel table value in another workbook

> ⚠ **IMPORTANT** Hiding or displaying a table's *Totals* row affects any links to a cell in that row. Hiding the *Totals* row causes references to that row to display a #REF! error message.

To create a link to a cell, cell range, or table on another worksheet

1. Start creating a formula that will include a value from a cell or cell range on another worksheet.

2. When you reach the portion of the formula in which you want to reference the external data, select the sheet tab of the worksheet that contains the data, select the cell or cells to include in the formula, and then press **Enter**.

To create a link to a cell or cell range in another workbook

1. Open the workbook where you want to create the formula that references an external cell or cell range.

2. Open the workbook that contains the cell or cell range you want to include in your formula.

3. Switch back to the first workbook and start creating a formula that will include a value from a cell or cell range in the other workbook.

4. When you reach the portion of the formula in which you want to reference the external data, switch to the workbook that contains the data, display the worksheet, select the cell or cells to include in the formula, and then press **Enter**.

To open the source of a linked value

1. Open a workbook that contains a link to an external cell or cell range.

2. On the **Data** tab of the ribbon, in the **Queries & Connections** group, select the **Edit Links** button.

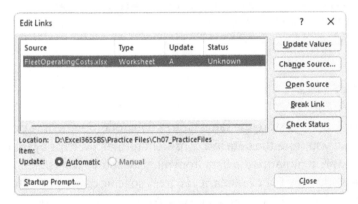

Manage workbook links from the Edit Links dialog

3. In the **Edit Links** dialog, select the link you want to work with.

4. Select the **Open Source** button.

To fix a link that returns an error because it references the wrong workbook

1. Select the **Edit Links** button.

2. In the **Edit Links** dialog, select the link that returns an error.

3. Select **Change Source**.

4. Select the workbook that contains the correct source value.

5. If the **Select Sheet** dialog appears, select the worksheet that contains the correct source value, and select **OK**.

6. Select **Close**.

To break a link

1. In a workbook that contains a link to a cell on another worksheet or in another workbook, select the **Edit Links** button.

2. In the **Edit Links** dialog, select the link you want to edit.

3. Select the **Break Link** button.

4. When prompted, select **Break Links** to confirm that you want to break the link.

5. Select **Close**.

 TIP If you can't easily fix a link that returns an error, the best choice is often to delete the link from the formula and re-create it.

Consolidate multiple sets of data

One common use for Excel is to store the same type of data for different time periods or different products. If you store the data in a consistent format, perhaps by using a template, you can easily summarize the data from multiple source worksheets or workbooks into one worksheet. For example, if you track specific data by month, you can quickly summarize the data for an entire year. You achieve this by using the Consolidate Data tool.

When summarizing data, you can perform any of the following operations on it: Sum, Count, Average, Max, Min, Product, Count Numbers, StdDev, StdDevp, Var, and Varp. Thus, you could quickly report on the total sales for the year, the average monthly sales for the year, and so on.

	Call Center	Hour					
		9:00 AM	10:00 AM	11:00 AM	12:00 PM	1:00 PM	2:00 PM
4	Northeast	23091	30290	30480	41357	36313	31119
5	Atlantic	43825	35597	29315	32345	41246	23518
6	Southeast	16865	23607	34813	21760	36645	33407
7	North Central	33834	40303	35109	32258	36446	29803
8	Midwest	40340	24713	31320	26938	40510	38271
9	Southwest	26196	31866	36182	34617	26181	35644
10	Mountain West	35134	38888	15112	42592	21838	28247
11	Northwest	37632	33481	26690	26472	37654	27450
12	Central	36516	32200	28779	46406	30739	35836
13	**Total**	**293,433**	**290,945**	**267,800**	**304,745**	**307,572**	**283,295**

Q1 Total January February March +

Data consolidation from three worksheets

The important requirement for consolidating data is that every source data range must have the same number of rows and columns. Excel consolidates the data by relative location in the range, performing the selected summary operation on the upper-left cells of every source range, and so on.

A workbook can contain only one data consolidation. If you want to perform multiple summary operations, you can do so by saving the consolidations in separate workbooks.

To consolidate cell ranges from multiple worksheets or workbooks

1. Open the workbook into which you want to consolidate your data (the target workbook) and the workbooks supplying the data for the consolidated range (the source workbooks).

2. Ensure that the data is arranged identically in each source.

3. In the target workbook, position the insertion point in the upper-left corner of the consolidation area.

4. On the **Data** tab, in the **Data Tools** group, select the **Consolidate** button.

5. In the **Consolidate** dialog, in the **Function** list, select the function you want to perform when consolidating the source data.

189

6. For each data source you want to consolidate, do the following:

   a. Activate the **Reference** field.

   b. If you're consolidating data from a different worksheet, on the **View** tab, in the **Window** group, select **Switch Windows**, and then select the workbook.

   c. Activate the source worksheet, and then drag to select the source data range.

   d. Select **Add** to add the range to the All References list.

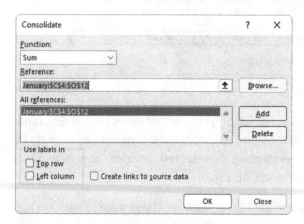

Add data ranges to create a consolidation range

7. After you add all the source ranges, select **OK** to generate the consolidated data.

Skills review

In this chapter, you learned how to:

- Look up data from other locations
- Link to data in other locations
- Consolidate multiple sets of data

Practice tasks

Before you can complete these tasks, you must copy the book's practice files to your computer. The practice files for these tasks are in the **Excel365SBS\Ch07** folder. You can save the results of the tasks in the same folder.

Look up data from other locations

Open the **LookupData** workbook in Excel, and then perform the following tasks:

1. Sort the values in the first table column in ascending order.

2. In cell C3, create a formula that finds the CustomerID value for a shipment ID entered into cell B3.

3. Edit the formula so that it finds the DestinationPostalCode value for the same package.

Link to data in other locations

Open the **CreateDataLinks** and **FleetOperatingCosts** workbooks in Excel, and then perform the following tasks:

1. In the **CreateDataLinks** workbook, create links to the **FleetOperatingCosts** workbook that copy truck fuel, truck maintenance, airplane fuel, and airplane maintenance costs to the appropriate cells in column I on **Sheet1** of the **CreateDataLinks** workbook.

2. Close the **FleetOperatingCosts** workbook.

3. View the links in the **CreateDataLinks** workbook and show the source for one of the links.

4. Break the link to the airplane fuel source data cell.

Consolidate multiple sets of data

Open the **ConsolidateData** workbook in Excel, and then perform the following tasks:

1. On the **Q1** worksheet, create a consolidation target by using cells **C4:O12**.

2. Add call data from the **January, February,** and **March** worksheets as consolidation ranges, and then complete the consolidation.

Analyze alternative data sets

When you store data in an Excel workbook, you can use that data, either by itself or as part of a calculation, to discover important information about your organization.

The data in your worksheets is great for answering "what-if" questions, such as "How much money would we save if we reduced our labor to 20 percent of our total costs?" You can always save an alternative version of a workbook and create formulas that calculate the effects of your changes, but you can do the same thing in your existing workbooks by defining one or more alternative data sets. You can also create a data table that calculates the effects of changing one or two variables in a formula, find the input values required to generate the result you want, and describe your data statistically.

This chapter guides you through procedures related to defining scenarios that result in alternative data sets, forecasting data by using data tables, and using Goal Seek to identify the input necessary to achieve a specific result.

In this chapter

- Define and display alternative data sets
- Forecast data by using data tables
- Identify the input necessary to achieve a specific result

Define and display alternative data sets

When you save data in an Excel worksheet, you create a record that reflects the characteristics of an event or object. For example, that data could represent the number of deliveries in an hour on a specific day, the price of a new delivery option, the percentage of total revenue accounted for by a delivery option—the possibilities are endless. After the data is in place, you can create formulas to generate totals, find averages, and sort the rows in a worksheet based on the contents of one or more columns. However, if you want to perform a what-if analysis or explore the impact that changes in the data would have on any of the calculations in your workbooks, you must change the data. By doing so, you run the risk of losing the original data. If you only want to make temporary changes for forecasting purposes, you can safely do so by applying a scenario—a set of alternative values—to the original data set to create an alternative data set.

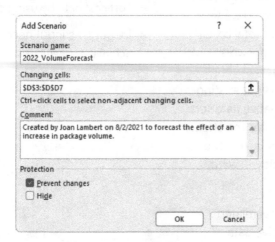

A scenario changes data in specific cells

Applying a scenario creates an alternative data set by replacing the values in the original data set with the alternative values defined in the scenario and recalculating any formulas that depend on those values. After you apply the scenario, you can return to the original data set by undoing the scenario.

> ⚠️ **IMPORTANT** It's important to revert to the original data set before you save and close the workbook, because the original data isn't stored anywhere. To avoid accidentally losing the original data, create a scenario that contains the original values or create a scenario summary.

Each scenario can change a maximum of 32 cells, so if you want to modify a lot of data, you will need to create multiple scenarios. You can create and apply as many scenarios as you want. (If multiple scenarios affect the same cell, the cell displays the value created by the most recently applied scenario.)

If you want to keep a record of the effect of various scenarios within a workbook, you can create a scenario summary worksheet that displays the effect of the scenarios on specific cells.

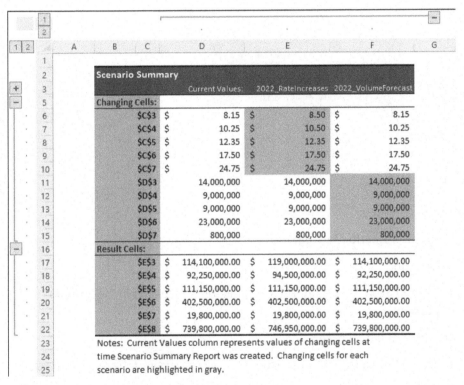

A scenario summary worksheet tracks the effects of all scenarios

As with other Excel tools, you can edit and delete the scenarios you create. Deleting a scenario does not undo the effects of the scenario on the worksheet data; it only removes the scenario from the Scenario Manager dialog.

To open the Scenario Manager dialog

- On the **Data** tab, in the **Forecast** group, select **What-If Analysis**, and then select **Scenario Manager.**

Manage and summarize scenarios

To define a scenario

1. Open the **Scenario Manager** dialog.

2. Select **Add.**

3. In the **Add Scenario** dialog, enter a name for the scenario in the **Scenario name** box.

4. Do either of the following:

   - In the **Changing cells** box, enter the cell references of the cell values you want to change.

   - Activate the **Changing cells** box and then, on the worksheet, select the cells in which you want to change the values.

 TIP When you select the cells on the worksheet, the dialog name changes from Add Scenario to Edit Scenario.

5. In the **Comment** box that contains your name and the date, append any notes that you might find useful later.

6. In the **Add Scenario** dialog, select **OK**.

7. In the **Scenario Values** dialog, replace the original values of each of the changing cells, and then select **OK**.

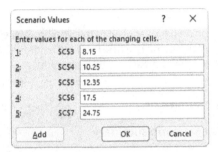

Enter alternative data in the Scenario Values dialog

To display an alternative data set

1. In the **Scenario Manager** dialog, select the scenario you want to apply, and then select **Show**.

2. To apply additional scenarios, repeat step 1.

To revert to the original data set

- Close the **Scenario Manager** dialog, and then do either of the following:

  - On the Quick Access Toolbar, select the **Undo** button.

  - Press **Ctrl+Z**.

To edit a scenario

1. In the **Scenario Manager** dialog, select the scenario you want to edit, and then select **Edit**.

2. In the **Edit Scenario** dialog, change any values in the **Scenario name**, **Changing cells**, or **Comment** boxes, and then select **OK**.

3. In the **Scenario Values** dialog, modify the new values for the changing cells, and then select **OK**.

8

To delete a scenario

■ In the **Scenario Manager** dialog, select the scenario you want to delete, and then select **Delete**.

To create a scenario summary worksheet

1. Revert any scenarios that have been applied to the original data set.

> ⚠ **IMPORTANT** Make sure there are no scenarios applied to the workbook when you create the summary worksheet. If a scenario is active, Excel will record the alternative data set as the original values, and the summary will be inaccurate.

2. In the **Scenario Manager** dialog, select **Summary**.

3. In the **Scenario Summary** dialog, select **Scenario summary**.

4. Do either of the following:

   • In the **Result cells** box, enter the cell references of the cell changes you want to summarize.

   • Activate the **Result cells** box and then, on the worksheet, select the cells whose changes you want to summarize.

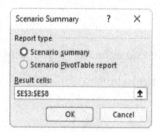

Summarize scenarios by using the Scenario Summary dialog

5. In the **Scenario Summary** dialog, select **OK**.

Forecast data by using data tables

Data tables are another useful data-forecasting tool in Excel. They let you clearly see the result of applying different patterns to existing data

	A	B	C	D
1	Revenue Forecast			
2				
3	Factor	Current	Increase	Revenue
4	Year	2021		$ 2,102,600.70
5	Increase	0%	2%	$ 2,144,652.71
6	Package Count	237,582	5%	$ 2,207,730.74
7	Average Rate	$ 8.85	8%	$ 2,270,808.76

Projecting different rates of increase on the current data

A data table can forecast changes to either one or two formula inputs. These are called the *variables*. To create a data table with one variable, you arrange the formula inputs—including the changing value, the variable values, and a summary formula—on a worksheet, leaving an area for the data table in the lower-right corner of the cell range. The variable values can be in a column (as shown here) or in a row.

8

D4 f_x =(1+B5)*(B6*B7)

	A	B	C	D
1	Revenue Forecast			
2				
3	Factor	Current	Increase	Revenue
4	Year	2021		$ 2,102,600.70
5	Increase	0%	2%	
6	Package Count	237,582	5%	
7	Average Rate	$ 8.85	8%	

Excel substitutes the variables for the changing value

In the example shown above, the formula inputs are in B5:B7, with the changing value in B5, the variables in C5:C7, and the summary formula (shown in the formula bar) in cell D4. Excel builds the data table in D5:D7 to reflect the effect of the variables on the summary formula.

To create a two-variable data table, arrange the formula inputs, including the two changing values, in the same way as for the one-variable table. Place one set of variable values in a column and another in a row, again leaving an area for the data table in the lower-right corner. Place the summary formula at the junction of the column and the row.

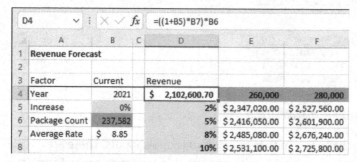

Two-variable data tables generate multiple outcomes

In this example, the variables in D5:D8 represent the rate increase and the variables in E4:F4 represent the package count increase.

To create a one-variable data table

1. On a worksheet, enter the following information, and arrange it as shown and described above:

   - A summary formula

   - The input values for the summary formula

   - A column (or row) of alternative values for one of the input values

2. Select the cells representing the variables and the summary formula, and the cells in which the data table displaying the alternative formula results should appear.

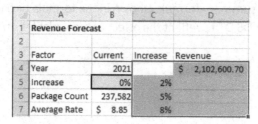

Identify the input and output cells for the data table

3. On the **Data** tab, in the **Forecast** group, select **What-If Analysis**, and then select **Data Table**.

4. In the **Data Table** dialog, do either of the following:

   - If the variables are in a row, enter the cell reference of the changing value in the **Row input cell** box.

   - If the variables are in a column, enter the cell reference of the changing value in the **Column input cell** box.

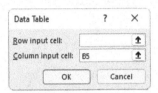

Identify the changing value

5. Select **OK**.

To create a two-variable data table

1. On a worksheet, enter the following information, and arrange it as shown and described above:

   - A summary formula

   - The input values for the summary formula

   - A column of alternative values for one input value

   - A row of alternative values for another input value

2. Select the cells representing the variables and the summary formula, and the cells in which the data table displaying the alternative formula results should appear.

3. On the **What-If Analysis** menu, select **Data Table**.

4. In the **Data Table** dialog, in the **Row input cell** box, enter the cell reference of the cell whose alternative values are in a row.

5. In the **Column input cell** box, enter the cell reference of the cell whose alternative values are in a column.

8

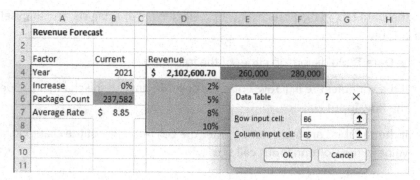

Identify both changing values

6. Select **OK**.

Identify the input necessary to achieve a specific result

When you run an organization, you must track how every element performs, both in absolute terms and in relation to other parts of the organization. There are many ways to measure your operations, but one useful technique is to limit the percentage of total costs contributed by a specific item.

As an example, consider a worksheet that displays the actual costs and percentage of total costs for several production input values.

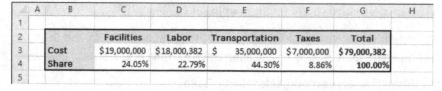

A worksheet that contains formulas that calculate the percentage of total costs for each of four categories

Under the current pricing structure, transportation represents 44.3 percent of the total cost of creating the product. If you want to get the transportation costs below 35 percent of the total, you can manually change the cost until you find the number you want. Alternatively, you can use Excel's Goal Seek feature to find the solution for you. You simply tell Goal Seek your target value for the cell and the value you want to change to get there.

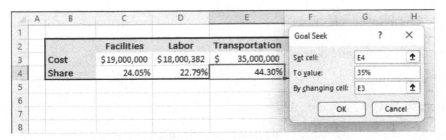

Identify the cell that contains the formula you want to use to generate a target value

Goal Seek finds the closest solution it can without exceeding the target you set and provides a suggested value. You can accept the suggestion to replace the original value or reject it to revert to the original value.

A worksheet in which Goal Seek found a solution to a problem

To find a target value by using Goal Seek

1. On the **Data** tab, in the **Forecast** group, select **What-If Analysis**, and then select **Goal Seek**.

2. In the **Goal Seek** dialog, in the **Set cell** box, enter the cell whose value you want to change.

3. In the **To value** box, enter the target value for the cell.

4. In the **By changing cell** box, enter the cell that contains the value you want to vary to produce the result you want.

5. Select **OK**.

> ⚠ **IMPORTANT** Saving a workbook with the results of a Goal Seek calculation in place overwrites the original workbook values. Consider running Goal Seek calculations on copies of the original data or reverting calculations immediately so you don't accidentally save or autosave them.

8

Skills review

In this chapter, you learned how to:

- Define and display alternative data sets
- Forecast data by using data tables
- Identify the input necessary to achieve a specific result

Practice tasks

Before you can complete these tasks, you must copy the book's practice files to your computer. The practice files for these tasks are in the **Excel365SBS\Ch08** folder. You can save the results of the tasks in the same folder.

Define and display alternative data sets

Open the **CreateScenarios** workbook in Excel, and then perform the following tasks:

1. Create a scenario named Overnight that changes the Base Rate value for Overnight and Priority Overnight packages (in cells C6 and C7) to $18.75 and $25.50.

2. Apply the Overnight scenario and note its effects on the data.

3. Press **Ctrl+Z** to revert to the original data.

4. Create a scenario named HighVolume that increases the number of Ground packages to 17,000,000 and 3-Day packages to 14,000,000.

5. Create a scenario named NewRates that increases the Ground rate to $9.45 and the 3-Day rate to $12.

6. Create a scenario summary worksheet that displays the effects of the three scenarios.

7. Apply the HighVolume scenario and note its effects on the data.

8. Apply the NewRates scenario and note the additional changes.

Forecast data by using data tables

Open the **DefineDataTables** workbook in Excel, and then perform the following tasks:

1. On the **RateIncreases** worksheet, select cells **C4:D7**.

2. Perform the steps to create a data table in cells D5:D7, entering B5 as the **Column input cell**. Review the resulting data.

3. On the **RateAndVolume** worksheet, select cells **D4:F8**.

4. Perform the steps to create a data table in cells E5:F8, entering B6 as the **Row input cell** and B5 as the **Column input cell**. Review the resulting data.

Identify the input necessary to achieve a specific result

Open the **PerformGoalSeekAnalysis** workbook in Excel, and then perform the following tasks:

1. Select cell **C4**.

2. Open the **Goal Seek** dialog.

3. Verify that **C4** appears in the **Set cell** box.

4. In the **To value** box, enter 20%.

5. In the **By changing cell** box, enter C3.

6. Select **OK**.

Create charts and graphics

When you enter data into an Excel worksheet, you create a record of important events, whether they are individual sales, sales for an hour of a day, the price of a product, or something else entirely. What a list of values in cells can't communicate easily, however, are the overall trends in the data. The best way to communicate trends in a large collection of data is by creating a chart, which summarizes data visually. In addition to standard charts, with Excel for Microsoft 365 you can create compact charts called *sparklines*, which summarize a data series by using a graph contained within a single cell.

You have a great deal of control over the appearance of your charts. You can change the color of any chart element, choose a different chart type to better summarize the underlying data, and change the display properties of text and numbers in a chart. If the data in the worksheet used to create a chart represents a progression through time, such as sales over several months, you can have Excel extrapolate future sales and add a trendline to the graph representing that prediction.

This chapter guides you through procedures related to creating many kinds of charts, customizing chart elements, identifying data trends, summarizing data by using sparklines, illustrating processes and relationship in SmartArt graphics, and inserting and managing shapes.

In this chapter

- Create standard charts
- Create combo charts
- Create specialized charts
- Customize chart appearance
- Identify data trends
- Summarize data by using sparklines
- Illustrate processes and relationships
- Insert and manage shapes

Create standard charts

You can create a chart from numeric data in a data range or table. Excel supports a wide variety of charts, with the most common being column charts, bar charts, line charts, and pie charts.

Choosing the correct chart for your data is important. When you start creating a chart, Excel evaluates the data and recommends the types of charts that would express it well. The Recommended Charts tab of the Insert Chart dialog shows you exactly how each of the recommended charts will display the data.

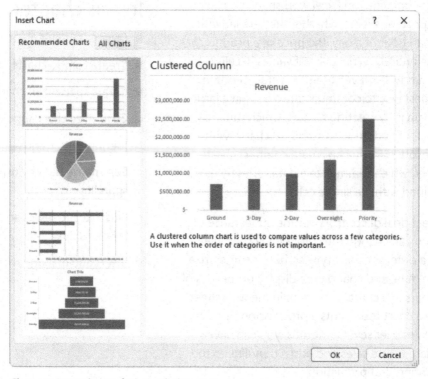

Chart recommendations for a simple data range

If the recommended charts aren't precisely what you want, you can preview your data presented in all the other chart types. Most chart types have multiple two- and three-dimensional layouts from which you can choose.

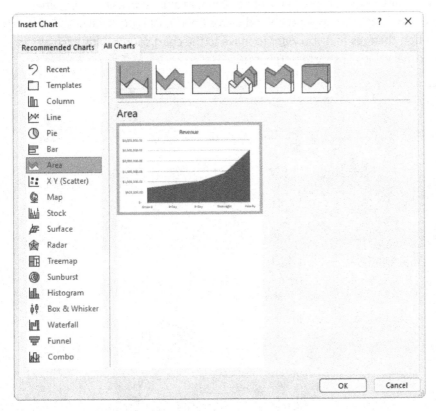

Preview thumbnails of all available charts

If you already know what type of chart you want to use, you can bypass the recommended charts and select your preferred chart type directly from the ribbon. For any chart type, you can preview your data in each of the available layouts before creating the chart. The ability to quickly preview data as it would appear in a chart simplifies the process of selecting the correct data and choosing a chart type. It can also bring to your attention changes that you want to make to the chart source data, such as removing decimal values or shortening names.

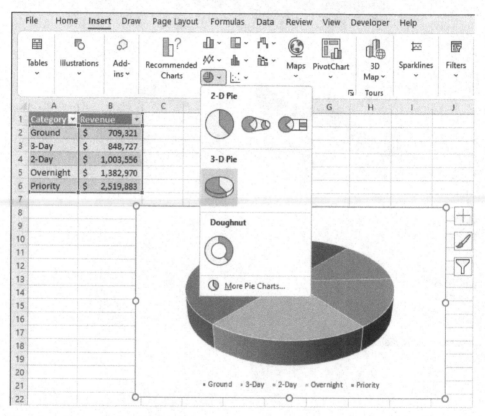

Most charts have multiple layouts

If Excel doesn't plot the data the way you want it to, you can change the axis on which Excel plots a data column. The most common reason for incorrect data plotting is that the column to be plotted on the horizontal axis contains numeric values instead of text. For example, if your data includes a *Year* column and a *Volume* column, instead of plotting volume data for each consecutive year along the horizontal axis, Excel plots both of those columns in the body of the chart and creates a sequential series to provide values for the horizontal axis.

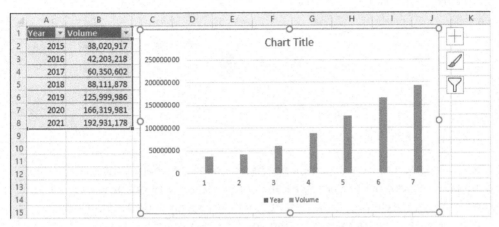

A chart with horizontal axis labels plotted as data

You can specify which data Excel should plot on the horizontal axis (the *x-axis*) and on the vertical axis (the *y-axis*). If Excel has swapped the axis values, you can simply switch the row and column data to update the chart. If the problem is a little more involved, you can help Excel to correctly interpret the source data.

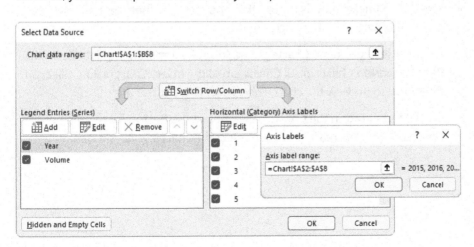

Change how Excel plots your data

After you identify the cell range that provides the values for the axis labels, Excel will revise your chart.

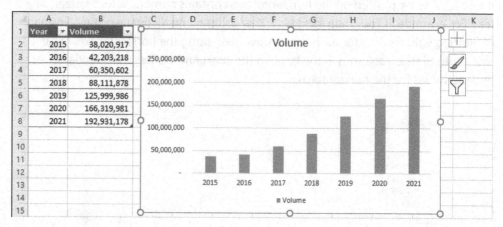

The replotted chart

After you create a chart, you can change its size to reflect whether the chart should dominate the worksheet or simply be an informative element on the worksheet. You can also move the chart to its own chart sheet. This is a particularly good idea for complex charts, because the chart is the only item on the sheet.

To create a chart

1. Select the data you want to chart.

2. Do one of the following:

   - Select the **Quick Analysis** button that appears, and then on the **Chart** tab, select the chart you want to create.

   - On the **Insert** tab, in the **Charts** group, select **Recommended Charts**. On the **Recommended Charts** or **All Charts** tab of the **Insert Chart** dialog, select any thumbnail to preview the chart. Then select **OK** to insert the chart.

   - On the **Insert** tab, in the **Charts** group, select the button for the type of chart you want to create, and then select the chart layout you want.

To create a chart of the default type

1. Select the data you want to chart.

2. Do either of the following:

   - Press **F11** to create the chart on a new chart sheet.

   - Press **Alt+F1** to create the chart on the active worksheet.

To switch row and column values

1. Select the chart you want to edit.

2. On the **Chart Design** tool tab, in the **Data** group, select the **Switch Row/ Column** button.

To change how Excel plots the data in a chart

1. Select the chart.

2. On the **Chart Design** tool tab, in the **Data** group, choose **Select Data**.

3. In the **Select Data Source** dialog, do any of the following:

   - Delete a **Legend Entries (Series)** data set by selecting the series and then selecting the **Remove** button.

   - Add a **Legend Entries (Series)** data set by selecting the **Add** button and, in the **Edit Series** dialog that appears, selecting the cells that contain the data you want to add, and then selecting **OK**.

   - Edit a **Legend Entries (Series)** data set by selecting the series you want to edit and then selecting the **Edit** button. In the **Edit Series** dialog, select the cells that provide values for the series, and then select **OK**.

   - Change the order of **Legend Entries (Series)** data sets by selecting the series you want to move and then selecting either the **Move Up** or **Move Down** button.

   - Switch the row and column data series by selecting the **Switch Row/ Column** button.

   - Change the values used to provide **Horizontal (Category) Axis Labels** by selecting that section's **Edit** button and then, in the **Axis Labels** dialog that appears, selecting the cells to provide the label values and then **OK**.

9

To resize a chart

- Select the chart, and then do one of the following:

    - Drag the sizing handles on the sides of the chart to change the height or width.

    - Drag the sizing handles on the corners of the chart to change the height and width at the same time.

    - Hold down the **Shift** key while dragging a sizing handle to maintain the aspect ratio of the chart while resizing it.

    - On the **Format** tool tab, in the **Size** group, enter or select values in the **Shape Height** and **Shape Width** boxes.

To move a chart within a worksheet

- Select the chart, and then drag it to the new location.

To move a chart to another sheet

1. Select the chart, and then do either of the following:

    - Right-click the chart, and then on the context menu, select **Move Chart**.

     TIP To display a context menu, right-click or long-press (tap and hold) the element.

    - On the **Chart Design** tool tab, in the **Location** group, select the **Move Chart** button.

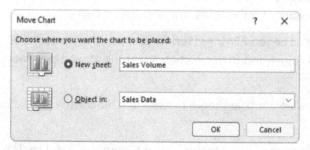

Moving a chart to its own sheet

2. In the **Move Chart** dialog, do either of the following:

   - To move the chart to an existing worksheet, select **Object in**, and then in the list, select the sheet to which you want to move the chart.

   - To move the chart to its own chart sheet, select **New sheet** and enter a name for the chart sheet.

3. In the **Move Chart** dialog, select **OK**.

Create combo charts

The Excel charting engine is powerful, but it does have its quirks. Some data collections you might want to summarize in Excel will have more than one value related to each category. For example, each regional center for a package-delivery company could have both overall package volume and revenue for the year. You can restructure the data in your Excel table to create a combo chart, which uses two vertical axes to show both value sets in the same chart.

9

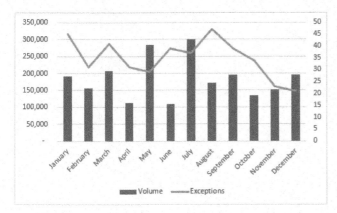

A combo chart with two vertical axes

 TIP A Pareto chart, discussed later in this chapter, is a type of dual-axis chart.

To create a dual-axis chart

1. Select the data you want to visualize.

2. On the **Insert** tab, in the **Charts** group, select the **Insert Combo Chart** button.

3. Do either of the following:

- Select the type of combo chart you want to create.

- Select **Create Custom Combo Chart** and use the settings in the **Combo** category of the **All Charts** tab to define your combo chart.

Create specialized charts

Excel for Microsoft 365 has four categories of charts for presenting business intelligence data for analysis: hierarchy charts, statistic charts, scatter charts, and stock charts.

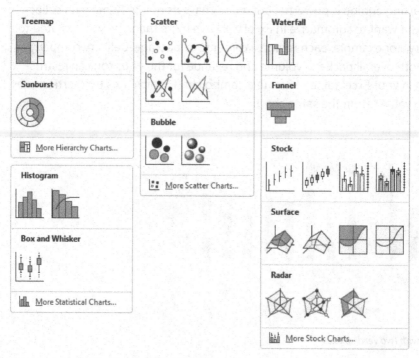

Present analytical data in specialized charts

These types of charts are generally used to represent financial and statistical data. Most people who use these charts on a regular basis have extensively studied the data types represented by the charts. This topic provides an overview of these charts and of the 2D Map chart in which you can present geographical statistics.

Hierarchy charts

This category includes treemap and sunburst charts.

Treemap charts divide data into categories, which are represented by colors, and represent the hierarchy of values within each category by the size of the rectangles in that category.

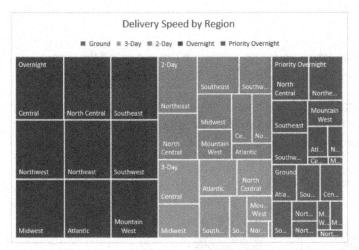

Treemap charts display contributions from elements of each data category

A sunburst chart breaks down a data set's hierarchy to an even deeper level, showing the details of how much each subcategory of data contributes to the whole.

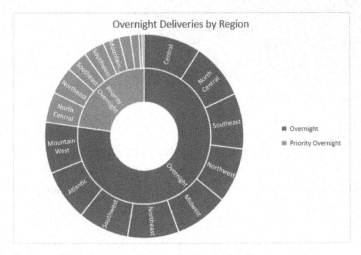

Sunburst charts show category contributions in detail

To create a hierarchy chart

1. Select the data you want to chart.

2. On the **Insert** tab, in the **Charts** group, select the **Insert Hierarchy Chart** button.

3. Point to the **Treemap** and **Sunburst** thumbnails to preview the data in each chart type, and then select the chart type you want to create.

Statistic charts

This category includes histogram charts and a variation thereof called the Pareto chart, and box-and-whisker charts.

Histograms count the number of occurrences of values within a set of ranges, where each range is called a *bin*. For example, a summary of daily package volumes for a delivery area could fall into several ranges.

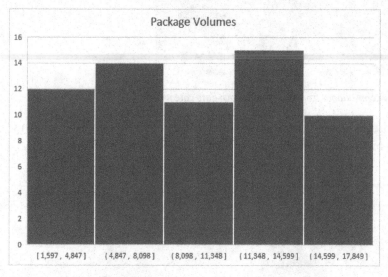

You can set the size of the bins to meet your needs

A Pareto chart combines a histogram and a line chart to show both the contributions of categories of values, such as package delivery options (for example, overnight, priority overnight, and ground) and the cumulative contributions after each category is counted.

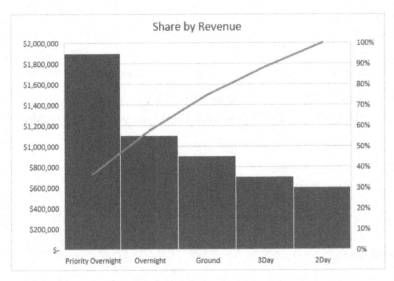

Pareto charts show category revenue and share of the total

A box-and-whisker chart combines several statistical measures, including the average (or mean), median, minimum, and maximum values for a data series, into a single chart. These charts provide a compact yet informative view of your data from a statistical standpoint.

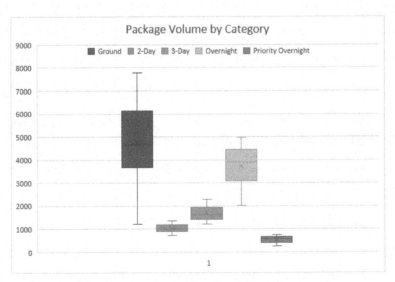

Box-and-whisker charts provide graphic statistical summaries

To create a statistical chart

1. Select the data you want to chart.

2. On the **Insert** tab, in the **Charts** group, select the **Insert Statistic Chart** button.

3. Point to the **Histogram**, **Pareto**, and **Box and Whisker** thumbnails to preview the data in each chart type, and then select the chart type you want to create.

Scatter charts

This category includes scatter charts and bubble charts.

Scatter charts compare and contrast two or more sets of values or pairs of data. Each data point represents an x,y value or a measurement. The chart shows the relationships between the value sets.

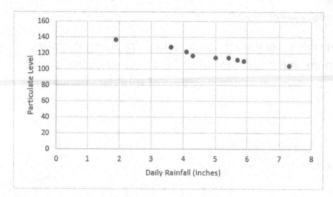

Scatter charts plot sets of values

Bubble charts compare and contrast three sets of values or pairs of data, in which one of the values can be used to determine the relative size of the bubble.

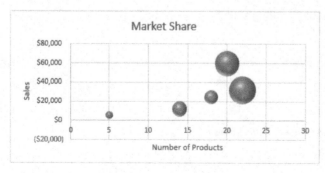

Bubble charts compare sets of values to a known whole

To create a scatter chart

1. Select the data you want to chart.

2. On the **Insert** tab, in the **Charts** group, select the **Insert Scatter Chart** button.

3. Point to each of the five scatter chart thumbnails and two bubble chart thumbnails to preview the data in each chart type, and then select the chart type you want to create.

Stock charts

This category includes waterfall and funnel charts, as well as stock, surface, and radar charts, which we don't cover in this book.

Waterfall charts summarize financial data by distinguishing increases from decreases and indicating whether a specific line item is an income or expense account, such as Sales Revenue, or a broader measure, such as Starting Balance or Ending Balance.

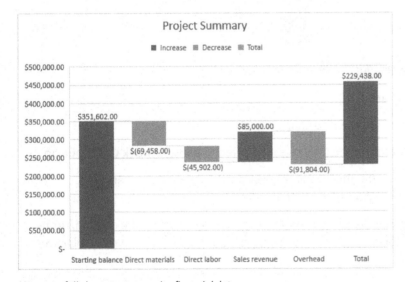

Use waterfall charts to summarize financial data

Excel doesn't automatically recognize which entries should be treated as totals, but you can identify any columns that represent totals (or subtotals) so Excel knows how to handle them.

A funnel chart shows how many items in a process continue to the next step. For example, a business might track sales leads, successful contacts, and customers who place an order. The top level of the funnel would depict the leads, the second the successful contacts, and the third customers who placed orders.

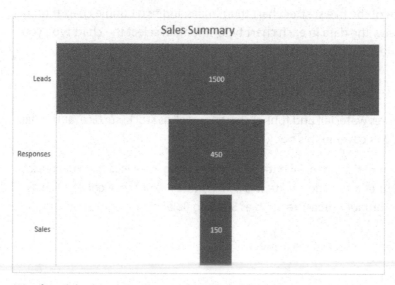

Use a funnel chart to summarize processes with declining values

To create a stock chart

1. Select the data you want to chart.

2. On the **Insert** tab, in the **Charts** group, select the **Insert Stock Chart** button.

3. Point to each of the thumbnails to preview the data in that chart type, and then select the chart type you want to create.

4. If necessary, identify a chart column as a total by selecting the column, right-clicking the selected column to display the context menu, and then selecting **Set as Total**.

Map charts

If you collect geographical data, such as customer locations, you can summarize that data on a map. You can mark states from which customers placed orders or use color or marker size to show the relative number or value of orders from those states. You can also use the Locations data type in Excel for Microsoft 365 to display statistical data about various regions.

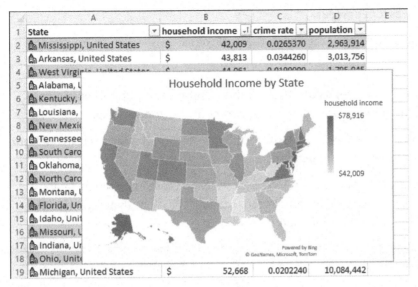

The table columns are:

	A	B	C	D	E
1	State	household income	crime rate	population	
2	Mississippi, United States	$ 42,009	0.0265370	2,963,914	
3	Arkansas, United States	$ 43,813	0.0344260	3,013,756	
4	West Virginia, United States	$ 44,061	0.0100000	1,705,045	
5	Alabama,				
6	Kentucky,				
7	Louisiana,				
8	New Mexico				
9	Tennessee				
10	South Carolina				
11	Oklahoma,				
12	North Carolina				
13	Montana,				
14	Florida, Un				
15	Idaho, Unit				
16	Missouri, U				
17	Indiana, Ur				
18	Ohio, Unite				
19	Michigan, United States	$ 52,668	0.0202240	10,084,442	

Chart geographic data on a 2D map

If you attempt to map data that does not include an identifiable geographic element, Excel displays an error message. For this reason, it's a good idea to tag the geographic elements as location data. When you enter a series of locations, Excel might prompt you to do so; if it doesn't, you can select the data type manually.

> **SEE ALSO** For information about creating a three-dimensional map chart of geographic statistics in Excel, see "Create 3D data maps" in Chapter 16, "Create forecasts and visualizations."

To create a 2D map chart

1. Select the data you want to chart.

2. On the **Insert** tab, in the **Charts** group, select the **Maps** button, and then select the **Filled Map** chart type.

3. When prompted, give Excel permission to upload your data to the internet to create the chart.

To tag an entry as location data

1. Enter the geographic locations on the worksheet.

2. Do either of the following:

   - If Excel recognizes a pattern (after three entries) and prompts you to convert the column to a location type, select the button to do so.

   - Select the cells that contain the locations. Then, on the **Data** tab, in the **Data Types** gallery, select **Locations**.

   Excel attempts to match the selected locations to those in its online database and displays an icon to the left of each location. Locations that have multiple matches display a question mark icon.

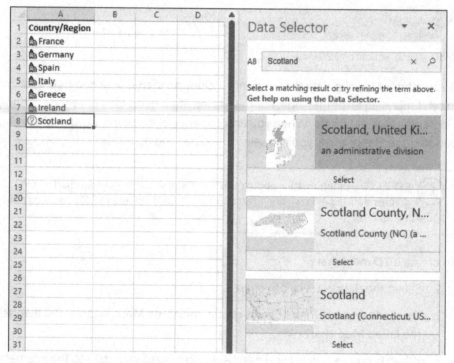

Resolving locations with multiple matches

3. For each unresolved location, do the following:

   a. Select the question mark icon to display the possible matches.

   b. In the **Data Selector** pane, select the intended location to display more information.

   c. To confirm the location and resolve it in the worksheet, choose **Select**.

To add location statistics to a table or data range

1. Do either of the following:

   • If the geographic locations are in a table, activate the table and then select the **Add Column** button that appears near the upper-right corner of the table.

   • If the geographic locations are in a data range, select one of the locations and then select the **Insert Data** button that appears near the upper-right corner of the cell.

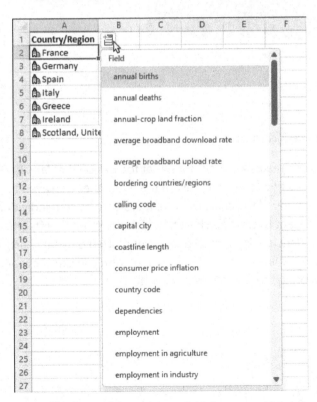

Some of the dozens of data points available for geographic locations

9

2. In the **Field** list that opens, select the data you want to insert on the worksheet.

    If you're working in a table, Excel inserts the column heading from the Field list and the corresponding data for all locations in the table.

Customize chart appearance

When you select a chart, three buttons appear near its upper-right corner: the Chart Elements, Chart Styles, and Chart Filter buttons.

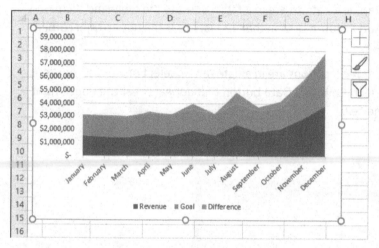

Quickly customize a chart by using the adjacent tools

When you create a chart, Excel creates a visualization that focuses on the data. In most cases, the chart includes a title, a legend (a list of the data series displayed in the chart), horizontal lines in the body of the chart to make it easier to discern individual values, and axis labels. If you want to create a chart that includes more or different elements, such as additional data labels for each data point plotted on your chart, you can do so by selecting a new layout. If it's still not quite right, you can show or hide individual elements by using the Chart Elements button.

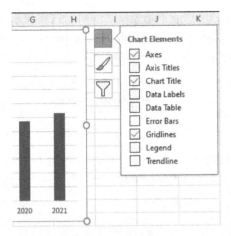

Display or hide elements in the active chart

After you select a chart element, you can change its size and appearance by using controls specifically created to work with that element type.

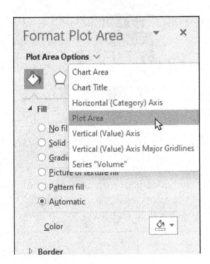

Format a chart element by using a pane designed for that element

If you want to change a chart's appearance, you can do so by using the Chart Styles button, which appears in a group of three buttons next to a selected chart. These buttons put chart formatting and data controls within easy reach.

9

Selecting the Chart Styles button opens a gallery that has two tabs: Style and Color. The Style tab contains 14 styles from which to choose, and the Color tab displays a series of color schemes you can select to change your chart's appearance.

 TIP If you prefer to work with commands on the ribbon, these same styles appear in the Chart Styles gallery on the Chart Design tab.

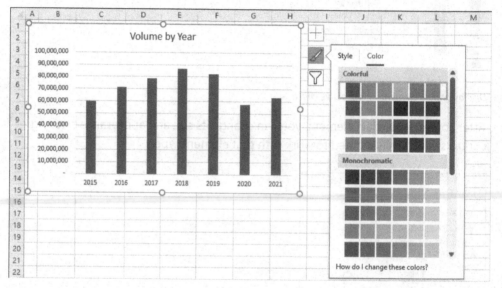

Select a color palette for your chart

 TIP The colors and styles in the Chart Styles gallery are tied to your workbook's theme. If you change your workbook's theme, Excel changes the colors available in the Chart Styles gallery, as well as your chart's appearance, to reflect the new theme's colors.

You can use the third button, Chart Filters, to focus on specific data in your chart. Selecting the Chart Filters button displays a filter interface that is very similar to that used to limit the data displayed in an Excel table.

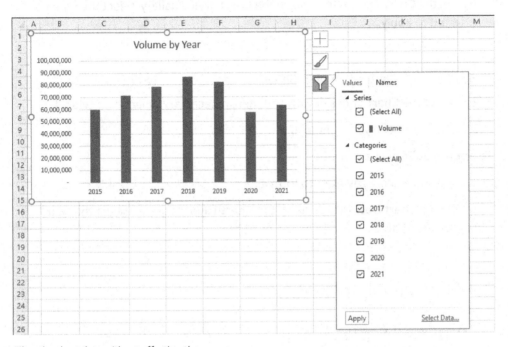

Filter the chart data without affecting the source

Selecting or clearing a checkbox displays or hides data related to a specific value within a series. You can also use the checkboxes in the Series section of the panel to display or hide entire data series.

If you think you'll want to apply the same set of changes to charts you create in the future, you can save your chart as a chart template. When you select the data you want to summarize visually and apply the chart template, you'll create consistently formatted charts in a minimum of steps.

To select a chart

- Click or tap near the chart border to select the chart and chart area.

- Display the Selection Pane, and then select the chart object.

To apply a built-in chart style

1. Select the chart you want to format.

2. On the **Chart Design** tool tab, in the **Chart Styles** gallery, select the style you want to apply.

Or

1. Select the chart you want to format.

2. Select the **Chart Styles** button and then, if necessary, select the **Style** tab.

3. Select the style you want to apply.

To apply a built-in chart layout

1. Select the chart you want to format.

2. On the **Chart Design** tool tab, in the **Chart Layouts** group, select the **Quick Layout** button.

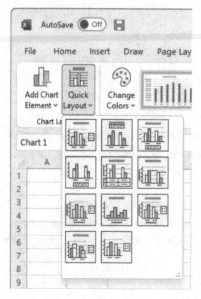

Select a new layout from the Quick Layout gallery

3. Select the layout you want to apply.

To change a chart's color scheme

1. Select the chart you want to format.

2. On the **Chart Design** tool tab, in the **Chart Styles** group, select **Change Colors**, and then select the color scheme you want to apply.

Or

1. Select the chart, and then select the adjacent **Chart Styles** button.

2. On the **Color** tab, point to any color scheme to preview its effect, and then select the color scheme you want to apply.

To select a chart element

■ Select the chart title, plot area, axis, series value, gridline, or other element.

Or

1. Select the chart.

2. On the **Format** tool tab, in the **Current Selection** group, select the **Chart Elements** arrow.

3. Select the desired chart element.

To format a chart element

1. Select the chart element, and then do either of the following:

    • Use the tools on the **Format** tool tab to change the element's formatting.

    • In the **Current Selection** group, select the **Format Selection** button to display the **Format *Chart Element*** pane.

2. Change the element's formatting.

To display or hide a chart element

■ Select the chart, and then do either of the following:

    • Select the **Chart Elements** button and select or clear the checkbox next to the element you want to show or hide.

    • On the **Chart Design** tool tab, in the **Chart Layouts** group, select the **Add Chart Element** button. Point to the element on the list and then select **None** to hide the element or one of the other options to show the element.

To create a chart filter

1. Select the chart, and then select the adjacent **Chart Filters** button.

2. On the **Values** tab, clear the checkboxes of series or categories you want to filter out.

To save a chart as a template

1. Right-click the chart, and then select **Save as Template**.

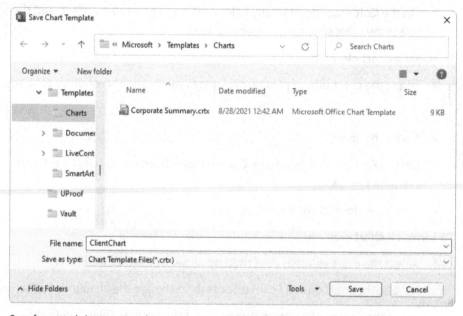

Save formatted charts as templates so you can quickly reproduce the formatting

2. In the **File name** box, enter a name for the template.

3. Select **Save**.

To apply a chart template

1. Select the chart to which you want to apply the template.

2. On the **Chart Design** tool tab, in the **Type** group, select **Change Chart Type**.

3. On the **All Charts** tab, select the **Templates** category.

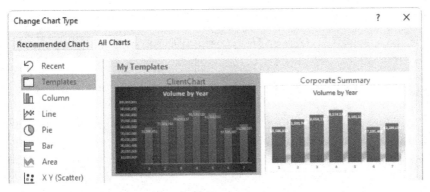

Apply a template to give charts a consistent appearance

4. Select the template you want to apply, and then select **OK**.

Identify data trends

You can use the data in Excel workbooks to discover how your business has performed in the past, but you can also have Excel estimate future performance based on the current trend. As an example, consider a line chart that shows the number of packages processed by our fictional shipping company from 2011 through 2021.

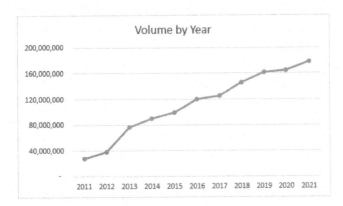

A line chart that shows data over time

The total has increased from 2011 to 2021, but the growth hasn't been uniform, so guessing how much package volume would increase if the overall trend continued would require detailed mathematical computations. Fortunately, Excel knows that math and can use it to add a trendline to your data.

9

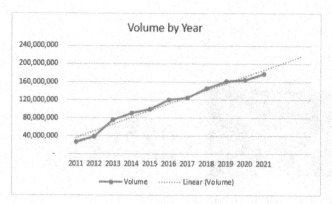

Create a trendline to forecast future data values

You can choose the data distribution that Excel should expect when it makes its projection. The right choice for most business data is Linear; other distributions (such as Exponential, Logarithmic, and Polynomial) are used for scientific and operations research applications. You can also tell how far ahead Excel should look. Looking ahead by zero periods shows the best-fit line for the current data set, whereas looking ahead two periods would project two periods into the future, assuming current trends continue.

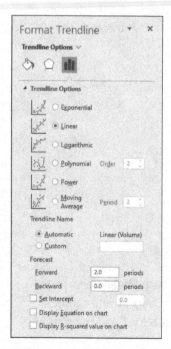

Change trendline characteristics by using the Format Trendline pane

As with other chart elements, you can double-click the trendline to open a formatting dialog and change the line's appearance.

To add a trendline to a chart

1. Select the chart to which you want to add a trendline.

2. On the **Chart Design** tool tab, in the **Chart Layouts** group, select the **Add Chart Element** button.

3. Point to **Trendline**, and then select the type of trendline you want to add.

To edit a trendline's properties and appearance

1. Select the chart that includes the trendline.

2. On the **Format** tool tab, in the **Current Selection** group, select the **Chart Elements** arrow.

3. Select the element that ends with the word *Trendline*.

4. Select **Format Selection**.

5. Use the controls in the **Format Trendline** pane to edit the trendline's properties and appearance.

To delete a trendline

- Select the trendline, and then press the **Delete** key.

9

Summarize data by using sparklines

You can create charts in Excel to summarize data visually in a separate window. Sparklines are miniature charts that fit within individual cells to provide a quick visual summary of data. Sparklines are commonly used to summarize the data in adjacent rows or columns, although you can reference data in any location, as you can with standard charts.

You can create three types of sparklines: line, column, and win/loss. The line and column sparklines are compact versions of the standard line and column charts. The win/loss sparkline indicates whether a cell value is positive (a win), negative (a loss), or zero (a tie).

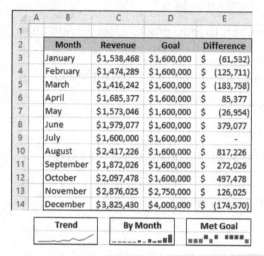

	A	B	C	D	E
1					
2		Month	Revenue	Goal	Difference
3		January	$1,538,468	$1,600,000	$ (61,532)
4		February	$1,474,289	$1,600,000	$ (125,711)
5		March	$1,416,242	$1,600,000	$ (183,758)
6		April	$1,685,377	$1,600,000	$ 85,377
7		May	$1,573,046	$1,600,000	$ (26,954)
8		June	$1,979,077	$1,600,000	$ 379,077
9		July	$1,600,000	$1,600,000	$ -
10		August	$2,417,226	$1,600,000	$ 817,226
11		September	$1,872,026	$1,600,000	$ 272,026
12		October	$2,097,478	$1,600,000	$ 497,478
13		November	$2,876,025	$2,750,000	$ 126,025
14		December	$3,825,430	$4,000,000	$ (174,570)

Trend	By Month	Met Goal

A data set summarized in different ways by line, column, and win/loss sparklines

> ✓ **TIP** Edward Tufte introduced sparklines in his book *Beautiful Evidence* (Graphics Press, 2006), with the goal of creating charts that imparted their information in approximately the same space as a word of printed text.

After you create a sparkline, you can change its appearance. Because a sparkline takes up the entire interior of a single cell, resizing the row or column that contains the cell resizes the sparkline. You can also change a sparkline's formatting, modify its labels, or delete it entirely.

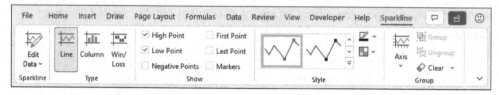

Modify and format sparklines from the Sparkline tool tab

> **TIP** Sparklines work best when displayed in compact form. If you find yourself adding markers and labels to a sparkline, you might consider using a regular chart to take advantage of its wider range of formatting and customization options.

To create a sparkline

1. Select the data you want to visualize.

2. On the **Insert** tab, in the **Sparklines** group, do one of the following:

   - Select the **Line** button.

   - Select the **Column** button.

   - Select the **Win/Loss** button.

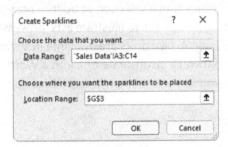

The data range and sparkline can be on different sheets

3. In the **Create Sparklines** dialog, verify that the data you selected appears in the **Data Range** box.

   If the wrong data appears, select the **Collapse Dialog** button next to the **Data Range** box, select the cells that contain your data, and then select the **Expand Dialog** button.

4. Do either of the following:

   - In the **Location Range** box, enter the cell in which you want to display the sparkline.

   - At the right end of the **Location Range** box, select the **Collapse Dialog** button. On the worksheet, select the cell in which you want to display the sparkline. Then in the dialog, select the **Expand Dialog** button.

5. In the **Create Sparklines** dialog, select **OK**.

9

To format a sparkline

1. Select the cell that contains the sparkline.

2. Use the tools on the **Sparkline** tool tab to format the sparkline.

To delete a sparkline

1. Select the cell that contains the sparkline.

2. On the **Sparkline** tool tab, in the **Group** group, select the **Clear** button.

Illustrate processes and relationships

Businesses define processes to manage product development, sales, and other essential functions. Excel for Microsoft 365 comes with a selection of built-in business diagrams, called SmartArt graphics, that you can use to illustrate lists, processes, cycles, hierarchies, and other relationships. SmartArt graphics are available in all the Microsoft 365 applications. It's more likely that you'll incorporate one into a Word document or PowerPoint presentation, but you can create them in any Office app and move them around as you like.

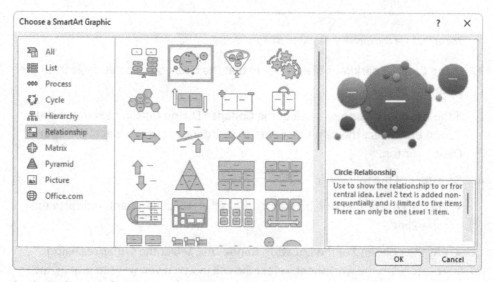

Previewing layouts before creating a SmartArt graphic

SmartArt graphics express the content of hierarchical bulleted lists as interrelated shapes. After creating a SmartArt graphic, you enter text either in list format within the Text pane or directly into the graphic shapes. Some shapes support only short text strings and others support more. The text size changes to accommodate the content. You can also format the shapes and text manually.

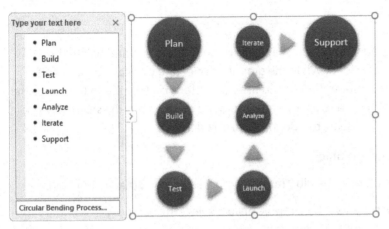

Illustrate relationships and processes by using SmartArt

SmartArt graphic layouts support from one to four hierarchical levels of information, so it's good to know the amount of content that you want to depict before creating the graphic. If necessary, you can change an existing SmartArt graphic to another layout in the same or a different category.

9

The following table describes the nine categories of SmartArt graphic layouts.

Diagram	Description
List	A series of items that typically require a large amount of text to explain
Process	A progression of sequential steps through a task, process, or workflow
Cycle	A process with a continuous cycle or relationships of core elements
Hierarchy	Hierarchical relationships, such as those within an organization chart
Relationship	Relationships between two or more items
Matrix	Relationship of components to a whole
Pyramid	Proportional, foundation-based, or hierarchical relationships such as a series of skills
Picture	Layouts that include one or more image placeholders and are also available within the other categories
Office.com	Layouts that are available to download from Office.com, which might change from time to time

> ✓ **TIP** Some types of SmartArt graphics can be used to illustrate several types of relationships. Examine all the options before you decide on the type of graphic to use to illustrate your point.

As with other drawing objects and shapes, you can move, copy, and delete the SmartArt graphic as needed. While the graphic is selected, you can add and edit text; add, edit, or reposition shapes; and use the buttons on the ribbon to change the shapes' formatting. To add text, you can either type directly into the shape or work in the Text pane, which appears beside the SmartArt diagram.

To create a SmartArt graphic

1. On the **Insert** tab, in the **Illustrations** group, select the **SmartArt** button.

2. In the **Choose a SmartArt Graphic** dialog, select the category from which you want to choose your graphic style.

3. Select any SmartArt layout to display information about it.

4. Select the SmartArt layout you want to create, and then select **OK**.

To select a SmartArt graphic

- Select near the edge of the SmartArt canvas.

To open and close the SmartArt Text pane

- Select the SmartArt graphic, and then do either of the following:

  - In the middle of the left side of the SmartArt canvas, select the **Text Pane** button.

  - On the **SmartArt Design** tool tab, in the **Create Graphic** group, select the **Text Pane** button.

To edit text in a SmartArt graphic

1. Select the SmartArt graphic.

2. Open the Text pane if necessary.

3. In the Text pane, do any of the following:

   - Edit the text in the bulleted list.

   - Press **Enter** at the end of a list item to create a new list item and shape.

- Press **Tab** at the beginning of a list item to indent the list item and demote the shape.

- Press **Shift+Tab** at the beginning of a list item to outdent the list item and promote the shape.

- Select multiple list items and press **Tab** or **Shift+Tab** to relevel them at the same time.

Or

1. On the SmartArt canvas, select the shape that contains the text you want to edit.

2. Edit the text, and then select away from the shape.

To add a shape to a SmartArt graphic

1. In the Text pane, position the insertion point at the end of the bulleted list item after which you want to insert a shape.

2. Press **Enter** to create a bulleted list item and shape at the same level as the original.

Or

1. On the SmartArt canvas, select the shape adjacent to which you want to insert the new shape.

2. On the **SmartArt Design** tool tab, in the **Create Graphic** group, select the **Add Shape** arrow (not the button), and then select **Add Shape After**, **Add Shape Before**, **Add Shape Above**, **Add Shape Below**, or **Add Assistant**.

> **TIP** Only the options that work with the current SmartArt graphic layout will be available.

To change the position of a shape within a SmartArt graphic

- In the Text pane, move the bulleted list item that corresponds to the shape.

Or

1. On the SmartArt canvas, select the shape you want to move.

2. On the **SmartArt Design** tool tab, in the **Create Graphic** group, select **Move Up** or **Move Down**.

9

To change the hierarchical level of a SmartArt graphic shape

1. In the Text pane, position the insertion point at the beginning of the bulleted list item corresponding to the shape.

2. Press **Tab** to demote the list item and shape or **Shift+Tab** to promote them.

Or

1. On the SmartArt canvas, select the shape whose level you want to change.

2. On the **SmartArt Design** tool tab, in the **Create Graphic** group, select **Promote** or **Demote**.

To remove a shape from a SmartArt graphic

- In the Text pane, delete the bulleted list item that corresponds to the shape.

- On the SmartArt canvas, select the shape, and then press the **Delete** key.

To change the layout of a SmartArt graphic

1. Select the SmartArt graphic.

2. On the **SmartArt Design** tool tab, in the **Layouts** group, select the **More** button to expand the **Layouts** gallery, which displays other layouts in the same category.

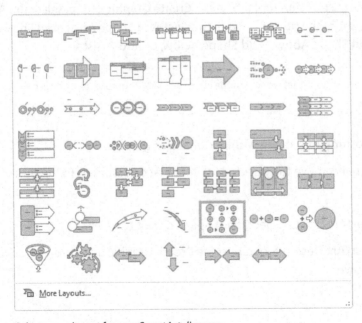

Select a new layout for your SmartArt diagram

3. Do either of the following:

- To use a layout from the same category, point to any layout in the gallery to preview the existing content in that layout. Then select the layout you want to use to apply it.

- To use a layout from another category, select **More Layouts** to open the Choose A SmartArt Graphic dialog. Select any layout in the dialog to display information about it, and then select **OK** to apply a layout.

 TIP If the original SmartArt graphic includes more levels of content than the new layout supports, the unsupported content is hidden.

To change the color scheme of a SmartArt graphic

1. Select the SmartArt graphic.

2. On the **SmartArt Design** tool tab, in the **SmartArt Styles** group, select the **Change Colors** button.

3. On the **Change Colors** menu, point to any color scheme to preview its effect on the SmartArt graphic.

4. Select a color scheme to apply it.

To apply a visual effect to a SmartArt graphic

1. Select the SmartArt graphic.

2. In the **SmartArt Styles** group, select the **More** button to expand the **SmartArt Styles** gallery.

3. Point to any style to preview its effect on the graphic.

4. Select the style you want to apply.

To format SmartArt graphic shape text

1. On the SmartArt canvas, select the shape that contains the text you want to format.

2. Use the tools on the Mini toolbar, in the **WordArt Styles** group on the **Format** tool tab, or in the **Font** group on the **Home** tab to format the text.

9

To format a SmartArt graphic shape

1. Select the shape you want to format.

2. Use the tools on the **Format** tool tab to change the shape's formatting.

To resize a SmartArt graphic or shape

- Select the SmartArt graphic or the individual shape, and then do either of the following:

  - Drag the sizing handles on the sides and corners.

  - On the **Format** tool tab, in the **Size** group, enter or select the **Height** and **Width**.

To delete a SmartArt graphic

- Select the graphic, and then press the **Delete** key.

- Right-click the graphic, and then select **Cut**.

Insert and manage shapes

With Excel, you can analyze your worksheet data in many ways, including summarizing your data and business processes visually by using charts and SmartArt. You can also augment your worksheets by adding objects such as geometric shapes, lines, flowchart symbols, and banners.

> **TIP** A SmartArt diagram is a collection of shapes that Excel treats as a collective unit. The shapes described in this topic are individual objects that Excel manages independently.

After you draw a shape on a worksheet, or select it after you've drawn it, you can use the controls on the Shape Format tool tab to change its appearance.

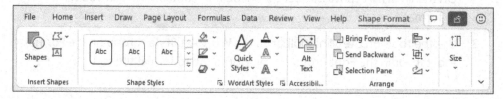

Shape and text formatting options on the Shape Format tool tab

TIP Holding down the Shift key while you draw a shape keeps the shape's height, width, and other characteristics equal. For example, selecting the Rectangle tool and then holding down the Shift key while you draw the shape causes you to draw a square.

After you create a shape, you can use the controls on the Shape Format tool tab to change its formatting. You can apply predefined styles or use the options accessible from the Shape Fill, Shape Outline, and Shape Effects buttons to change those aspects of the shape's appearance.

TIP When you point to a formatting option, such as a style or option displayed in the Shape Fill, Shape Outline, or Shape Effects lists, Excel displays a live preview of how your shape will appear if you apply that formatting option. You can preview as many options as you want before committing to a change.

If you want to use a shape as a label or header in a worksheet, you can add text to the shape's interior by selecting the shape and typing. If you want to edit a shape's text, point to the text. When the mouse pointer is in position, it will change from a white pointer with a four-pointed arrow to a black I-bar. You can then select the text to start editing it or change its formatting.

9

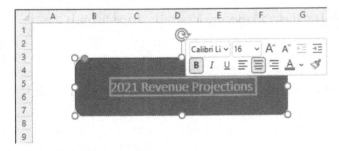

Add text to shapes to make labels stand out

You can move a shape within a worksheet by dragging it to a new position. If the worksheet contains multiple shapes, you can align and distribute them within the worksheet. Aligning shapes horizontally means arranging them so they are lined up by their top edge, bottom edge, or vertical center. Aligning them vertically means lining them up so that they have the same right edge, left edge, or horizontal center. Distributing shapes moves the shapes so they have a consistent horizontal or vertical distance between them.

When you insert multiple shapes on a worksheet, Excel arranges them in layers from front to back, placing newer shapes in front of older shapes. You can change the order of the shapes to create exactly the arrangement you want, whether by moving a shape one step forward or backward, or by moving it all the way to the front or back of the stack.

Layer shapes and icons to create custom labels

To insert a shape on a worksheet

1. On the **Insert** tab, in the **Illustrations** group, select the **Shapes** button.

2. On the **Shapes** menu, select the shape that you want to insert.

3. Do one of the following:

   - Click or tap anywhere on the worksheet to insert the shape there at the default size.

   - Drag on the worksheet to define the shape size and aspect ratio.

   - Hold down the **Shift** key while dragging to define a shape of equal height and width.

To move a shape

- Select the shape, and then drag it to its new location.

To resize a shape

- Select the shape, and then do one of the following:

   - Drag the sizing handles on the sides of the shape to change the height or width.

   - Drag the sizing handles on the corners of the shape to change the height and width at the same time.

- Hold down the **Shift** key while dragging a sizing handle to maintain the aspect ratio of the shape while resizing it.

- On the **Shape Format** tool tab, in the **Size** group, enter or select a value in the **Shape Height** and **Shape Width** boxes.

To rotate a shape

- Select the shape, and then do one of the following:

  - Drag the rotate handle (it looks like a clockwise-pointing circular arrow) above the shape to a new position.

  - On the **Shape Format** tool tab, in the **Arrange** group, select the **Rotate** button, and then select the rotate option you want.

  - On the **Shape Format** tool tab, in the **Arrange** group, select the **Rotate** button, and then select **More Rotation Options** to open the **Format Shape** pane in which you can precisely set the shape rotation.

To format a shape

- Select the shape, and then use the tools in the Shape Styles group on the **Shape Format** tool tab to change the fill and outline colors and to apply shadow, reflection, glow, soft edges, bevel, and 3-D rotation effects to the shape.

To add text to a shape

- Select the shape, and then type the text.

To edit shape text

- Point to the text in the shape. When the mouse pointer changes to a thin I-bar, click the text once.

To format shape text

1. Point to the text in the shape. When the mouse pointer changes to a thin I-bar, click the text once.

2. Select the text you want to format.

3. Use the tools on the Mini toolbar or on the **Home** tab to format the text.

To align shapes

1. Select the shapes you want to align.

2. On the **Shape Format** tool tab, in the **Arrange** group, select the **Align** button, and then select the alignment option that you want to apply.

9

To distribute shapes

1. Select three or more shapes.

2. On the **Shape Format** tool tab, in the **Arrange** group, select the **Align** button, and then do either of the following:

   - Select **Distribute Horizontally** to place the shapes on the worksheet with evenly spaced horizontal gaps between them.

   - Select **Distribute Vertically** to place the shapes on the worksheet with evenly spaced vertical gaps between them.

Insert mathematical equations

Excel and Microsoft 365 apps have a special toolset with which you can form complex mathematical equations. You can choose from a list of common equations, such as the Pythagorean theorem, or form equations by using built-in structures and symbols. You can enter an equation by typing or selecting buttons on a toolbar; Excel can also interpret handwritten equations.

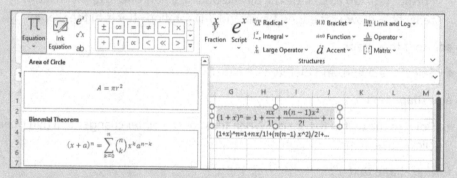

Building equations in Excel

When you create an equation in Excel, the equation is inserted into a text box that floats on the worksheet. You can copy the equation from the text box into a worksheet cell; when you do so, Excel converts the notation appropriately.

To begin entering an equation, display the Insert tab and then, in the Symbols group, select Equation.

To reorder shapes

1. Select the shape you want to move.

2. On the **Shape Format** tool tab, in the **Arrange** group, do either of the following:

   - Select the **Bring Forward** arrow, and then select **Bring Forward** or **Bring to Front**.

   - Select the **Send Backward** arrow, and then select **Send Backward** or **Send to Back**.

To delete a shape

- Select the shape, and then press **Delete**.

Skills review

In this chapter, you learned how to:

- Create standard charts
- Create combo charts
- Create specialized charts
- Customize chart appearance
- Identify data trends
- Summarize data by using sparklines
- Illustrate processes and relationships
- Insert and manage shapes

9

Practice tasks

Before you can complete these tasks, you must copy the book's practice files to your computer. The practice files for these tasks are in the **Excel365SBS\Ch09** folder. You can save the results of the tasks in the same folder.

Create standard charts

Open the **CreateCharts** workbook in Excel, and then perform the following tasks:

1. Using the values on the **Data** worksheet, create a column chart.

2. Change the column chart so it uses the Year values in cells A3:A9 as the horizontal (category) axis values, and the Volume values in cells B3:B9 as the vertical axis values.

3. Using the same set of values, create a line chart.

4. Using the Quick Analysis toolbar, create a pie chart from the same data.

Create combo charts

Open the **CreateComboCharts** workbook in Excel, and then perform the following tasks:

1. On the **Summary** worksheet, create a dual-axis chart that displays the Volume series as a column chart and the Exceptions series as a line chart.

2. Ensure that the Exceptions values are plotted on the minor vertical axis at the right edge of the chart.

Create specialized charts

Open the **CreateSpecialCharts** workbook in Excel, and then perform the following tasks:

1. Use the data on the **Funnel** worksheet to create a funnel chart.

2. Use the data on the **Mapping** worksheet to create a 2D map by state.

3. Use the data on the **Waterfall** worksheet to create a waterfall chart. Identify the **Starting Balance** and **Total** values as totals.

4. Use the data on the **Histogram** worksheet to create a histogram.

5. Use the data on the **Pareto** worksheet to create a Pareto chart.

6. Use the data on the **BoxAndWhisker** worksheet to create a box-and-whisker chart.

7. Use the data on the **Treemap** worksheet to create a treemap chart.

8. Use the data on the **Sunburst** worksheet to create a sunburst chart.

Customize chart appearance

Open the **CustomizeCharts** workbook in Excel, and then perform the following tasks:

1. On the **Presentation** worksheet, change the color scheme of the chart.

2. Change the same chart's layout.

3. On the **Yearly Summary** worksheet, change the chart's type to a line chart.

4. Move the chart from the **Yearly Summary** worksheet to a new chart sheet.

Identify data trends

Open the **IdentifyTrends** workbook in Excel, and then perform the following tasks:

1. On the **Data** worksheet, add a linear trendline to the chart that draws the best-fit line through the existing data.

2. Edit the trendline so it shows a forecast two periods into the future.

3. Delete the trendline.

Summarize data by using sparklines

Open the **CreateSparklines** workbook in Excel, and then perform the following tasks:

1. Using the data in cells C3:C14, create a line sparkline in cell G3.

2. Using the data in cells C3:C14, create a column sparkline in cell H3.

3. Using the data in cells E3:E14, create a win/loss sparkline in cell I3.

4. Change the color scheme of the win/loss sparkline.

5. Delete the sparkline from cell H3.

Illustrate processes and relationships

Open the **InsertSmartArt** workbook in Excel, and then perform the following tasks:

1. Create a SmartArt graphic that illustrates a process you perform on a regular basis.

2. Enter the steps into the shapes from the Text pane.

3. Add a shape to the process.

4. Change the place where one of the shapes appears in the diagram.

5. Change the diagram's color scheme.

6. Delete a shape from the diagram.

Insert and manage shapes

Open the **InsertShapes** workbook in Excel, and then perform the following tasks:

1. Create three shapes and add text to each of them.

2. Edit and format the text in one of the shapes.

3. Move the shapes so you can determine which is in front, which is in the middle, and which is in back.

4. Change the shapes' order and observe how it changes the appearance of the worksheet.

5. Align the shapes so their middles are on the same line.

6. Distribute the shapes evenly in the horizontal direction.

7. Delete one of the shapes.

Create PivotTables and PivotCharts

When you create Excel worksheets, you must consider how you want the data to appear when you show it to your colleagues. You can change the formatting of the data to emphasize the content of specific cells, sort and filter data based on the contents of specific columns, or hide rows containing data that isn't relevant to the point you're trying to make.

A limitation of the standard Excel worksheet is that you can't easily change how the data is organized on the page. Fortunately, there is an Excel tool with which you can easily display, sort, filter, and rearrange the aspects of the data that you want to focus on. That tool is the PivotTable.

This chapter guides you through procedures related to creating and managing PivotTables, filtering and slicing PivotTable data, formatting PivotTables, and presenting PivotTable data visually in PivotCharts.

In this chapter

- Analyze data dynamically in PivotTables
- Filter, show, and hide PivotTable data
- Edit PivotTables
- Format PivotTables
- Create dynamic PivotCharts

Analyze data dynamically in PivotTables

In Excel worksheets, you can gather and present important data, but the standard worksheet can't be easily changed from its original configuration. As an example, consider a worksheet that records monthly package volumes for each of nine distribution centers in the United States. The data in the worksheet is organized so that each row represents a distribution center, and each column represents a month of the year.

	A	B	C	D	E	F
1		January	February	March	April	May
2	Atlantic	6,042,842	3,098,663	3,210,406	3,002,529	3,368,888
3	Central	6,006,191	2,932,222	3,167,785	2,989,245	3,576,763
4	Midwest	5,720,977	3,456,904	3,046,753	3,125,231	3,280,768
5	Mountain West	5,872,046	2,935,951	3,265,252	3,071,049	3,159,233
6	North Central	6,236,863	3,785,068	2,929,397	2,677,853	3,079,267
7	Northeast	6,370,982	3,281,469	3,725,669	3,148,289	3,165,070
8	Northwest	6,108,382	4,216,668	3,640,750	2,997,048	3,236,144
9	Southeast	6,396,724	4,877,758	4,387,252	3,583,479	3,513,158
10	Southwest	5,949,454	4,413,610	3,226,583	3,006,170	3,019,311
11	Grand Total	54,704,461	32,998,313	30,599,847	27,600,893	29,398,602

Static tables summarize one aspect of the data

Such a neutral presentation of your data is useful but has limitations. First, although you can use sorting and filtering to restrict the rows or columns shown, it's difficult to change the worksheet's organization. For example, in this worksheet, you can't easily reorganize its contents so that the months are assigned to the rows and the distribution centers are assigned to the columns.

To reorganize and redisplay your data dynamically, you can create a PivotTable. In Excel, you can quickly create PivotTables from the Recommended PivotTables dialog.

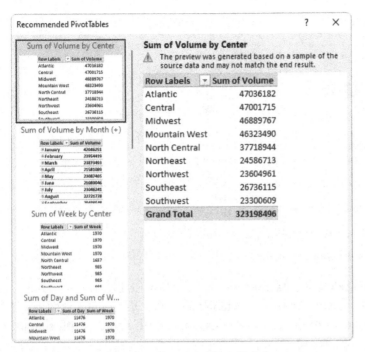

Excel analyzes your data and recommends PivotTable layouts

Pointing to a recommended PivotTable shows a preview of what that PivotTable would look like if you selected that option, so you can view several possibilities before deciding which one to create.

10

 TIP If Excel for Microsoft 365 shows no recommended PivotTables for your data, it gives you the option to create a blank PivotTable.

If none of the recommended PivotTables meet your needs, you can create a PivotTable by adding individual fields. For example, you can create a PivotTable with the same layout as the worksheet described previously, which emphasizes totals by month, and then change the PivotTable layout to have the rows represent the months of the year and the columns represent the distribution centers. The new layout emphasizes the totals by regional distribution center.

	A	B	C	D	E	F
1						
2						
3	Sum of Volume	Column Labels ▼				
4	Row Labels ▼	Atlantic	Central	Midwest	Mountain West	North Central
5	January	6042842	6006191	5720977	5872046	6236863
6	February	3098663	2932222	3456904	2935951	3785068
7	March	3210406	3167785	3046753	3265252	2929397
8	April	3002529	2989245	3125231	3071049	2677853
9	May	3368888	3576763	3280768	3159233	3079267
10	June	3208696	2973980	3035619	3063572	3040683
11	July	3115294	3364482	2945492	3456576	3521947
12	August	3237645	3191591	3441757	3371850	3166710
13	September	3072723	2807222	3166599	2942925	2996901
14	October	3261585	3362250	3333751	3182437	3125591
15	November	6137174	6083306	6236356	6121929	6026826
16	December	6279737	6546678	6099560	5880670	6093514
17	Grand Total	47036182	47001715	46889767	46323490	46680620

Reorganize your PivotTable by changing the order of fields

To create a PivotTable quickly, the data must be collected in a list. Excel tables mesh perfectly with PivotTable dynamic views. Excel tables include a well-defined column and row structure, and the ability to refer to an Excel table by its name greatly simplifies PivotTable creation and management.

In an Excel table used to create a PivotTable, each row of the table should contain a value representing the attribute described by each column. Columns could include data on distribution centers, years, months, days, weekdays, and package volumes, for example. Excel needs that data when it creates the PivotTable so that it can maintain relationships among the data.

> ⚠️ **IMPORTANT** It's OK if some cells in the source data list or Excel table are blank, but the source must not contain any blank rows. If Excel encounters a blank row while creating a PivotTable, it stops looking for additional data.

	A	B	C	D	E	F	G	H	I
1									
2		Center ▼	Date ▼	Year ▼	Month ▼	Week ▼	Day ▼	Weekday ▼	Volume ▼
3		Atlantic	1/1/2020	2020	January	1	1	Wednesday	120933
4		Atlantic	1/2/2020	2020	January	1	2	Thursday	52979
5		Atlantic	1/3/2020	2020	January	1	3	Friday	45683
6		Atlantic	1/4/2020	2020	January	1	4	Saturday	53152
7		Atlantic	1/5/2020	2020	January	1	5	Sunday	149776
8		Atlantic	1/6/2020	2020	January	1	6	Monday	108772
9		Atlantic	1/7/2020	2020	January	1	7	Tuesday	99919
10		Atlantic	1/8/2020	2020	January	2	8	Wednesday	138271

Use an Excel table or data range to create a PivotTable

After you organize the data you want to summarize, you can start creating the PivotTable. In most cases, the best choice is to place your new PivotTable on its own worksheet to avoid cluttering the display. If you do want to place it on an existing worksheet, perhaps as part of a summary worksheet with multiple visualizations, you can do so.

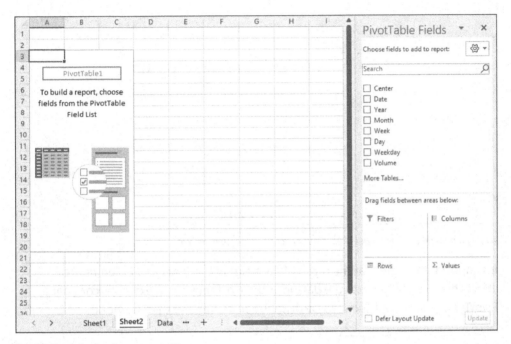

Specify the data structure you want to see

PivotTables include four areas where you can place fields: Rows, Columns, Values, and Filters. To define the PivotTable's data structure, drag field names from the PivotTable field list to any of those four areas at the bottom of the PivotTable Fields pane.

10

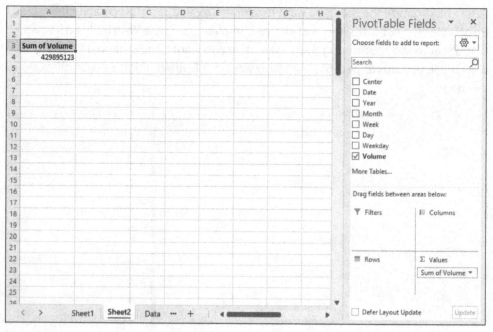

Adding a data field to the Values area summarizes all values in that field

It's important to note that the order of the fields in the Rows and Columns areas affects how Excel organizes the data in your PivotTable. As an example, consider a PivotTable that groups the rows by distribution center and then by month.

	A	B
3	**Row Labels** ▼	**Sum of Volume**
4	⊟ **Atlantic**	**47036182**
5	January	6042842
6	February	3098663
7	March	3210406
8	April	3002529
9	May	3368888
10	June	3208696
11	July	3115294
12	August	3237645
13	September	3072723
14	October	3261585
15	November	6137174
16	December	6279737
17	⊟ **Central**	**47001715**
18	January	6006191
19	February	2932222
20	March	3167785

A PivotTable with data arranged by distribution center and then by month

The same PivotTable data could also be organized by month and then by distribution center. In other words, you could *pivot* the data to display different information.

	A	B
3	Row Labels	Sum of Volume
4	⊟ January	54704461
5	Atlantic	6042842
6	Central	6006191
7	Midwest	5720977
8	Mountain West	5872046
9	North Central	6236863
10	Northeast	6370982
11	Northwest	6108382
12	Southeast	6396724
13	Southwest	5949454
14	⊟ February	32998313
15	Atlantic	3098663
16	Central	2932222
17	Midwest	3456904

A PivotTable with package volume data arranged by month and then by distribution center

In the preceding examples, all the field headers are in the Rows area. If you move the Center header from the Rows area to the Columns area in the PivotTable Fields pane, the PivotTable reorganizes (pivots) its data to form a different configuration.

10

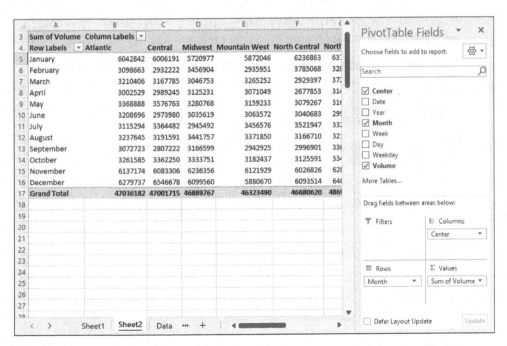

A PivotTable arranged in cross-tabular format

If your data set is large or if you based your PivotTable on a data collection on another computer, it might take some time for Excel to reorganize the PivotTable after a pivot. You can have Excel delay redrawing the PivotTable until you're ready for Excel to display the reorganized contents.

If you expect the PivotTable source data to change, such as when you link to an external database, you should ensure that your PivotTable summarizes all the available data. To do that, you can refresh the connection between the PivotTable and its data source to have Excel update the PivotTable contents with any new or changed data.

To organize data for use in a PivotTable

- Do either of the following:

  - Create an Excel table.

  - Create a data range that contains no blank rows or columns and has no adjacent data.

To create a recommended PivotTable

1. Select a cell in the Excel table or data range you want to summarize.

2. On the **Insert** tab, in the **Tables** group, select **Recommended PivotTables**.

3. In the **Recommended PivotTables** dialog, review the data structures of the recommended PivotTables, and then select the one you want to create.

4. Select **OK** to create the recommended PivotTable on a new worksheet.

To create a PivotTable

1. Select a cell in the Excel table or data range you want to summarize.

2. On the **Insert** tab, in the **Tables** group, select the **PivotTable** button (not the arrow) to open the PivotTable From Table Or Range dialog.

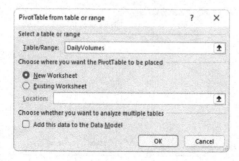

Verify the data source and target location of your PivotTable

3. In the **Table/Range** box, verify that Excel has correctly identified the data source you want to use.

4. In the **Choose where you want the PivotTable to be placed** section, do either of the following:

   - To create the PivotTable on its own worksheet, select **New Worksheet**.

   - To add the PivotTable to the same worksheet as the data, select **Existing Worksheet**, and then in the **Location** box enter or select the cell in which you want to place the upper-left corner of the PivotTable.

5. Select **OK** to create the PivotTable.

To activate a PivotTable for editing

- Select any cell in the body of the PivotTable.

To display or hide the PivotTable Fields pane

1. Select a cell in the body of the PivotTable.

2. On the **PivotTable Analyze** tool tab, in the **Show** group, select the **Field List** button.

 TIP You can close the PivotTable Fields pane by selecting the Close button in the upper-right corner of the pane.

10

To add fields to a PivotTable

1. Activate the PivotTable and display the **PivotTable Fields** pane.

2. In the pane, drag a field header from the field list to the **Filters**, **Columns**, **Rows**, or **Values** quadrant at the bottom of the pane.

To remove a field from a PivotTable

- In the **PivotTable Fields** pane, drag a field header from the **Filters**, **Columns**, **Rows**, or **Values** area to the field list.

To pivot a PivotTable

- In the **PivotTable Fields** pane, drag a field header from the **Filter**, **Columns**, **Rows**, or **Values** area to another area.

To defer PivotTable updates

1. In the **PivotTable Fields** pane, select the **Defer Layout Update** checkbox.

Defer PivotTable updates that might take a while to execute

2. When you want to update the PivotTable, select **Update**.

3. To turn automatic updating back on, clear the **Defer Layout Update** checkbox.

Filter, show, and hide PivotTable data

PivotTables often summarize huge data sets in a relatively small worksheet. The more details you can capture and write to a table, the more flexibility you have in analyzing the data. As an example, consider a table in which each row contains a value representing the distribution center, date, year, month, week, day, weekday, and volume for every day of the year. You could filter this data to display only values for Mondays.

	Center	Date	Year	Month	Week	Day	Weekday	Volume
8	Atlantic	1/6/2020	2020	January	1	6	Monday	108772
15	Atlantic	1/13/2020	2020	January	2	13	Monday	146927
22	Atlantic	1/20/2020	2020	January	3	20	Monday	86771
29	Atlantic	1/27/2020	2020	January	4	27	Monday	110649
36	Atlantic	2/3/2020	2020	February	1	3	Monday	87675
43	Atlantic	2/10/2020	2020	February	2	10	Monday	63424
50	Atlantic	2/17/2020	2020	February	3	17	Monday	63439
57	Atlantic	2/24/2020	2020	February	4	24	Monday	60790

Filter Excel tables to focus on relevant data

Each column, in turn, contains numerous values: There are nine distribution centers, data from two years, 12 months in a year, seven weekdays, and as many as five weeks and 31 days in a month. Just as you can filter the data that appears in an Excel table or other data collection, you can filter the data displayed in a PivotTable by selecting which values you want the PivotTable to include.

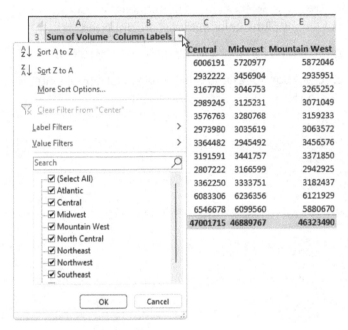

Filter a PivotTable by selecting a filter arrow

 SEE ALSO For more information about filtering an Excel table, see "Filter data ranges and tables" in Chapter 5, "Manage worksheet data."

Selecting the column header in the PivotTable displays several sorting options, commands for various categories of filters, and a list of items that appear in the field you want to filter. Every list item includes a checkbox next to it. Items with selected checkboxes are currently displayed in the PivotTable, and items with cleared checkboxes are hidden.

The first entry at the top of the item list is the Select All checkbox. The Select All checkbox can have one of three states:

- **Checked** If the Select All checkbox displays a check mark, the PivotTable displays every item in the list.

- **Displaying a black square** If the Select All checkbox contains a black square, it means that some, but not all, of the items in the list are displayed.

- **Cleared** If the Select All checkbox is empty, no filter items are selected.

Selecting only the Northwest checkbox, for example, leads to a PivotTable configuration in which only the data for the Northwest center is displayed.

	A	B	C
3	Sum of Volume	Column Labels 🔽	
4	Row Labels 🔽	Northwest	Grand Total
5	⊟ 2020	23604961	23604961
6	January	3023030	3023030
7	February	1662538	1662538
8	March	1708446	1708446
9	April	1648903	1648903
10	May	1607655	1607655
11	June	1373976	1373976
12	July	1570950	1570950
13	August	1767367	1767367
14	September	1582032	1582032
15	October	1744048	1744048
16	November	2982666	2982666
17	December	2933350	2933350
18	⊟ 2021	25028389	25028389
19	January	3085352	3085352
20	February	2554130	2554130
21	March	1932304	1932304

Limit data by using selection filters

If you'd rather display PivotTable data on the entire worksheet, you can hide the PivotTable Fields pane and filter the PivotTable by using the filter arrows on the Row Labels and Column Labels headers within the body of the PivotTable. Excel indicates that a PivotTable has filters applied by placing a filter indicator next to the Column Labels or Row Labels header, as appropriate, and next to the filtered field name in the PivotTable Fields pane.

So far, all the fields by which we've talked about filtering the PivotTable will change the organization of the data in the PivotTable. Adding some fields to a PivotTable, however, might create unwanted complexity. For example, you might want to filter a PivotTable by month, but adding the Month field to the body of the PivotTable expands the table unnecessarily.

	A	B	C	D	E	F	G
3	Sum of Volume	Column Labels					
4	Row Labels	January	February	March	April	May	June
5	⊟2020	27109328	15143659	15795737	14061629	15172813	13386192
6	Atlantic	3076578	1556937	1522379	1557093	1838569	1482926
7	Central	2863187	1524882	1573351	1441040	1763017	1542462
8	Midwest	2946100	1410456	1445833	1729429	1751682	1577610
9	Mountain West	2929502	1383853	1624226	1417220	1642780	1511853
10	North Central	3126629	1521920	1376048	1201665	1554219	1504845
11	Northeast	3297909	1473017	2020459	1632875	1684026	1432470
12	Northwest	3023030	1662538	1708446	1648903	1607655	1373976
13	Southeast	2926429	2888829	2945358	1952239	1763780	1587372
14	Southwest	2919964	1721227	1579637	1481165	1567085	1372678
15	⊟2021	27595133	17854654	14804110	13539264	14225789	13587254
16	Atlantic	2966264	1541726	1688027	1445436	1530319	1725770
17	Central	3143004	1407340	1594434	1548205	1813746	1431518
18	Midwest	2774877	2046448	1600920	1395802	1529086	1458009

Adding multiple fields to an area substantially expands PivotTables

Instead of adding the Month field to the Rows or Columns area, adding the field to the Filters area leaves the body of the PivotTable unchanged, but adds a new filter control above the PivotTable in its worksheet. When you select the filter arrow of a field in the Filters area, Excel displays a list of the values in the field. You can choose to filter based on one or more values.

10

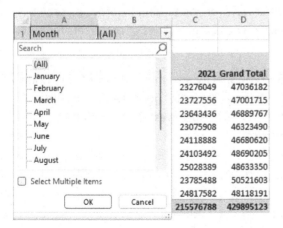

Add a field to the Filter area to filter a PivotTable without changing its organization

If your PivotTable has more than one field in the Rows area of the PivotTable Fields pane, you can filter values in a PivotTable by hiding and collapsing levels of detail within the report. To do that, you select the Hide Detail control (which looks like a box with a minus sign in it) or the Show Detail control (which looks like a box with a plus sign in it) next to a header.

	A	B
3	**Row Labels** ▾	**Sum of Volume**
4	⊞ 2020	214318335
5	⊟ 2021	215576788
6	Atlantic	23276049
7	Central	23727556
8	Midwest	23643436
9	Mountain West	23075908
10	North Central	24118888
11	Northeast	24103492
12	Northwest	25028389
13	Southeast	23785488
14	Southwest	24817582
15	**Grand Total**	429895123

Summarize levels of data by using the Show Detail and Hide Detail controls

> ✅ **TIP** If a PivotTable area, such as Rows or Columns, contains more than one field, you can select the field by which to filter by selecting the Select Field arrow and then selecting the field you want.

Excel for Microsoft 365 provides two other ways for you to filter PivotTables: search filters and slicers. By using a search filter, you can enter a series of characters for Excel to use to filter that field's values.

Search filters look for the character string you specify anywhere within a field's value, not only at the start of the value. When filtering the Center field, the search string "no" filters the list to *North Central*, *Northeast*, and *Northwest*. The search string "cen" would return both *Central* and *North Central*.

Filter a PivotTable field by using a search filter

When filtering by using the Sort & Filter button, the only visual indicator that a field is filtered is the changed icon on the field's filter button. The icon indicates that the field has an active filter but provides no information about which values are displayed and which are hidden. An alternative when filtering PivotTables is to use *slicers*. Slicers provide a visual interface from which users can filter tables and quickly see what filters are applied. Slicers display the results of all filters, whether they were applied by using the slicer or by using the standard field filter.

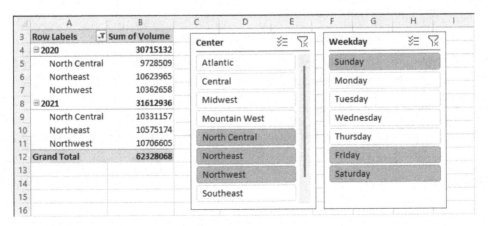

Slicers provide an attractive visual filter interface

10

A slicer displays the values within the PivotTable field you identified. Any value displayed in color (or gray if you use a gray-and-white color scheme) is active in the PivotTable. Values displayed in light gray or white are hidden.

Selecting a field value in a slicer alternately removes or includes it in the visible data. As with other objects in an Excel workbook, you can use the Shift key to select multiple contiguous slicer elements and the Ctrl key to select multiple noncontiguous slicer elements. You can also turn on multiselect by selecting the Multi-Select button, which looks like a three-item checklist, on the slicer title bar. When multi-select is on, Excel adds each item that you select to the slicer instead of replacing the original selection.

As with other drawing objects in Excel, you can move and resize slicers. When you're done filtering values, you can clear the slicer filter or delete it entirely.

To filter a PivotTable by a field value

1. In the body of a PivotTable, select the filter arrow at the right edge of a field header.

2. Use the controls in the filter list to create your filter.

3. Select **OK**.

Or

1. Display the **PivotTable Fields** pane.

2. Drag a field to the **Filters** area.

3. In the **Filter** area of the PivotTable, select the field's filter arrow.

4. Do either of the following:

   • Select the value by which you want to filter.

   • Select the **Select Multiple Items** checkbox and select the checkboxes next to the items you want to appear in the PivotTable.

To hide or show a level of detail in a PivotTable

■ Select the **Hide Detail** or **Show Detail** control next to the PivotTable field's row header.

To add a slicer to a PivotTable

1. Activate the PivotTable.

2. On the **PivotTable Analyze** tool tab, in the **Filter** group, select the **Insert Slicer** button.

3. In the **Insert Slicers** dialog, select the checkbox next to each field for which you want to create a slicer.

You can display slicers for any fields in the source data

4. Select **OK**.

To select multiple values in a slicer filter

1. On the slicer title bar, select the **Multi-Select** button.

2. Select each value that you want to appear in the PivotTable.

To filter a field by using a slicer

- In the body of the slicer, do any of the following:

  - Select any one value that you want to display.

  - Hold down the **Ctrl** key and select each value that you want to display.

  - Select one value, hold down the **Shift** key, and then select a second value to display the two values and all values between them.

To clear the filter in a slicer

- On the slicer title bar, select the **Clear Filter** button.

10

To change the appearance of a slicer

- Select the slicer and then, on the **Slicer** tool tab, select a style in the **Slicer Styles** gallery.

Or

1. Right-click the slicer's title bar and then on the context menu, select **Size and Properties**.

> **TIP** To display a context menu, right-click or long-press (tap and hold) the element.

2. Use the settings in the **Format Slicer** pane to change the slicer's appearance.

3. Select the pane's **Close** button to close it and apply the changes.

To remove a slicer from a PivotTable

- Right-click the slicer and then select **Remove** *field*.

Edit PivotTables

When you create a PivotTable, Excel assigns it a name, such as *PivotTable1*. The default name doesn't help you or your colleagues understand the data the PivotTable contains, particularly if you use the PivotTable data in a formula on another worksheet. You can provide more information about your PivotTable and the data it contains by changing its name to something more descriptive.

When you create a PivotTable with at least one field in the Rows area and one field in the Columns area of the PivotTable Fields pane, Excel adds a grand total row and column to summarize your data. You can control which totals and subtotals appear, and where they appear, to best suit your data and analysis goals.

After you create a PivotTable, Excel determines the best way to summarize the data in the column you assign to the Values area. For numeric data, for example, Excel uses the SUM function, but you can change the function used to summarize your data.

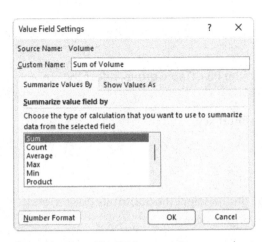

Control how your PivotTable summarizes your values

You can also change how the PivotTable displays the data in the Values area. Some of these methods include displaying each value as a percentage of the grand total, row total, or column total, or as a running total.

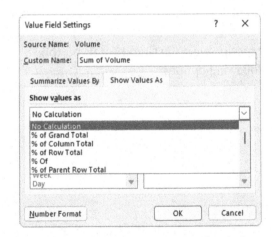

You can change how Excel summarizes values in the body of a PivotTable

If you want, you can create a formula that incorporates a value from a PivotTable cell. When you get to a point in your formula where you want to use PivotTable data, select the cell that contains the value you want to include in the formula. When you do, a GETPIVOTDATA formula appears in the formula bar of the worksheet that contains the PivotTable. When you press the Enter key, Excel creates the GETPIVOTDATA formula and displays the contents of the PivotTable cell in the target cell.

10

To rename a PivotTable

1. Activate the PivotTable.

2. On the **PivotTable Analyze** tool tab, in the **PivotTable** group, select the current name in the **PivotTable Name** box.

3. Replace the name, and then press the **Enter** key.

To show or hide PivotTable subtotals

1. Activate the PivotTable.

2. On the **Design** tool tab, in the **Layout** group, select the **Subtotals** button, and then in the list, select one of the following options:

   - **Do Not Show Subtotals**

   - **Show all Subtotals at Bottom of Group**

   - **Show all Subtotals at Top of Group**

To show or hide PivotTable grand totals

1. Activate the PivotTable.

2. On the **Design** tool tab, in the **Layout** group, select the **Grand Totals** button, and then in the list, select one of the following options:

   - **Off for Rows and Columns**

   - **On for Rows and Columns**

   - **On for Rows Only**

   - **On for Columns Only**

To open the Value Field Settings dialog

- Select any data cell in the PivotTable, and then do either of the following:

   - On the **PivotTable Analyze** tool tab, in the **Active Field** group, select **Field Settings**.

   - In the **PivotTable Fields** pane, in the **Values** quadrant, select the arrow at the right end of the summary field, and then select **Value Field Settings**.

To change the summary operation for the Values area

1. Open the **Value Field Settings** dialog.

2. On the **Summarize Values By** tab, in the **Summarize value field by** list, select the calculation you want to use to summarize the PivotTable data.

3. Select **OK**.

To change how Excel displays data in the Values area

1. Open the **Value Field Settings** dialog.

2. On the **Show Values As** tab, in the **Shows values as** list, select the calculation you want to use.

3. If the **Base field** and **Base item** lists activate, select the values on which you want to base the calculation.

4. Select **OK**.

To use PivotTable data in a formula

1. Start entering a formula in a cell.

2. When you reach the point in your formula where you want to use data from a PivotTable cell, select the PivotTable cell that contains the data you want to use.

3. Complete the formula and press **Enter**.

10

Format PivotTables

PivotTables are the ideal tools for summarizing and examining data in very large data tables. Although PivotTables often end up as compact summaries, you should do everything you can to make your data more comprehensible. One way to improve the data's readability is to apply a number format to the PivotTable Values field.

 SEE ALSO For more information about selecting and defining cell formats in the Format Cells dialog, see "Format cells" in Chapter 4, "Change workbook appearance."

Analysts often use PivotTables to summarize and examine organizational data for the purpose of making important decisions about the company. Excel extends the capabilities of your PivotTables by enabling you to apply a conditional format to the PivotTable cells. Additionally, you can choose whether to apply the conditional format to every cell in the Values area, to every cell at the same level as the selected cell (that is, a regular data cell, a subtotal cell, or a grand total cell), or to every cell that contains or draws its values from the selected cell's field.

	A	B
3	**Row Labels** ▼	**Sum of Volume**
4	⊟ 2020	
5	Atlantic	23,760,133
6	Central	23,274,159
7	Midwest	13,291,030
8	Mountain West	10,026,974
9	North Central	22,561,732
10	Northeast	24,586,713
11	Northwest	23,604,961
12	Southeast	26,736,115
13	Southwest	23,300,609
14	⊟ 2021	
15	Atlantic	23,276,049
16	Central	21,332,335
17	Midwest	18,889,907

Summarize values visually by adding a conditional format

Excel offers three options for applying a conditional format to a PivotTable:

- **Selected cells** Applies the conditional format to the selected cells only

- **All cells showing "Value Field" values** Applies the conditional format to every cell in the body of the PivotTable that contains data, regardless of whether the cell is in the data area, a subtotal row or column, or a grand total row or column

- **All cells showing "Value Field" values for "Row Field"** Applies the conditional format to every cell at the same level (for example, data cell, subtotal, or grand total) as the selected cells

 SEE ALSO For more information about creating conditional formats, see "Change the appearance of data based on its value" in Chapter 4, "Change workbook appearance."

You can take full advantage of Excel's enhanced formatting capabilities to apply existing formats to your PivotTables. Just as you can create Excel table formats, you can also create your own PivotTable formats to match your organization's preferred color scheme. After you give the new style a name, you can format each element of PivotTables to which you apply the style.

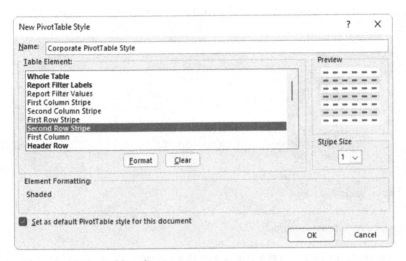

Define custom PivotTable styles

 SEE ALSO For more information about creating custom table styles, see "Apply and modify table styles" in Chapter 4, "Change workbook appearance."

The Design tool tab contains many other tools you can use to format your PivotTable, but one of the most useful is the Banded Columns checkbox. If you select a PivotTable style that offers banded rows as an option, selecting the Banded Rows checkbox turns on banding. If you prefer not to have Excel band the rows in your PivotTable, clearing the checkbox turns off banding.

To apply a number format to PivotTable data

1. Open the **Value Field Settings** dialog.

2. In the lower-left corner of the dialog, select **Number Format**.

3. On the **Number** tab of the **Format Cells** dialog, select or define a number format for the value field.

4. Select **OK** to close the Format Cells dialog, and then select **OK** to close the Value Field Settings dialog and apply the number format.

To apply a conditional format to a PivotTable

1. Activate the PivotTable.

2. On the **Home** tab, in the **Styles** group, select the **Conditional Formatting** button, and define the conditional format you want to apply.

3. Select the **Formatting Options** button that appears to the right of the active cell.

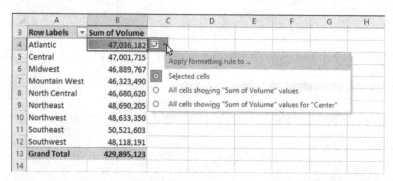

Options for applying conditional formatting

4. In the **Apply formatting rule to** list, do one of the following:

   - Select **Selected cells** to apply the conditional format only to the cell you selected before creating the format.

   - Select **All cells showing "Sum of *field*" values** to format all data cells, including subtotals and grand totals.

   - Select **All cells showing "Sum of *field*" values for "*Field1*"** to format all data cells that are not subtotals or grand totals.

To apply an existing PivotTable style

1. Activate the PivotTable.

2. On the **Design** tool tab, in the **PivotTable Styles** group, select the style you want to apply.

To create a new PivotTable style

1. Activate the PivotTable.

2. On the **Design** tool tab, in the **PivotTable Styles** group, select the **More** button to expand the **PivotTable Styles** gallery.

3. At the bottom of the menu, below the gallery, select **New PivotTable Style**.

4. In the **New PivotTable Style** dialog, in the **Name** box, enter a name for the style.

5. For each table element that you want to define, do the following:

   a. In the **Table Element** list, select the element.

   b. Select the **Format** button.

   c. In the **Format Cells** dialog, define the font, border, and fill settings for the element, and then select **OK**.

6. If you want to apply the new style to all PivotTables in the current workbook, select the **Set as default PivotTable style for this document** checkbox.

7. In the **New PivotTable Style** dialog, select **OK** to close the dialog and apply the style.

To apply banded rows to a PivotTable

1. Apply a PivotTable Style that includes a first- or second-row stripe.

2. On the **Design** tool tab, in the **PivotTable Style Options** group, select the **Banded Rows** checkbox.

Create dynamic PivotCharts

Just as you can create a PivotTable that you can reorganize whenever you want to emphasize different aspects of the data in a list, you can also create a dynamic chart, or PivotChart, to reflect the contents and organization of a PivotTable.

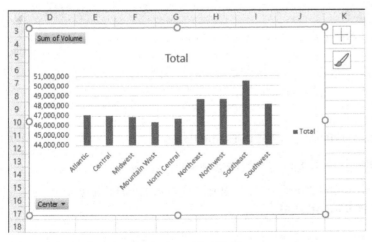

Summarize your data visually by using a PivotChart

Any changes to the PivotTable on which the PivotChart is based are reflected in the PivotChart. For example, applying a PivotTable filter that limits the data displayed to values for the year 2020 focuses the chart on that data.

You can also filter a PivotChart by using tools available in the body of the PivotChart or change the PivotChart's chart type to represent your data differently.

You can create a PivotTable and its associated PivotChart at the same time, or you can create a PivotChart from an existing PivotTable. If you create the PivotTable and PivotChart at the same time, blank outlines for each appear in your worksheet.

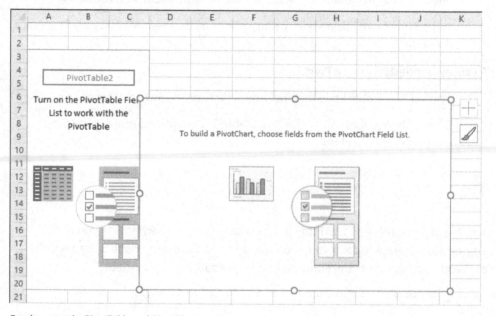

Excel creates the PivotTable and PivotChart on the same sheet

> **IMPORTANT** If your data is of the wrong type to be represented by the chart type you select, Excel displays an error message.

To create a PivotTable and PivotChart at the same time

1. Select a cell in the Excel table or data range you want to summarize.

2. On the **Insert** tab, in the **Charts** group, select the **PivotChart** arrow, and then select **PivotChart & PivotTable**.

3. In the **Create PivotTable** dialog, in the **Table/Range** box, verify that Excel has correctly identified the data source you want to use.

Select the data and location for the PivotTable and associated PivotChart

4. In the **Choose where you want the PivotTable report to be placed** section, do either of the following:

   - To create the PivotTable and PivotChart on their own worksheet, select **New Worksheet**.

   - To add the PivotTable and PivotChart to the same worksheet as the data, select **Existing Worksheet**, and then in the **Location** box, enter or select the cell in which you want to place the upper-left corner of the PivotTable.

5. Select **OK** to create the PivotTable and PivotChart.

To create a PivotChart from an existing PivotTable

1. Activate the PivotTable, and then do either of the following to open the Insert Chart dialog:

   - On the **Insert** tab, in the **Charts** group, select the **PivotChart** button.

   - On the **PivotTable Analyze** tab, in the **Tools** group, select the **PivotChart** button.

2. On the **All Charts** tab, select any thumbnail to preview the chart as it will appear. Then select **OK** to insert the chart.

10

3. Select the chart layout you want to use, and then select **OK** to create the PivotChart.

 TIP Excel doesn't recommend PivotChart layouts in the same way that it recommends standard chart layouts.

To change the chart type of a PivotChart

1. Activate the PivotChart.

2. On the **Design** tool tab, in the **Type** group, select **Change Chart Type**.

3. In the **Change Chart Type** dialog, select the category of chart you want to create.

4. If necessary, select the subtype of chart you want to create.

5. Select **OK**.

To change the data shown in a PivotChart

- In the lower-left corner of the chart canvas, select the category by which you want to filter the chart, and then select or clear values.

Skills review

In this chapter, you learned how to:

- Analyze data dynamically in PivotTables
- Filter, show, and hide PivotTable data
- Edit PivotTables
- Format PivotTables
- Create dynamic PivotCharts

Practice tasks

Before you can complete these tasks, you must copy the book's practice files to your computer. The practice files for these tasks are in the **Excel365SBS\Ch10** folder. You can save the results of the tasks in the same folder.

Analyze data dynamically in PivotTables

Open the **CreatePivotTables** workbook in Excel, and then perform the following tasks:

1. Select a cell in the Excel table on **Sheet1** and create a PivotTable based on that data.

2. In the **PivotTable Fields** pane, add the **Year** field to the **Columns** area, the **Center** field to the **Rows** area, and the **Volume** field to the **Values** area.

3. Pivot the PivotTable so the **Year** field is above the **Center** field in the **Rows** area.

Filter, show, and hide PivotTable data

Open the **FilterPivotTables** workbook in Excel, and then perform the following tasks:

1. Using the **Month** field, create a selection filter that displays data for **January**, **April**, and **July**.

2. Remove the filter.

3. Add the **Weekday** field to the **Filters** area and limit the data shown to **Tuesday**.

4. Change the **Weekday** field's filter to include multiple values, and then set it to display values for **Tuesday** and **Wednesday**.

5. Create a slicer for the **Month** field, and then display values for the month of **December**.

6. Change the slicer filter to allow multiple selections, and then display values for **January** and **December**.

7. Clear the slicer filter, and then delete the slicer.

Edit PivotTables

Open the **EditPivotTables** workbook in Excel, and then perform the following tasks:

1. On the **PivotTable** worksheet, change the name of the PivotTable to PackageVolume.

2. Change the PivotTable's subtotals so they appear at the bottom of each group.

3. Change the summary function for the body of the PivotTable from **Sum** to **Average**.

4. In cell **E3**, create a formula that displays the data from cell B5 (the **Sum of Volume** value for the Atlantic center).

Format PivotTables

Open the **FormatPivotTables** workbook in Excel, and then perform the following tasks:

1. Change the format of the **Volume** field, currently providing data for the **Values** area, so that the numbers are displayed in the **Comma** number format with no digits after the decimal point.

2. Select any cell in the data area of the PivotTable, and then create a conditional format that changes the fill color of cells that contain a value that is above average for the field.

3. Apply a different PivotTable style to the PivotTable.

4. Create a new PivotTable style and apply it.

Create dynamic PivotCharts

Open the **CreatePivotCharts** workbook in Excel, and then perform the following tasks:

1. On the **Data** sheet, create a clustered column PivotChart from the data in the table, with the **Center** field in the **Legend (Series)** area and **Volume** (which will be displayed as *Sum of Volume*) in the **Values** area.

2. Remove the **Center** field from the body of the PivotTable, and then drag the **Year** field to the **Axis (Category)** area.

3. Change the chart type of the PivotChart to a line chart.

4. Add the **Center** field to the **Legend (Series)** area.

Part 3

Collaborate and share in Excel

Print worksheets and charts

Excel for Microsoft 365 gives you a wide range of tools with which to create and manipulate your data. By using filters, by sorting, and by creating PivotTables and charts, you can change your worksheets so that they convey the greatest possible amount of information.

After you configure your worksheet so that it shows your data to its best advantage, you can print your Excel documents for use in a presentation or a report. You can choose to print all or part of any of your worksheets, change how your data and charts appear on the printed page, and even hide any error messages that might appear in your worksheets.

This chapter guides you through procedures related to adding headers and footers to your worksheets, preparing your worksheets for printing, printing all or part of a worksheet, and printing charts.

In this chapter

- Add headers and footers to printed pages
- Prepare worksheets for printing
- Print worksheets
- Print parts of worksheets
- Print charts

Add headers and footers to printed pages

If you want to display information in the top or bottom margin of printed pages, you can do so by using headers or footers. The header appears at the top of the printed page; the footer appears at the bottom of the printed page. Business documents commonly display information such as the file name, page number, author, or date in the header or footer to identify the printed document and its source.

| | | Orders | | | Page 1 |
Order ID	Employee	Customer	Order Date	Shipped Date	Ship Via
30	Anne Hellung-Larsen	Company AA	1/15/2021	1/22/2021	Shipping Company B
31	Jan Kotas	Company D	1/20/2021	1/22/2021	Shipping Company A
32	Mariya Sergienko	Company L	1/22/2021	1/22/2021	Shipping Company B
33	Michael Neipper	Company H	1/30/2021	1/31/2021	Shipping Company C
34	Anne Hellung-Larsen	Company D	2/6/2021	2/7/2021	Shipping Company C
35	Jan Kotas	Company CC	2/10/2021	2/12/2021	Shipping Company B

Headers and footers provide space to add information about your workbook

Worksheet page headers and footers are visible in Page Layout view. Page Layout view shows you exactly how a workbook will look when printed, while still enabling you to edit the file. (Another way to see exactly how a workbook will look when printed is to display it in Print Preview. However, Print Preview mode does not allow you to edit the file.)

> **SEE ALSO** For information about Print Preview, see "Prepare worksheets for printing" later in this chapter.

Excel divides the page headers and footers into left, middle, and right sections. When you point to an editable header or footer section, Excel highlights the section to indicate that selecting it will open that header or footer section for editing.

> **TIP** If a chart is selected when you select the Header & Footer button on the Insert tab, Excel displays the Header/Footer page of the Page Setup dialog instead of opening a header or footer section for editing.

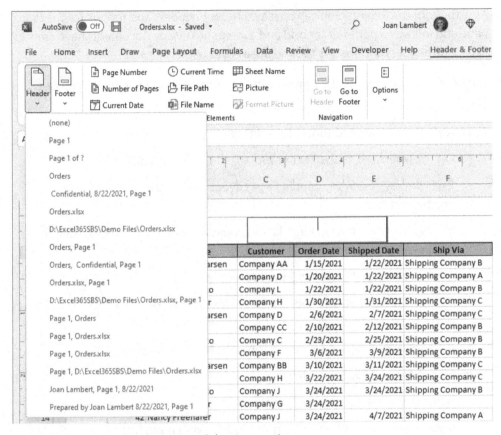

Excel generates headers based on your worksheet's properties

Excel makes it easy to insert standard information—such as the file name, sheet name, page number, author, or date—into the page header or footer. You can choose from suggestions that are based on the actual worksheet data and properties. If these aren't what you want, you can insert text or an image of your choosing. For example, you might insert your company logo in the header of each worksheet for consistency with other corporate documents that you intend to distribute in a printed report.

After inserting an image in a header or footer, you can change its size and apply color effects to it, such as grayscale and washout. This is the method for creating image-based page backgrounds or custom watermarks. (A watermark is a logo, image, or text on the page background, behind the document content.)

As with Word documents, you can display different headers and footers for the first page and following pages or for odd and even pages. Many documents have empty first-page headers and footers to simulate a cover page.

The header and footer are the same width as the printed worksheet, but you can adjust their heights.

To activate the header and footer for editing

- On the **Insert** tab, in the **Text** group, select **Header & Footer**.

  Excel displays the worksheet in Page Layout view and activates the center header section.

- Display the worksheet in **Page Layout** view, and then select the header or footer cell you want to edit.

To switch between the header and the footer

- On the **Header & Footer** tool tab, in the **Navigation** group, select **Go to Footer** or **Go to Header**.

- In **Page Layout** view, scroll to the top or bottom of the page.

To insert header and footer content

1. Activate the header or footer cell you want to edit.

2. If you want to insert text, use any of the following methods:

   - Type or paste text into the section.

   - Select preconfigured text sets from the **Header** or **Footer** menu on the **Header & Footer** tool tab.

   - Insert file properties from the **Header & Footer Elements** group.

> ⚠ **IMPORTANT** The text options on the Header and Footer menus specify entries for the left, middle, and right sections of the header or footer, and replace any content that is already there.

3. If you want to insert an image, on the **Header & Footer** tool tab, in the **Header & Footer Elements** group, select **Picture**.

   From the Insert Pictures dialog that opens, you can insert a picture from a file or from your connected OneDrive folder, or search for an image by using Bing Search.

To edit an image in a header or footer

1. Activate the header or footer section that contains the **&[Picture]** code.

2. On the **Header & Footer** tool tab, in the **Header & Footer Elements** group, select **Format Picture** to open the **Format Picture** dialog.

3. On the **Size** tab, adjust the size either to fit into the header/footer area or to flow into the page area as a background image.

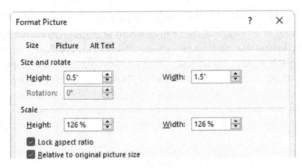

Size the image to fit the space

4. On the **Picture** tab, crop the inserted image so that only a portion of it is visible, and modify the color, brightness, and contrast of the image.

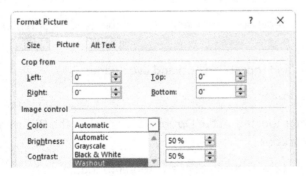

When using a picture as a background image, select the Washout option to mute its colors so the worksheet content is readable

11

5. On the **Alt Text** tab, provide a meaningful description of the image in case the image fails to render when a user displays it online or a person is using a screen reader to navigate the worksheet content.

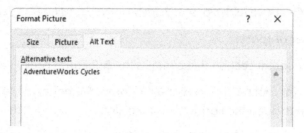

Provide alternative text descriptions for all images

> ✓ **TIP** The picture formatting options for header and footer images do not yet support the marking of an image as decorative, which tells screen readers to skip over it. For a background image that doesn't provide information, you can use the alt text "Decorative background image." For an image that provides a watermark, use the watermark text, such as "Draft document watermark" or "This document is marked as a draft."

6. Select **OK**.

To display a different header on the first printed page

1. Activate the header or footer.

2. On the **Header & Footer** tool tab, in the **Options** group, select the **Different First Page** checkbox.

3. Display the first page of the worksheet and configure the header content as you want it.

To display different headers and footers on odd and even pages

1. Activate the header or footer.

2. On the **Header & Footer** tool tab, in the **Options** group, select the **Different Odd & Even Pages** checkbox.

3. Display an odd page and create the header and footer for odd pages.

4. Display an even page and create the header and footer for even pages.

To change the vertical size of headers and footers

1. On the **Page Layout** tab, in the **Page Setup** group, select **Margins**, and then select **Custom Margins**.

2. On the **Margins** tab of the **Page Setup** dialog, enter or select the **Header** and **Footer** heights and if necessary, the **Top** and **Bottom** margins.

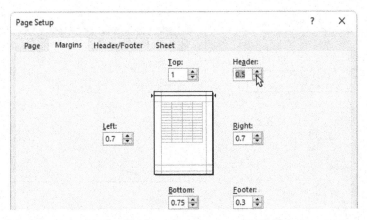

The lines on the thumbnail indicate the element you're modifying

Prepare worksheets for printing

When you're ready to print your workbook, you can change the workbook's properties to ensure that your worksheets display all your information and that printing is centered on the page. In Excel, all these printing functions are gathered together in one place: the Backstage view.

11

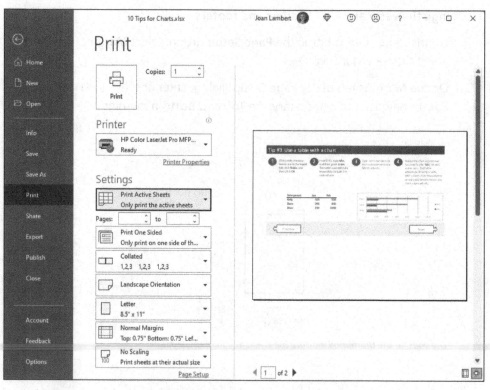

You can configure most aspects of your printed worksheet in the Backstage view

You can change the number of copies to print, the printer to which you will send the file, whether Excel should print the page in landscape or portrait orientation, which paper size to use, which margin settings you want, and whether to scale the worksheet's contents so they fit on a specific number of printed pages.

Fit your worksheet contents to the printed page

Excel for Microsoft 365 has three standard page margin settings: Normal, Wide, and Narrow. Normal, which is the default, leaves 0.75 inches clear on the top and bottom of the page and 0.7 inches on the left and right sides. Narrow has the same top and bottom margins but leaves only 0.25 inches clear on the left and right sides. Wide leaves 1 inch clear all the way around. If none of these meet your needs, you can set custom margins. The margins are visible in Page Layout view.

Order ID	Employee	Customer	Order Date	Shipped Date	Ship Via	Ship Name
30	Anne Hellung-Larsen	Company AA	1/15/2021	1/22/2021	Shipping Company B	Karen Toh
31	Jan Kotas	Company D	1/20/2021	1/22/2021	Shipping Company A	Christina Lee
32	Mariya Sergienko	Company L	1/22/2021	1/22/2021	Shipping Company B	John Edwards
33	Michael Neipper	Company H	1/30/2021	1/31/2021	Shipping Company C	Elizabeth Andersen
34	Anne Hellung-Larsen	Company D	2/6/2021	2/7/2021	Shipping Company C	Christina Lee
35	Jan Kotas	Company CC	2/10/2021	2/12/2021	Shipping Company B	Soo Jung Lee
36	Mariya Sergienko	Company C	2/23/2021	2/25/2021	Shipping Company B	Thomas Axen
37	Laura Giussani	Company F	3/6/2021	3/9/2021	Shipping Company B	Francisco Pérez-Olaeta
38	Anne Hellung-Larsen	Company BB	3/10/2021	3/11/2021	Shipping Company C	Amritansh Raghav
39	Jan Kotas	Company H	3/22/2021	3/24/2021	Shipping Company C	Elizabeth Andersen
40	Mariya Sergienko	Company J	3/24/2021	3/24/2021	Shipping Company B	Roland Wacker

Set page margins to control the space available for printed content

A potential issue with printing worksheets is that the data in worksheets tends to be wider than a standard sheet of paper. If that's the case, you can change the alignment of the rows and columns on the page. When the columns parallel the long edge of a piece of paper, the page is laid out in portrait mode; when the columns parallel the short edge of a piece of paper, it is in landscape mode. Changing between portrait and landscape mode might result in a better fit.

If you can't fit your worksheet on a single page by changing its orientation, you can change its scale. Scaling a worksheet for printing lets you specify the number of printed pages the worksheet will take up. You can scale your worksheet until everything fits on a specified number of printed pages, specify the number of printed pages on which the columns will appear, or specify the number of printed pages on which the rows will appear. For example, if you have a list of data that's 15 columns wide and 100 rows long, you could scale it so the columns all fit on each page of your printout.

The Print page of the Backstage view displays a preview that accurately represents the appearance of the worksheet when printed with the current settings.

> **TIP** When you preview a multipage worksheet on the Print page of the Backstage view, you can move through the pages by selecting the Previous and Next arrows flanking the page counter below the preview, move forward by pressing the Page Down key or backward by pressing the Page Up key, enter a page number in the Current Page box and then press Enter to move directly to a page, or scroll through the pages by dragging the vertical scroll bar to the right of the preview.

11

To display the print preview of a worksheet

- Select the **File** tab, and then select **Print** to display the Print page of the Backstage view.

- Press **Ctrl+P**.

To specify the print orientation of a worksheet

- On the **Page Layout** tab, in the **Page Setup** group, select **Orientation**, and then select either **Portrait** or **Landscape**.

Or

1. Display the print preview of the worksheet.

2. On the **Print** page, in the **Settings** area, select the **Orientation** button.

3. Select either **Portrait Orientation** or **Landscape Orientation**.

To scale a worksheet for printing

1. On the **Print** page of the Backstage view, in the **Settings** area, select the **Scaling** button.

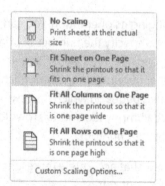

Select a scaling option to print your worksheet on a set number of pages

2. Select the scaling option you want.

Change page breaks in a worksheet

Another way to affect how your worksheet will appear on the printed page is to change where Excel assigns its page breaks. A *page break* is the point at which Excel prints all subsequent data on a new sheet of paper. You can make these changes indirectly by modifying a worksheet's margins, but you can also do so directly. In Page Break Preview mode, the dashed blue lines in the window represent the page breaks.

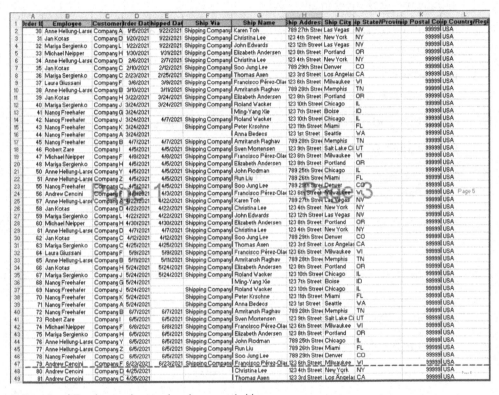

In Page Break Preview mode, page breaks appear in blue

To split data gracefully between multiple pages, you can move existing page breaks or insert manual page breaks on a worksheet.

To display the Page Break Preview of a worksheet

- On the **View** tab, in the **Workbook Views** group, select the **Page Break Preview** button.

11

To insert a page break on a worksheet

1. Display the Page Break Preview of the worksheet.

2. Select the row or column header before which you want to insert the page break, and then select **Insert Page Break**.

Or

1. Display the worksheet in any view.

2. Select the row or column header before which you want to insert the page break.

3. On the **Page Layout** tab, in the **Page Setup** group, select **Breaks**, and then select **Insert Page Break**.

To insert vertical and horizontal page breaks at the same time

1. Display the Page Break Preview of the worksheet.

2. Select the cell before which you want to insert the page breaks, and then select **Insert Page Break**.

Or

1. Display the worksheet in any view.

2. Select the cell before which you want to insert the page breaks.

3. On the **Page Layout** tab, in the **Page Setup** group, select **Breaks**, and then select **Insert Page Break**.

To move a page break

1. Display the Page Break Preview of the worksheet.

2. Drag the page break to its new position.

To remove a page break

1. Select the row header, column header, or cell after the page break.

2. On the **Page Layout** tab, in the **Page Setup** group, select **Breaks**, and then select **Remove Page Break**.

To reset all page breaks

- On the **Page Layout** tab, in the **Page Setup** group, select **Breaks**, and then select **Reset All Page Breaks**.

Change the page printing order for worksheets

When you display a worksheet in Page Break Preview mode, Excel indicates the order in which the pages will be printed with light gray words on the worksheet pages. (These indicators appear only in Page Break Preview mode; they don't show up when the worksheet is printed.) Depending on the organization of data on the worksheet, you might want to change the order in which Excel prints the worksheet pages, to keep related information on consecutive pages.

The default page printing order is down, then over, meaning that Excel prints all the rows in the first page width of columns, then all the rows in the second page width of columns, and so on. You can change the print order to over, then down, so that Excel prints all the columns in the first page height of rows, then all the columns in the second page height, and so on.

Print worksheet pages in a logical order

To open the Page Setup dialog

- On the **Page Layout** tab, select the **Page Setup** dialog launcher (the arrow in the lower-right corner of the group).

To change the order in which worksheet pages are printed

1. Open the **Page Setup** dialog and display the **Sheet** tab.

2. In the **Page order** section, select either **Down, then over** or **Over, then down**. The thumbnail image for each option illustrates the print order.

3. In the **Page Setup** dialog, select **OK**.

Print worksheets

When you're ready to print a worksheet, you can specify the printer to which you want to send the print job, which worksheets to print, whether to print single- or double-sided (if your printer supports duplex printing), how many copies of the job to print, and whether to collate them (print all pages of each copy together instead of all copies of each page).

11

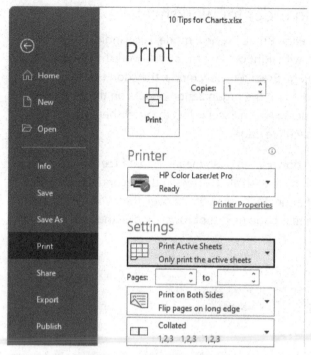

Control your print job from the Print page of Backstage view

Some worksheets you print could be works in progress, where some of the formulas might display errors because of missing values. You can select how Excel will print any errors in your worksheet: printing it as it normally appears in the worksheet, printing a blank cell in place of the error, or choosing one of two other indicators that are not standard error messages.

To display the print preview of a worksheet

- Display the **Print** page of the Backstage view.

- Press **Ctrl+P**.

To print a worksheet

1. Display the print preview of the worksheet you want to print.

2. On the **Print** page of the Backstage view, select the options you want to apply to the print job, and then select the **Print** button.

To print multiple worksheets

1. Display the first worksheet you want to print.

2. Hold down the **Ctrl** key and select the tabs of the other worksheets you want to print.

3. Display the selected worksheets in Print Preview mode.

4. On the **Print** page of the Backstage view, select the options you want to apply to the print job, and then select the **Print** button.

To print multiple copies

1. On the **Print** page of the Backstage view, in the **Copies** box, enter or select the number of copies you want to print.

2. In the **Settings** section of the page, in the **Collated** list, do either of the following:

    *   To print all pages of each copy together, select **Collated**.

    *   To print all copies of each page together, select **Uncollated**.

To control how Excel prints worksheet errors

1. Open the **Page Setup** dialog and display the **Sheet** tab.

2. In the **Cell errors as** list, select the option representing how you want errors to be printed.

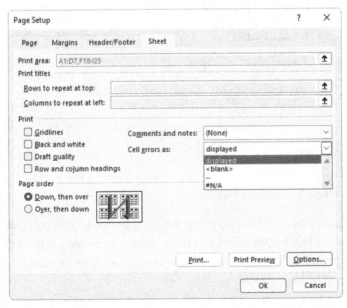

Specify how Excel should print worksheet errors

3. Select **OK**.

Print parts of worksheets

Just as you can control what your worksheets look like when printed, you can also specify which sheet content you want to print. For example, you can choose which pages of a multipage worksheet you want to print. If you want to print a portion of a worksheet instead of the entire worksheet, you can define the area or areas you want to print and use the Center on Page controls on the Margins tab of the Page Setup dialog to specify how Excel should position the area on the printed page.

 TIP You can include noncontiguous groups of cells in the area to be printed by holding down the Ctrl key as you select the cells.

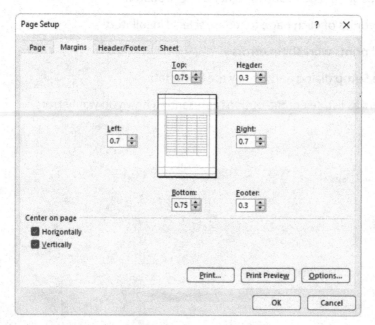

Center printed items on the page horizontally and vertically

If the contents of a worksheet will take up more than one printed page, you can have Excel repeat one or more rows at the top of the page or columns at the left of the page as column headers. Repeating the header row makes it easier to read data when a multipage workbook is printed.

To print specific pages

1. On the **Print** page of the Backstage view, in the first **Pages** box, enter or select the page number of the first page you want to print.

2. In the second **Pages** box, enter or select the page number of the last page you want to print.

3. Select the **Print** button.

To define a print area

1. Select the cell range you want to print.

2. If you want to print multiple regions, hold down the **Ctrl** key and select each of the other cell ranges. Excel prints each noncontiguous region on a separate page.

3. On the **Page Layout** tab, in the **Page Setup** group, select **Print Area**. Then, on the menu, select **Set Print Area**.

> **TIP** When you select Print in the Backstage view, the preview area displays the content you've chosen to print and updates to reflect any changes you make in the Settings area.

To add a print area

1. Select the cell range you want to add to the print area.

2. On the **Page Layout** tab, in the **Page Setup** group, select **Print Area**, and then on the menu, select **Add to Print Area**.

   If the new print area is next to an existing print area, Excel extends the first print area to encompass both.

To clear the defined print area

- On the **Page Layout** tab, in the **Page Setup** group, select **Print Area**. Then, on the menu, select **Clear Print Area**.

11

To position printed material on the page

1. Open the **Page Setup** dialog, and display the **Margins** tab.

2. In the **Center on page** section, do one of the following:

   - Select the **Horizontally** checkbox to center the printed content between the left and right page margins.

   - Select the **Vertically** checkbox to center the printed content between the top and bottom page margins.

   - Select both checkboxes to print the content in the center of the page.

   The thumbnail on the Margins tab updates to reflect your selection.

To repeat rows at the top of each printed page

1. On the **Page Layout** tab, in the **Page Setup** group, select **Print Titles**.

2. On the **Sheet** tab of the **Page Setup** dialog, at the right edge of the **Rows to repeat at top** box, select the **Collapse Dialog** button to expose the worksheet.

3. Select the row or rows you want to print at the top of each page.

4. Select the **Expand Dialog** button, and then select **OK**.

To repeat columns at the left of each printed page

1. On the **Page Layout** tab, in the **Page Setup** group, select **Print Titles**.

2. On the **Sheet** tab of the **Page Setup** dialog, at the right edge of the **Columns to repeat at left** box, select the **Collapse Dialog** button to expose the worksheet.

3. Select the column or columns you want to print on the left side of each page.

4. Select the **Expand Dialog** button, and then select **OK**.

Print charts

With charts, which are graphic representations of your Excel data, you can communicate a lot of information with a single picture. Depending on your data and the type of chart you make, you can show trends across time, indicate the revenue share for various departments in a company for a month, or project future sales by using trendline analysis. After you create a chart, you can print it to include it in a report or use it in a presentation.

If you embed a chart in a worksheet, the chart will probably obscure some of your data unless you move the chart to a second page in the worksheet. Fortunately, you can print a chart by itself without changing the layout of your worksheet.

Select a chart in your worksheet to print it by itself on a page

To print a chart

1. On the worksheet or chart sheet, select the chart.

2. Display the print preview of the chart.

3. In the **Settings** section of the **Print** page of the Backstage view, verify that **Print Selected Chart** is selected.

4. In the **Printer** list, select your preferred printer. Then select the **Print** button.

Skills review

In this chapter, you learned how to:

- Add headers and footers to printed pages

- Prepare worksheets for printing

- Print worksheets

- Print parts of worksheets

- Print charts

Practice tasks

Before you can complete these tasks, you must copy the book's practice files to your computer. The practice files for these tasks are in the **Excel365SBS\Ch11** folder. You can save the results of the tasks in the same folder.

Add headers and footers to printed pages

Open the **AddHeaders** workbook in Excel, and then perform the following tasks:

1. Enter the text Q1 365 in the center section of the header, and press **Enter**.

2. Add a code to display the name of the current file, followed by a comma and a space, and then add a control to display the current date.

3. Create separate headers for odd and even pages.

4. In the middle section of the footer, add the ConsolidatedMessenger.png file, and then select any worksheet cell above the footer to view what the image looks like in the footer.

5. Edit the image so it is 80 percent of its original size.

6. Change the margins for both the header and footer so they are 0.5 inches high.

Prepare worksheets for printing

Open the **PrepareWorksheets** workbook in Excel, and then perform the following tasks:

1. Change the orientation of the **JanFeb** worksheet to **Landscape**.

2. Change the scale of the **JanFeb** worksheet to 80 percent.

3. On the **JanFeb** worksheet, set a horizontal page break above row 38.

4. Set the margins of the **MarJun** worksheet to the **Wide** preset values.

5. For the **MarJun** worksheet, change the page print order to **Over, then down**.

Print worksheets

Open the **PrintWorksheets** workbook in Excel, and then perform the following tasks:

1. Configure the worksheet so cell errors are displayed as blank cells.

2. Select the **Summary** and **Northwind** sheets and display them on the **Print** page of the Backstage view.

3. If you want, select the **Print** button to print your worksheets on your local printer.

Print parts of worksheets

Open the **PrintParts** workbook in Excel, and then perform the following tasks:

1. Set the print titles of the worksheet so that columns A and B are repeated at the left edge of each printed page.

2. Change the printer properties so Excel will print only pages 1 and 2 of the worksheet.

3. Scale the worksheet so its columns will fit on one page when printed.

4. Preview what the worksheet will look like when printed.

5. Define a multiregion print area including cells **A2:E9** and **A39:E46**.

6. Center the regions on the printed page.

7. Print the page.

Print charts

Open the **PrintCharts** workbook in Excel, and then perform the following tasks:

1. Select the Revenue chart.

2. Continue as if you will print only the Revenue chart, and then change the settings on the **Print** page of the Backstage view to print the entire worksheet.

Automate tasks and input

Many tasks you perform in Excel, such as entering data or creating formulas, you do only once. However, there are probably one or two tasks you perform frequently that require a lot of steps to accomplish. To save time, you can create a macro, which is a recorded series of actions, to perform the steps for you. You can create various short-cuts for running the macro, including buttons on the Quick Access Toolbar or on a worksheet.

If you create workbooks for other people to use, you can provide macros that perform specific tasks for the work-book users, and form fields that guide the data-entry process. You control where the form fields store the data they collect, and you can reference those data-storage locations in your macros.

This chapter guides you through procedures related to defining macro security settings; displaying macros in the Visual Basic Editor; running, creating, and modifying macros; creating buttons on the Quick Access Toolbar and in the workbook to easily run macros; and inserting and configuring form controls.

In this chapter

- Enable and examine macros
- Create and modify macros
- Run macros
- Present information and options as form controls

Enable and examine macros

Macros are powerful tools that let you automate tasks in Excel (and other Office apps) by writing or recording a series of Visual Basic for Applications (VBA) commands. Each action that you perform in a workbook or document—such as searching for a specific term, moving three cells to the right, or applying bold formatting—can be expressed by an equivalent VBA command, such as the following:

- `Sheet1.Find("packages")`
- `Cells(1,1).Offset(0,3).Select`
- `Selection.Font.Bold = True`

Desktop publishers (people who create useful things in Word, Excel, and PowerPoint, for example) use macros to perform routine tasks such as deleting unused styles from documents, applying series of styles, or clearing input cells in workbooks. Any repetitive task that you perform routinely by selecting a series of commands in Excel workbooks or Word documents is an excellent candidate for automation through a VBA macro.

Macros can also be written for nefarious purposes. Because of this, Excel (and all other Office apps) disables them by default in a couple different ways. First, Excel can ensure that a macro won't run unless you allow it. And second, certain Excel file types don't allow you to save Excel workbooks that contain a macro. The exception to this is that several file storage locations on your computer, in which Office stores the configuration files it needs to make your life more pleasant, are trusted by default.

Excel for Microsoft 365 supports many different file types. The native Excel file types have differing levels of macro support. The following table summarizes the macro capabilities of the native Excel file types.

Type	Extension	Macro
Excel Workbook	.xlsx	Stores data in XML format. You can create and run macros in this type of workbook, but you can't save the file if it contains macros.
Excel Macro-Enabled Workbook	.xlsm	You can create, save, and run macros in this type of workbook.
Excel Binary Workbook	.xlsb	Stores data in binary format and allows macros.

Type	Extension	Macro
Excel Template	.xltx	Macros are disabled.
Excel Macro-Enabled Template	.xltm	Macros are enabled.

For the security of your files, your computer, and your organization's systems, if you want to run macros you must modify the Excel security settings for a specific work-book, for workbooks saved in a specific location, or for the app. You can select the appropriate security level for your organization.

Set macro security levels in Excel

When you open a macro-enabled workbook, Excel checks the security settings to determine what to do. The default settings prevent the workbook from running the macro code. When that happens, Excel displays a security warning on the message bar.

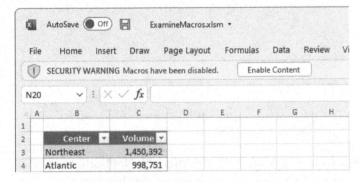

Macro security settings help reduce outside threats

Selecting the Enable Content button allows you to run macros in the workbook. However, it doesn't start running any of the macros unless the workbook contains a macro that is set to run automatically. Before you choose to enable macro content, con-sider whether you trust the workbook's source, whether you expected the workbook to contain macros, and whether you need to run one or more macros at this time. You can work normally in a workbook without enabling macros.

If you decide to not enable the macros in a workbook, you can close the message bar without enabling the content or leave the message bar open to decide later. You will be able to edit the workbook as usual, but macros and other active content will not be available.

12

If the workbooks you use often contain useful macros, you might choose to change your app-level macro security settings, which—along with many other security and privacy settings—are managed in the Trust Center dialog.

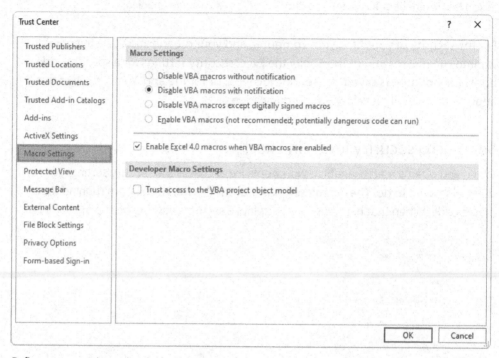

Define macro security settings in the Trust Center dialog

The Excel default macro security level is Disable VBA Macros with Notification, which means that Excel displays the security warning on the message bar but allows you to enable the macros manually. Other options automatically disable all or most macros. If you work in an environment in which workbooks contain macros that have been verified with digital signatures, you can choose to allow those to run without explicit permission.

You also have the option of enabling all macros. However, because it is possible to write macros that act as viruses, potentially causing harm to your computer and spreading copies of themselves to other computers, you should never choose this option, even if you have virus-checking software installed on your computer.

Other Trust Center pages that might be helpful if you frequently work with documents and workbooks that contain macros are the Trusted Publishers, Trusted Locations, and Trusted Documents pages. On these pages, you can specify file sources and storage locations from which Microsoft 365 apps can open macro-enabled files without your explicit permission. Microsoft 365 apps automatically add many of their own program file locations to this list.

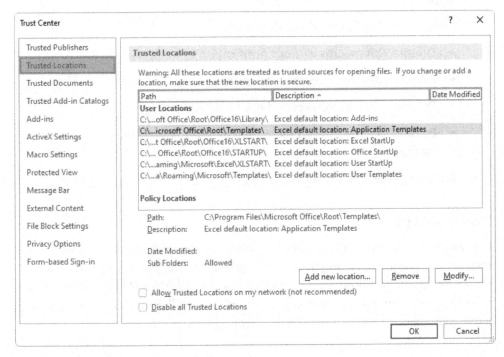

Files from trusted locations are automatically trusted

> ✅ **TIP** Each Microsoft 365 desktop app has a link to the Trust Center from its Options dialog. However, the macro settings that you configure within the Trust Center apply specifically to that app.

To open the Excel Options dialog

- Select the **File** tab to display the Backstage view of Excel, and then at the bottom of the left pane, select **Options**.

To open the Trust Center dialog

1. Open the **Excel Options** dialog.

2. At the bottom of the left pane, select **Trust Center**.

3. On the Trust Center page, select **Trust Center Settings**.

To change the macro security settings for Excel

1. Open the **Trust Center** dialog.

2. In the left pane, select **Macro Settings**.

3. Select one of the following security levels:

   - **Disable VBA macros without notification**

   - **Disable VBA macros with notification**

   - **Disable VBA macros except digitally signed macros**

   - **Enable VBA macros (not recommended; potentially dangerous code can run)**

4. Select **OK** in each of the open dialogs.

Examine macros

One way to gain an understanding of how macros work, and hopefully become comfortable with the idea of trying them out, is to examine the VBA code of an existing macro. You display and edit the code of VBA macros in the Visual Basic Editor, which you can access from the Macro dialog or from the Excel ribbon. This program is built into Excel; you don't need to install any other program or add-on.

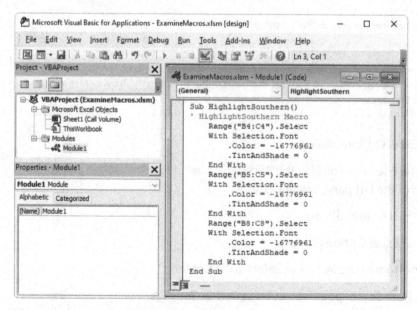

View and edit macros in the Visual Basic Editor

If you have programming experience, you will find this macro easy to read.

- The first line of the macro defines it as a subroutine (a macro) named HighlightSouthern.

- The second line is a comment from the developer. Developers often leave explanatory comments in code; in VBA, comments start with an apostrophe (').

- In the body of the code, beginning with Range ("B4:C4"), the macro selects three different cell ranges and sets the font color of the cell content. Notice that the color (-16776961) is the same for each of the three cell ranges.

You can move through a macro one step at a time to observe the effect of each line of code, run the macro up to a specific point (called a *breakpoint*), or run the macro the whole way through.

To display the Developer tab on the ribbon

1. Display the **Customize Ribbon** page of the **Excel Options** dialog.

2. In the pane below the **Customize the Ribbon** list, select the **Developer** checkbox.

3. Select **OK**.

To open the Macro dialog

- On the **View** tab, in the **Macros** group, select the **Macros** button.

- On the **Developer** tab, in the **Code** group, select **Macros**.

- Press **Alt+F8**.

To examine a macro

1. Open the **Macro** dialog.

2. Select the macro you want to examine, and then select **Edit** to open the **Visual Basic Editor** and display the macro.

3. Examine the macro's code.

To move through a macro one step at a time

1. Open the **Macro** dialog.

2. Select the macro you want to step through, and then select **Step Into** to display the macro in the Visual Basic Editor. An arrow and yellow highlighting indicate where the process will start.

12

3. Arrange the **Visual Basic Editor** and the worksheet so you can observe the macro effects as you step through it.

4. In the **Visual Basic Editor**, on the **Debug** menu, select **Step Into** to run the highlighted step. The highlight moves to the next instruction, and the worksheet changes to reflect the action that resulted from executing the preceding instruction.

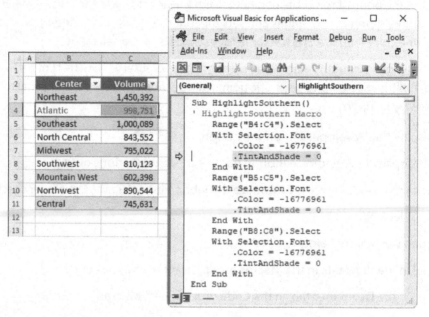

Step through a macro one instruction at a time

5. Do one of the following:

- Press **F8** (the keyboard shortcut for the Step Into command on the Debug menu) until you have moved through the entire macro.

- Press **F5** (the keyboard shortcut for the Run Macro command on the Run menu) to run the remaining steps without stopping.

- On the **Visual Basic Editor** toolbar, select the **Reset** button to stop stepping through the macro.

To close the Visual Basic Editor and return to Excel

- On the **File** menu, select **Close and Return to Microsoft Excel**.

- Press **Alt+Q**.

To open the Visual Basic Editor directly

- On the **Developer** tab, in the **Code** group, select **Visual Basic**.

- Press **Alt+F11**.

Create and modify macros

The first step in creating a macro is to carefully plan the process you want to automate. Think through each step, any decisions that must be made, any conditions that must be evaluated, and so on. It can be helpful to draw a simple process flowchart to make sure you're not missing anything.

After you plan your process, you can create your macro by using one of two methods:

- You can write the macro from scratch in the Visual Basic Editor.

- You can record yourself performing all the steps and then touch up the macro in the Visual Basic Editor.

The second method is by far the easiest. Recording a macro enters the VBA code for each action you perform into the Visual Basic Editor interface. You can record all the actions at one time, or record actions independently and then combine them. Using this method, you can build a library of VBA code that you can combine in different ways to create many different and useful macros.

To open the Record Macro dialog

- On the **View** tab, in the **Macros** group, select the **Macros** arrow (not the button), and then select **Record Macro**.

- On the **Developer** tab, in the **Code** group, select the **Record Macro** button.

- Near the left end of the status bar, select the **Macro Recording** button.

To record a macro

1. Open the **Record Macro** dialog.

2. In the **Macro name** box, enter a meaningful name for the macro.

3. If you want to assign a keyboard shortcut to run the macro, enter a letter or number in the **Shortcut key** box. Take care that you don't select a keyboard shortcut that already performs a task.

12

> **SEE ALSO** For a complete list of Excel keyboard shortcuts, see the appendix, "Keyboard shortcuts."

4. In the list, do one of the following:

   - Select **This Workbook** to save the macro with the current file. You'll need to save the file as a macro-enabled Excel workbook. The macro will be available to anyone using the workbook.

   - Select **New Workbook** to save the macro with a blank workbook. You will save that file as a macro-enabled Excel workbook and can run the macro from any other workbook while the new file is open.

   - Select **Personal Macro Workbook** to save the macro in a workbook that you designate for this purpose. This is a good choice if you intend to run the same macros in multiple workbooks.

5. In the **Description** box, enter any information that will be helpful for you or other macro users when locating the macro. You can also add this information after you create the macro.

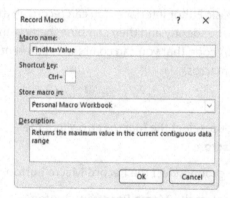

Choose a name that describes the macro's purpose

6. Select **OK**.

7. Perform the steps you want to record in your macro.

8. When you finish, do one of the following to stop recording:

   - On the **View** tab, select the **Macros** arrow, and then select **Stop Recording**.

   - On the **Developer** tab, select **Stop Recording**.

   - On the status bar, select the **Macros Recording** button.

To edit a macro

1. Open the **Macro** dialog.

2. Select the macro you want to edit, and then select **Edit**.

3. In the **Visual Basic Editor**, modify the macro code in the way that you want.

4. Press **Ctrl+S** to save your changes.

5. In the **Visual Basic Editor**, select **File**, and then select **Close and Return to Microsoft Excel**.

To delete a macro

1. Open the **Macro** dialog.

2. Select the macro you want to delete, and then select **Delete**.

3. In the confirmation dialog that appears, select **Yes**.

Or

1. Display the macro in the **Visual Basic Editor**.

2. Select the entire subroutine (from Sub to End Sub), and then press the **Delete** key.

Run macros

When you want to run a macro, you can do so from the Developer tab of the ribbon. However, the Developer tab is hidden by default. And besides, even when the Developer tab is visible, it can be time-consuming to open the Macro dialog, locate the macro you want to run, and then start it.

If you assign a shortcut key to the macro when you create it, and you can remember the shortcut key, you can run the macro more quickly. An even easier solution is to add a button for the macro to either the Quick Access Toolbar or to a worksheet, or to have one or more macros run automatically when the workbook opens. The best solution will depend on whether the macro is for your use only or if you want to make it available to other workbook users.

12

Assign a macro to a Quick Access Toolbar button

In "Customize the Excel app window" in Chapter 1, "Set up a workbook," you learned about adding existing commands to the Quick Access Toolbar. Adding a macro button follows a similar process. Because each macro is unique, you'll need to specify a display name and choose from 180 icons that are available to represent the macro. (The icon is optional, but choosing one is the fun part.) If you're adding the button for yourself to use on one computer, you can add it to your standard Quick Access Toolbar. If you'd like the button to travel with the workbook, you can add it to the workbook-specific Quick Access Toolbar.

To add a macro button to the Quick Access Toolbar

1. Display the **Quick Access Toolbar** page of the **Excel Options** dialog.

2. In the **Choose commands from** list in the upper-left corner of the page, select **Macros**.

3. If you want to add the macro to a Quick Access Toolbar that stays with the workbook, select the **Customize Quick Access Toolbar** arrow, and then select **For** *WorkbookName*.

4. Do either of the following for each macro you want to add to the Quick Access Toolbar:

   - In the left pane, select the macro name. Then in the center, select **Add** to show the command in the right pane.

   - In the left pane, double-click the macro name.

5. For each macro, do the following:

   a. In the right pane, select the macro name. Then below the right pane, select **Modify**.

   b. In the **Modify Button** dialog, select the icon you want to display on the button.

   c. In the **Display name** box, enter a meaningful name for the Quick Access Toolbar button.

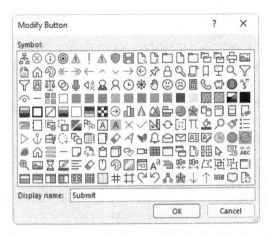

You can specify an icon and name for any Quick Access Toolbar button

    d. Select **OK** to close the **Modify Button** dialog and assign the name and icon to the Quick Access Toolbar button.

6. When you finish, select **OK** to close the **Excel Options** dialog and add the macro(s) to the Quick Access Toolbar.

To run a macro assigned to a Quick Access Toolbar button

■ Select the Quick Access Toolbar button to which the macro has been assigned.

To change the name or icon of a macro button on the Quick Access Toolbar

1. Display the **Quick Access Toolbar** page of the **Excel Options** dialog.

2. In the **Customize Quick Access Toolbar** list, select the Quick Access Toolbar that contains the macro.

3. In the right pane, select the display name of the macro button you want to modify. Then below the right pane, select **Modify**.

4. In the **Modify Button** dialog, change the icon or display name of the macro button.

5. Select **OK** in the **Modify Button** dialog and in the **Excel Options** dialog.

12

Assign a macro to a shape

If you want to make a macro available from a location on a worksheet, you can add a button to the worksheet in one of two ways: as a form control or as a graphic such as a shape or icon. Both options provide the same functionality. However, using a shape enables you to be more visually expressive thanks to various shape options, colors, and visual effects. Alternatively, you can choose any of the professional-looking icons supplied with Excel (and other Microsoft 365 apps) as your button.

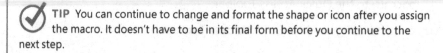 **SEE ALSO** You'll learn about buttons and other form controls in "Present informa- tion and options as form controls" later in this chapter. For information about inserting and recoloring icons, inserting and formatting shapes, and editing the text displayed within a shape, see Chapter 9, "Create charts and graphics."

To assign a macro to a shape or icon

1. Locate the area of the worksheet where you want the shape or icon to appear. Then insert the shape or icon to which you want to assign the macro.

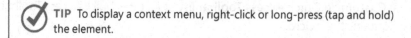 **TIP** You can continue to change and format the shape or icon after you assign the macro. It doesn't have to be in its final form before you continue to the next step.

2. Right-click the shape or icon, and then select **Assign Macro** from the context menu.

TIP To display a context menu, right-click or long-press (tap and hold) the element.

3. In the **Assign Macro** dialog, select the name of the macro you want to assign to the shape or icon. Then select **OK**.

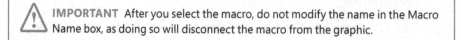 **IMPORTANT** After you select the macro, do not modify the name in the Macro Name box, as doing so will disconnect the macro from the graphic.

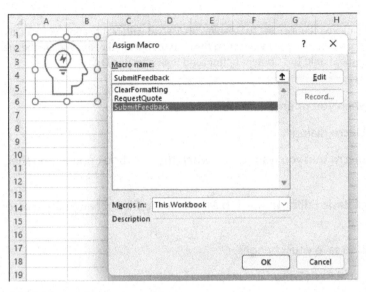

Select a shape or icons

To run a macro assigned to a shape

- Select the shape to which the macro has been assigned.

To edit a shape to which a macro has been assigned

1. Right-click the shape you want to edit.

2. In the shortcut menu, select **Format Shape**.

3. Use the tools in the **Format Shape** pane to change the shape's formatting.

4. Select the **Close** button to close the **Format Shape** pane.

Run a macro when a workbook opens

If you have a macro that you want to run every time you open a workbook—for example, to clear the data or formatting from specific cells—you can have Excel run the macro automatically. This functionality is based on the macro name, so you can select this option for only one macro per workbook.

12

> **TIP** If your macro security is set to Disable VBA Macros with Notification, you can allow the Auto_Open macro to run by selecting the Options button that appears on the message bar, selecting the Enable This Content option, and then selecting OK.

To run a macro when you open a workbook

1. Open the **Macro** dialog.

2. Select the macro that you want to run when the workbook opens, and then select **Edit**.

3. In the **Visual Basic Editor**, in the **Sub** *MacroName()* line, change the macro name to Auto_Open().

4. Press **Ctrl+S** to save your changes.

5. Close the Visual Basic Editor and return to Excel.

Present information and options as form controls

Earlier in this chapter, you learned how to assign a macro to a Quick Access Toolbar button or to a shape. You can also provide access to a macro through a button on a worksheet. While a button is essentially just a rectangle shape with a macro assigned to it, Excel provides many other form controls that you can use on worksheets. You can also use form controls to create professional-looking forms with which to gather data.

Form control management takes place on the Developer tab, which is hidden by default. To work with form controls, you must first display it on the ribbon.

Manage macros, form controls, and other advanced elements from the Developer tab

The following table identifies the form controls you can insert and configure from the Controls group of the Developer tab.

Icon	Name
▭	Button
▤	Combo Box
☑	Check Box
⬍	Spin Button
▤	List Box
◉	Option Button
ᵡʸᶻ	Group Box
Aa	Label
▤	Scroll Bar

Form controls provide interactivity and guidance for workbook users. You can use form controls to specify the options a user can select, to collect input in a controlled manner, and to provide easy access to macros.

 TIP The form controls described in this chapter mimic controls such as list boxes, checkboxes, and option buttons that are available in many Excel dialogs.

Two form controls, the list box and the combo box, display lists of values from a cell range you define. The difference between the list box and the combo box is that a list box displays all the values at the same time, and a combo box displays an arrow that you select to display the values from which you can choose.

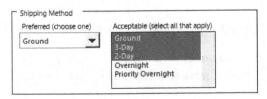

A group box that contains a list box and a combo box, both with labels

TIP Hiding the gridlines on a worksheet that hosts form controls provides a more professional and less cluttered appearance.

After you add a list box or combo box to your worksheet, you configure the settings in the Format Control dialog to identify the cells that provide values for the control, the cell that displays the control's value, and other properties.

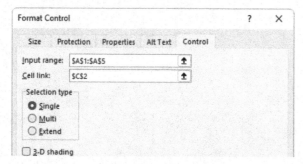

Set form control parameters in the Format Control dialog

 TIP The cells that provide values for your list box or combo box don't have to be on the same worksheet as the form control. Putting the values on another worksheet lets you reduce the clutter in the worksheet that contains the form control. Hiding the worksheet that contains the source data also helps prevent users from changing those values.

Another form control, the spin button, lets you change numerical values in increments. For example, you could use spin buttons to increase or decrease the pounds and ounces representing a package's weight.

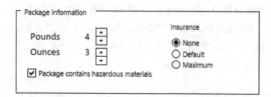

A group box that contains two spin buttons, a checkbox, and three option buttons with a label

Spin buttons are effective presentation tools. You can enter a specific value or change a value up or down in increments that you define, to show how formula results change.

Spin buttons use slightly different parameters than combo boxes or list boxes. Rather than identifying the cell range that provides values for the control, you specify the maximum value, minimum value, increment (the number of units by which the value changes—usually 1), and which worksheet cell displays the spin button's value.

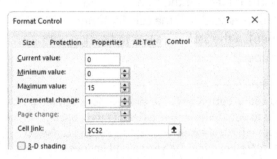

Change a spin button's values in the Format Control dialog

> ⚠ **IMPORTANT** The maximum, minimum, and increment values must be whole numbers. If you want to use a spin button to change a percentage, for example, you'll need to create a formula in another cell that divides the spin button's value by 100.

The button form control, also referred to as a command button, runs a macro when selected. When you add a button to a worksheet, Excel prompts you to assign a macro to it. If you don't yet have the macro, you can cancel out of the dialog and assign one later.

The Assign Macro dialog for a newly created command button

When you first insert a button, it is labeled Button followed by a number. You then edit the button label to reflect the action or process the button calls.

12

The next two form controls, the checkbox and option button, let users turn specific options on or off. For example, a package-delivery company could allow customers to waive a signature when a package is dropped off. If the Signature Required option button (the first option button in the group) is selected, the cell displaying the option button's value would contain the number 1. If the Signature Waived option button is selected, the cell would contain the number 2.

 TIP Even though the checkbox and option button serve the same purpose, you should consider using both types of controls to distinguish among different sets of options. When implemented correctly, option buttons represent exclusive options—the user can select only one from the group—and checkboxes represent nonexclusive or on/off options.

You can have a cell display whether a checkbox or option button is selected or define a control group that contains the possible options.

TIP Control groups can contain either option buttons or checkboxes, but you can't mix them in the same group.

After you add your controls to your worksheet, you can move, align, edit, and delete them, just as you can other shapes. One important element to edit is the control's caption, or label, which indicates the type of value the control represents. For example, an option button could have the label Signature Required, indicating that selecting that option requires the delivery person to have the recipient sign for the package.

To display the Developer tab on the ribbon

1. Right-click an empty area of the ribbon, and then select **Customize the Ribbon** to display the **Customize Ribbon** page of the **Excel Options** dialog.

2. In the pane below the **Customize the Ribbon** list, select the **Developer** checkbox.

3. Select **OK**.

To display options in a list box

1. Enter the list box values in a column on any worksheet in the workbook.

2. On the **Developer** tab, in the **Controls** group, select **Insert**.

3. In the **Form Controls** section of the **Insert** menu, select the **List Box (Form Control)** button.

4. In the body of the worksheet, select and drag to draw the list box.

5. Right-click the list box, and then select **Format Control** to display the **Control** tab of the **Format Control** dialog.

6. In the **Input range** box, enter or select the cells that contain the list box values you defined in step 1.

7. In the **Cell link** box, enter or select the cell in which you want to display the value(s) corresponding to the list box selection(s).

8. In the **Selection type** group, do one of the following:

   - Select **Single** to restrict the list box selection to only one option.

   - Select **Multi** to allow the user to select multiple options by selecting each.

   - Select **Extend** to allow the user to select multiple contiguous options by dragging across them and select noncontiguous options by holding down the Ctrl key and selecting the options.

9. Select **OK** to close the **Format Control** dialog.

 TIP If you want a control to appear slightly three-dimensional, select the 3-D shading checkbox on the Control tab of the Format Control dialog.

To display options in a combo box

1. Enter the combo box values in a column on any worksheet in the workbook.

2. On the **Developer** tab, in the **Controls** group, select **Insert**.

3. In the **Form Controls** section of the **Insert** menu, select the **Combo Box (Form Control)** button.

4. In the body of the worksheet, drag to draw the combo box.

5. Right-click the combo box, and then select **Format Control** to display the **Control** tab of the **Format Control** dialog.

6. In the **Input range** box, enter or select the cells that contain the list box values you defined in step 1.

7. In the **Cell link** box, enter or select the cell in which you want to display the value(s) corresponding to the list box selection(s).

8. In the **Drop down lines** box, enter the number of values in the list so the list displays all the values when the user selects the combo box arrow.

9. Select **OK** to close the **Format Control** dialog.

12

To display numeric options in a spin box

1. On the **Developer** tab, in the **Controls** group, select **Insert**.

2. In the **Form Controls** section of the **Insert** menu, select the **Spin Button (Form Control)** button.

3. In the body of the worksheet, drag to draw the spin control.

4. Right-click the spin control, and then select **Format Control** to display the **Control** tab of the **Format Control** dialog.

5. In the **Current value** box, enter the control's initial (default) value.

6. In the **Minimum value** box, enter the smallest value allowed in the spin control.

7. In the **Maximum value** box, enter the largest value allowed in the spin control.

8. In the **Incremental change** box, enter the increment by which the value should increase or decrease.

9. In the **Cell link** box, enter or select the cell in which you want to display the value corresponding to the spin button selection.

10. Select **OK** to close the **Format Control** dialog.

To provide macro access through a button

1. On the **Developer** tab, in the **Controls** group, select **Insert**.

2. In the **Form Controls** section of the **Insert** menu, select the **Button (Form Control)** button.

3. In the body of the worksheet, drag to draw the button.

4. In the **Assign Macro** dialog, select the macro you want to run when the button is selected. Then select **OK**.

5. Right-click the button, select **Edit Text** to activate the default button label for editing, and then enter a descriptive button label.

> **TIP** Changing the button label also changes the alt text—the description of the form control that provides the information a user would need if they couldn't see the control. If necessary, you can update the alt text to provide a more informative description.

6. Do either of the following to deactivate the text-editing feature:

   - Right-click the button, and then select **Exit Edit Text**.

   - Click away from the button.

7. If you want to modify the appearance of the button label text, select and hold (or right-click) the button, and then select **Format Control**.

   > ⚠ **IMPORTANT** If you select Format Control while the text is active for editing, the Format Control dialog displays only the Font tab. If you select Format Control after exiting the Edit Text feature, the Font, Alignment, Size, Protection, Properties, Margins, and Alt Text tabs are available.

8. In the **Format Control** dialog, do any of the following:

   - On the **Font** tab, change the label font, font size, or font color; apply bold or italic formatting; or underline, double-underline, or strike through the text.

   - On the **Alignment** tab, change the horizontal or vertical alignment of the text, rotate the text vertically, or set the text to change size automatically to fit the button. You can also change the reading direction of the text, which is useful when working with right-to-left languages such as Arabic.

   - On the **Margins** tab, specify how much space should be left around the button label.

   > **TIP** If the button label doesn't change to reflect the formatting that you apply, try moving the button on the worksheet to force the change.

12

9. When you finish adjusting the button properties, select **OK** to close the **Format Control** dialog.

To display a two-state option as a checkbox

1. On the **Developer** tab, in the **Controls** group, select **Insert**.

2. In the **Form Controls** section of the **Insert** menu, select the **Check Box (Form Control)** button.

3. In the body of the worksheet, drag to insert the checkbox and its label.

4. Select the default label and replace it with a meaningful label.

5. Right-click the checkbox, and then select **Format Control** to display the **Control** tab of the **Format Control** dialog.

6. In the **Value** group, indicate whether the checkbox should initially be selected, cleared, or mixed.

7. In the **Cell link** box, enter or select the cell in which you want to display the value corresponding to the checkbox state.

8. Select **OK** to close the **Format Control** dialog.

To display unique options as option buttons

1. On the **Developer** tab, in the **Controls** group, select **Insert**.

2. In the **Form Controls** section of the **Insert** menu, select the **Option Button (Form Control)** button.

3. In the body of the worksheet, drag to insert the option button and label.

4. Select the default label and replace it with a meaningful label.

5. Right-click the option button, and then select **Format Control** to display the **Control** tab of the **Format Control** dialog.

6. In the **Value** group, indicate whether the option button should initially be selected or unselected.

7. Select in the **Cell link** box, and then select the cell where you want to display the control's value.

8. Select **OK** to close the **Format Control** dialog.

To select form controls

- To select one form control, right-click the control to display the sizing handles and context menu. Then press **Esc** to close the context menu.

- To select multiple form controls, first select one control, then hold down the **Ctrl** key and select each additional control you want to select. To remove a control from the selection, hold down the **Ctrl** key and right-click the control.

To move a form control

- Select the control, and then do either of the following:

  - To move the control to another location on the same worksheet, click away from the context menu to close it, and then drag the control.

  - To move the control to a different sheet, select **Cut**, switch sheets, right-click the new sheet, and then select **Paste**.

To align form controls

1. Select the controls that you want to align.

2. On the **Shape Format** tool tab, in the **Arrange** group, select the **Align Objects** button, and then do any of the following:

    *   To vertically align the controls, select **Align Left**, **Align Center**, or **Align Right**.

    *   To horizontally align the controls, select **Align Top**, **Align Middle**, or **Align Bottom**.

    *   To evenly space the controls in the area defined by the selected controls, select **Distribute Horizontally** or **Distribute Vertically**.

To visually group form controls

1. On the **Developer** tab, in the **Controls** group, select **Insert**.

2. In the **Form Controls** section of the **Insert** menu, select the **Group Box (Form Control)** button.

3. In the body of the worksheet, draw the group box around the items you want to include in the group.

4. In the upper-left corner of the group box, select the default group box name and replace it with a meaningful name.

> ⚠ **IMPORTANT** The group box control is essentially just an outline. You can't assign specific controls to the group box or use it to select or work with multiple controls at one time.

To functionally group form controls

1. Select the form controls that you want to group.

2. Do either of the following:

    *   Right-click any of the selected controls, expand the **Group** submenu, and then select **Group**.

    *   On the **Shape Format** tool tab, in the **Arrange** group, select the **Group** button, and then select **Group**.

12

> ⚠ **IMPORTANT** Grouped controls have a separate dashed selection indicator. You can select a group of controls to move and format the controls together and set their common properties, or you can select and modify an individual control from within the group.

To precisely resize a form control

1. Right-click the control, and then select **Format Control**.

2. On the **Size** tab, set the height and width of the control. Then select **OK**.

To manually resize a form control

- Select the control, and then drag the sizing handles on the sides and corners of the control.

To prevent a form control from shifting size and position

1. Right-click the control, and then select **Format Control**.

2. On the **Properties** tab, select **Don't move or size with cells**. Then select **OK**.

To provide alternative text for a form control

1. Right-click the control, and then select **Format Control**.

2. On the **Alt Text** tab, enter a description of the form control that provides the information a user would need if they couldn't see the control. Then select **OK**.

To delete a form control

- Right-click the control, and then select **Cut**.

- With the control selected, press **Delete**.

Skills review

In this chapter, you learned how to:

- Enable and examine macros

- Create and modify macros

- Run macros

- Present information and options as form controls

Practice tasks

Before you can complete these tasks, you must copy the book's practice files to your computer. The practice files for these tasks are in the **Excel365SBS\Ch12** folder. You can save the results of the tasks in the same folder.

Enable and examine macros

Open the **ExamineMacros** workbook in Excel, and then perform the following tasks:

1. Enable macros in this workbook.

2. Display the **Macro** dialog, and then open the **HighlightSouthern** macro for editing.

3. Press **F8** to step through the first three macro steps, and then press **F5** to run the rest of the macro without stopping.

4. Close the **Visual Basic Editor** to return to Excel.

Create and modify macros

Open the **RecordMacros** workbook in Excel, and then perform the following tasks:

1. Record a macro that removes bold formatting from cells **C4:C5**. (Leave the values in cells **C6:C7** bold.)

2. Restore bold formatting to cells **C4:C5**, and then run the macro.

3. Restore bold formatting to cells **C4:C5** again, and then edit the macro so it removes bold formatting from cells **C4:C7**.

4. Run the macro you created.

5. Delete the macro.

Run macros

Open the **AssignMacros** workbook in Excel, and then perform the following tasks:

1. Assign the **SavingsHighlight** macro to a button on the Quick Access Toolbar. Choose an icon for the button, and display the name Highlight Savings.

2. Run the **SavingsHighlight** macro by selecting the Quick Access Toolbar button.

3. Assign the **EfficiencyHighlight** macro to the **Show Efficiency** shape in the worksheet.

4. Run the **EfficiencyHighlight** macro.

Present information and options as form controls

Open the **InsertFormControls** workbook in Excel, and then perform the following tasks:

1. In cell A2, create a spin button that initially displays the number 0 and lets the user enter a value from 0 to 70 pounds, in increments of 1 pound.

2. In cell B2, create a spin button that initially displays the number 0 and lets the user enter a value from 0 to 16 ounces, in increments of 1 ounce.

3. Add a label that reads Pounds for the first spin button and one that reads Ounces for the second spin button.

4. Position the labels above their respective spin buttons, and top-align them.

5. Create a combo box that derives its values from cells A2:A6 on the **ServiceLevels** worksheet and assign its output to cell C2.

6. Create the label Method for the combo box.

7. Create two option buttons labeled Signature Required and Signature Waived. Assign the value of the Signature Required option button to cell D2 and the value of the Signature Waived option button to cell E2.

8. Create a group that allows either the Signature Required or Signature Waived option button to be selected, but not both.

Work with other Microsoft 365 apps

By itself, Excel provides a broad range of tools so that you can store, present, and summarize data. These capabilities interact gracefully with other Microsoft 365 apps such as Word, PowerPoint, and Outlook. For example, you can create an illustration in PowerPoint and insert it on an Excel worksheet or link from an Excel worksheet to a report that you wrote in Word. Similarly, you can paste a chart created in Excel into an Outlook email message, insert a link to an Excel workbook into a Word document, or embed an Excel workbook onto a PowerPoint slide and update the workbook content from within PowerPoint.

Excel also integrates well with the web. If you know of a web-based resource that would be helpful to a workbook user, you can create a hyperlink from any workbook cell to a file stored on the computer or in a network location or to an online file or webpage. Anyone with access to the hyperlink target location can connect to the file or webpage. You can also create hyperlinks to other cells or sheets in the same workbook and create hyperlinks that create new Office documents or email messages.

This chapter guides you through procedures related to combining Excel, Word, and PowerPoint content; creating hyperlinks; and incorporating Excel charts in other files.

In this chapter

- Combine Excel, Word, and PowerPoint content

- Create hyperlinks from worksheets

- Copy or link to charts

Combine Excel, Word, and PowerPoint content

One benefit of working with Microsoft 365 apps is that you can combine data from Excel with information in Word and PowerPoint to create more-informative workbooks, documents, and presentations. Just as you do when you combine data from more than one Excel workbook, when you combine information from multiple Microsoft 365 apps you can either embed one file into the other or create a link between the two files. When you embed and link a file, you can open and update the original file from within the host file.

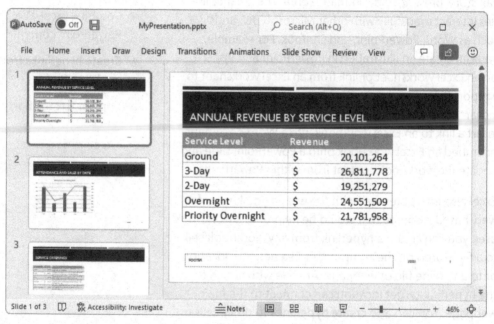

Embed Excel workbook content on PowerPoint slides

Link from Excel to a document or presentation

There are two advantages to creating a link between an Excel workbook and another file instead of copying the file into the workbook:

- Linking to the other file helps minimize the Excel workbook file size.

- Any changes to the linked file are available in the Excel workbook.

You have three options for linking to another Microsoft 365 document:

- Link to the file object and display its content in a window on the Excel worksheet. The initial link is in a very small container that you can resize to display the portion of the content you want visible on the worksheet. Selecting the container opens the linked file in its native app. This is a good option for local and network files.

- Link to the file object and display an icon on the Excel worksheet. Selecting the icon opens the file in its native app. This is also a good option for local and network files.

- Link to the file by using a hyperlink. Selecting the hyperlink opens the file in the online version of its native app (Word Online or PowerPoint Online). This is the best option to use when linking to a document or presentation that is stored in OneDrive or SharePoint, because Excel can sometimes experience trouble rendering online content.

You create a link between an Excel workbook and another Office document by identifying the file, specifying how to connect to it, and choosing how to display the file within your workbook. After you define this connection, you can edit the file by opening it from within Excel or in the app in which the file was created.

When you link to a file object, you can display either a simple link or an icon on the Excel worksheet. The simple link appears as a very small object that represents the upper-left corner of the linked file. You can increase the size of the object to display the linked file content. If displaying the content isn't important to you, you can instead display the icon, or you can create a hyperlink to the file.

To create a link to a file

1. On the **Insert** tab, in the **Text** group, select **Object** to open the **Object** dialog.

2. Select the **Create from File** tab.

3. In the **Create from File** page, select **Browse**.

4. In the **Browse** dialog, browse to the directory that contains the file you want to insert, select it in the file list, and then select **Insert**.

5. Select the **Link to file** checkbox.

6. Select **OK** to create a link from your workbook to the presentation.

13

To edit a file from its link in an Excel workbook

1. Select the linked file in your Excel workbook, point to **ObjectType**, and then select **Edit**.

2. Edit the file in the other app.

3. Save and close the file.

Embed file content

The preceding section described how to link to another file from within an Excel workbook. As mentioned, the advantages of linking to a file are that the workbook remains small, and any changes in the linked file will be reflected in your workbook. The disadvantage is that the linked file must be copied with the workbook or be on a network-accessible computer. If Excel can't find or access the file where the link says it is located, Excel can't display it. You can still open your workbook, but you won't be able to view the linked file's contents.

If file size isn't an issue and you want to ensure that the information in the file is always available, you can embed the file in your workbook. Embedding a file means that the file is saved as part of the workbook, so the embedded file is available wherever the workbook is. However, the embedded version of the file is no longer linked to the original file, so changes in one aren't reflected in the other.

 IMPORTANT To display a linked or embedded file in Excel, the native app must be installed on the computer on which you open the workbook.

Similarly, you can embed, as well as link, an Excel workbook in a document or presentation by inserting the workbook as an object. When doing so, you have the option of linking to the workbook so that updates are reflected in both files.

If you don't want to display the workbook content on the page or slide where you embed it, you can have the other app display an icon that represents the workbook.

To embed a file on an Excel worksheet or a worksheet on a Word document page

1. On the **Insert** tab, in the **Text** group, select the **Object** button.

2. In the **Object** dialog, select the **Create from File** tab.

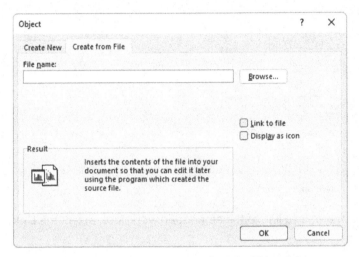

Identify the file to include in your workbook from the Object dialog

3. To the right of the **File name** box, select **Browse**.

4. Navigate to the folder that contains the file you want to embed, select the file, and then select **Insert**.

5. In the **Object** dialog, select **OK**.

To embed an Excel workbook on a PowerPoint slide

1. Open the PowerPoint presentation and position the insertion point on the slide where you want to embed the workbook.

2. On the **Insert** tab, select the **Object** button.

> ⚠️ **IMPORTANT** Microsoft Word has an Object button and an Object arrow. If you're embedding the workbook on a Word document page, select the button or select the arrow and then select Object.

3. In the **Insert Object** dialog, select the **Create from File** option, and then select **Browse**.

13

4. In the **Browse** dialog, navigate to the workbook you want to embed. Select the workbook, and then select **OK** to return to the Insert Object dialog.

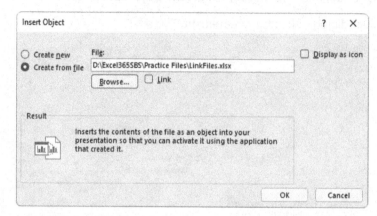

Insert workbook content onto a slide

5. If you want to maintain a link to the embedded workbook, select the **Link** checkbox.

6. If you want to display an icon instead of the workbook content, select the **Display as icon** checkbox.

7. Select **OK** to close the dialog and embed the workbook.

Create hyperlinks from worksheets

When you're browsing the internet, the links that you select on one webpage to open another webpage are *hyperlinks*. Excel workbooks can also contain hyperlinks. Like those on the internet, hyperlinks from an Excel worksheet can connect you to webpages. They can also connect you to cells or sheets in the current workbook (or in another workbook) and to local and network documents, and they can provide a method for workbook users to create new workbooks, documents, presentations, and email messages.

A hyperlink functions much like a link between two cells or between two files, but hyperlinks can reach any computer on the Internet, not only those on a corporate network. Hyperlinks that haven't been selected usually appear as underlined blue text, and hyperlinks that have been selected appear as underlined purple text, but you can change the default appearance settings.

You can create a hyperlink from the text in a cell or from an image; the process for doing either is the same.

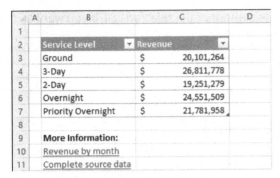

Link from a worksheet to additional resources

You can choose one of four types of targets, or destinations, for the hyperlink:

- An existing file or webpage
- A cell, sheet, or named entity in the current workbook
- A new workbook, document, or presentation
- A new email message with the recipient and subject prefilled

To create a hyperlink to a recently opened Excel, Word, or PowerPoint file

1. Select the cell in which you want the hyperlink to appear.

2. On the **Insert** tab, in the **Links** group, select the **Link** arrow (not the button), and then select the file to which you want to link.

   Excel inserts the target file name in the cell as a hyperlink.

To open the Insert Hyperlink dialog

- On the **Insert** tab, in the **Links** group, select the **Link** button (not the arrow).
- On the **Insert** tab, in the **Links** group, select the **Link** arrow, and then select **Insert Link**.
- Press **Ctrl+K**.

To create a hyperlink to an existing file

1. Select the cell in which you want the hyperlink to appear.

2. Open the **Insert Hyperlink** dialog.

13

3. In the **Link to** list, select **Existing File or Web Page**.

4. In the **Look in** area, navigate to the existing file and select the file name.

5. The **Text to display** box displays the content of the selected cell. If you want to change the display text, replace it.

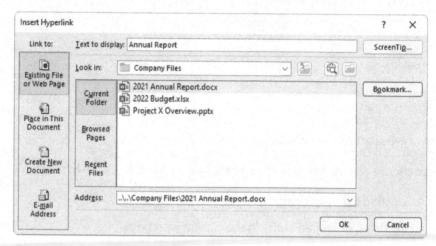

Create a link to an existing file or webpage

6. If you want to display other text in a tooltip when a workbook user points to the hyperlink, select **ScreenTip**. In the **Set Hyperlink ScreenTip** dialog, enter the text in the **ScreenTip text** box, and then select **OK**.

7. In the **Insert Hyperlink** dialog, select **OK** to close the dialog and insert the hyperlinked text.

To create a hyperlink to a webpage

1. Select the cell in which you want the hyperlink to appear.

2. Open the **Insert Hyperlink** dialog.

3. In the **Link to** list, select **Existing File or Web Page**.

4. Do one of the following:

   - In the **Address** box, enter the URL of the webpage to which you want to link.

   - Select the **Address** box arrow, and then from the list, select a webpage you've recently accessed from Excel.

   - In the **Look in** area, select the **Browsed Pages** button, and then select a recently visited webpage.

5. If you want to change the display text, replace it in the **Text to display** box.

6. If you want to display other text in a tooltip when a workbook user points to the hyperlink, select **ScreenTip**. In the **Set Hyperlink ScreenTip** dialog, enter the text in the **ScreenTip text** box, and then select **OK**.

7. In the **Insert Hyperlink** dialog, select **OK**.

To create a hyperlink to a cell, sheet, or named entity in the current workbook

1. Select the cell in which you want the hyperlink to appear.

2. Open the **Insert Hyperlink** dialog.

3. In the **Link to** list, select **Place in This Document**.

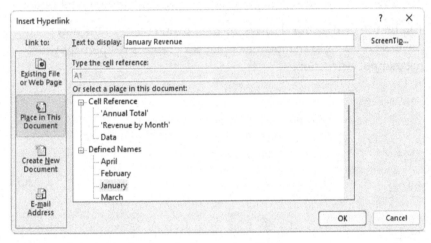

Create hyperlinks that lead to places in the current workbook

4. Do either of the following:

   - Enter the cell reference in the **Type the cell reference** box.

   - Select the link target in the **Or select a place in this document** box.

5. The **Text to display** box displays the name of the cell or place you're linking to. If you want to change the display text, replace it.

6. If you want to display other text in a tooltip when a workbook user points to the hyperlink, select **ScreenTip**. In the **Set Hyperlink ScreenTip** dialog, enter the text in the **ScreenTip text** box, and then select **OK**.

7. In the **Insert Hyperlink** dialog, select **OK**.

13

To create a hyperlink that creates a Word document or PowerPoint presentation

1. Select the cell in which you want the hyperlink to appear.

2. Open the **Insert Hyperlink** dialog.

3. In the **Link to** list, select **Create New Document**.

4. In the **Name of new document** box, enter a file name and extension for the new document.

5. If you want to create the document in a folder other than the one shown in the Full path area, select the **Change** button, navigate to the folder, and then select **OK**.

6. In the When to edit area, select the **Edit the new document later** option.

7. The **Text to display** box displays the path to and name of the new document. If you want to change the display text, replace it—perhaps with a meaningful instruction.

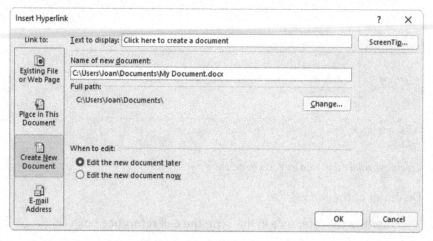

Enable workbook users to create documents

8. In the **Insert Hyperlink** dialog, select **OK**.

To create a hyperlink that creates an email message

1. Select the cell in which you want the hyperlink to appear.

2. Open the **Insert Hyperlink** dialog.

3. In the **Link to** list, select **E-mail Address**.

4. In the **Text to display** box, enter the hyperlink text that you want to display in the selected cell.

5. Do either of the following:

    • In the **E-mail address** box, enter the message recipient's email address.

    • In the **Recently used e-mail addresses** box, select the email address you want to use.

> **TIP** You can select only one email address. If you want to address the message to multiple recipients, separate them with semicolons. For example, Name1@email.com;Name2@email.com.

6. In the **Subject** box, enter a subject for the email message.

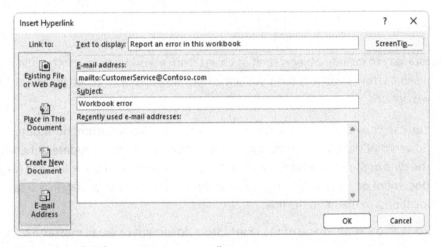

Create a hyperlink that generates a new email message

13

> **TIP** When you leave the E-mail Address text box, Excel inserts *mailto:* before the email address(es).

7. In the **Insert Hyperlink** dialog, select **OK**.

To display the target of a hyperlink

■ Point to the hyperlink. When the cursor shape changes to a pointing hand, select the hyperlink.

To edit a hyperlink

1. Right-click the hyperlink, and then select **Edit Hyperlink** from the context menu.

> **TIP** To display a context menu, right-click or long-press (tap and hold) the element.

2. In the **Edit Hyperlink** dialog, change any aspect of the hyperlink, and then select **OK**.

To delete a hyperlink

- Right-click the hyperlink, and then select **Remove Hyperlink** from the context menu.

Copy or link to charts

One more way to include objects such as charts from a workbook in another file is to copy the chart from Excel and then paste it into its new location. When you do so, you have two options:

- You can copy the chart in Excel and paste it into a Word document or onto a PowerPoint slide. This retains a link to the chart, so the chart updates whenever the data in the source workbook changes. The source workbook and the target document or presentation must retain the same relationship (stay in the same locations) to maintain the link.

- You can paste an image of the chart into a document or email message or onto a slide. This doesn't maintain a link to the original data, but it does provide an accurate picture of the chart's appearance when you captured the image.

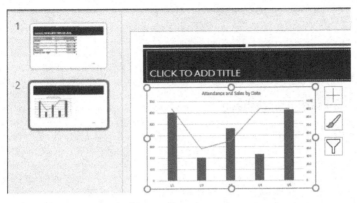

Link to a live chart or embed it as a picture

To paste a linked chart or chart image into a document or presentation

1. In Excel, use any method to copy the chart to the Clipboard.

2. Display the document or presentation into which you want to paste the chart.

3. Position the insertion point in the location where you want to paste the linked chart or chart image.

4. Press **Ctrl+V** or select the **Paste** button in the **Clipboard** group on the **Home** tab.

5. If you want to paste an image instead of a linked chart, select the **Paste Options** button adjacent to the lower-right corner of the pasted chart, and then select the **Picture** button.

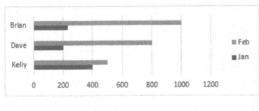

Paste a picture of a chart

Skills review

In this chapter, you learned how to:

- Combine Excel, Word, and PowerPoint content
- Create hyperlinks from worksheets
- Copy or link to charts

Practice tasks

Before you can complete these tasks, you must copy the book's practice files to your computer. The practice files for these tasks are in the **Excel365SBS\Ch13** folder. You can save the results of the tasks in the same folder.

 IMPORTANT You must have PowerPoint installed on your computer to complete some of the following procedures.

Combine Excel, Word, and PowerPoint content

Open the **LinkFiles** workbook in Excel and the **LinkWorkbooks** presentation in PowerPoint, and then perform the following tasks:

1. On the **Summary** worksheet, create a link from cell **B3** to the **LinkWorkbooks** PowerPoint presentation.

2. Display the linked file as an icon in your workbook.

3. From the workbook, open the **LinkWorkbooks** presentation for editing from within Excel, edit the presentation, save your changes, and close the presentation.

4. Switch to the **LinkWorkbooks** presentation and display the second slide.

5. Embed the **EmbedWorkbook** Excel workbook in the practice files folder in the PowerPoint presentation.

6. Edit the embedded file from within PowerPoint and save the presentation.

7. Open the **EmbedWorkbook** workbook in Excel and compare it with your changed file.

Create hyperlinks from worksheets

Open the **CreateHyperlinks** workbook in Excel, and then perform the following tasks:

1. Display the **Revenue by Level** worksheet, create a hyperlink from cell **E2** to the **LevelDescriptions** workbook in the practice files folder.

2. Create a hyperlink from the **Notes** text in cell **B11** to the **Notes** worksheet.

3. Create a mailto hyperlink in cell **C11** that does the following:

   - Displays Information about service levels in the cell.

   - Creates an email message addressed to you, with the subject Test from Excel.

4. On the **Notes** worksheet, delete the hyperlink from cell **B2**.

Copy or link to charts

Open the **LinkCharts** workbook in Excel and the **ReceiveLinks** and **LinkWorkbooks** presentations in PowerPoint, and then perform the following tasks:

1. Paste the chart from the **LinkCharts** workbook into the **ReceiveLinks** presentation.

2. Paste an image of the chart from the **LinkCharts** workbook into the **LinkWorkbooks** presentation.

Collaborate with colleagues

Many individuals provide input into business decisions. You and your colleagues can enhance the Excel workbook data you share by adding comments that offer insight into the information the data represents. If the workbook in which those projections and comments are stored is available on a network, you can allow more than one user to access the workbook at a time by turning on workbook sharing, and you can track changes.

If you prefer to limit the number of colleagues who can view and edit your workbooks, you can add password protection to a workbook, worksheet, cell range, or even an individual cell. You can also hide formulas used to calculate values. If you work in an environment in which you exchange files frequently, you can use a digital signature to help verify that your workbooks and any macros they contain are from a trusted source. Finally, if you want to display information on a website, you can do so by saving a workbook as a webpage.

This chapter guides you through procedures related to managing comments in workbooks, protecting workbooks and worksheets from unwanted changes, finalizing workbooks, saving workbook content as PDF files, and creating and distributing workbook templates.

In this chapter

- Manage comments
- Protect workbooks and worksheets
- Finalize workbooks
- Save workbook content as a PDF file
- Create and distribute workbook templates

Manage comments

Excel makes it easy for you and your colleagues to insert comments in workbook cells, adding insights that go beyond the cell data. When you add a comment to a cell, a flag appears in the upper-right corner of the cell. Depending on the settings, the comment is shown in a box adjacent to the cell or in the Comments pane. In either location, the comment indicates who created the comment and when it was entered.

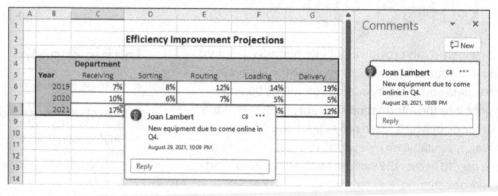

Comment display options

Normally, Excel displays a cell's comment only when you point to the cell. You can change that behavior to display an individual comment or to show all comments within a worksheet. If you want to edit a comment, you can do so. You can also delete a comment from your workbook.

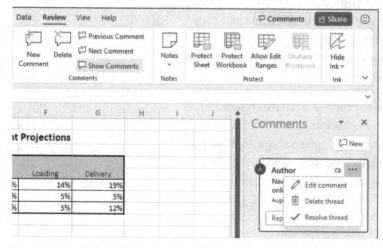

Manage comments on the Review tab and in the Comments pane

IMPORTANT When someone other than the original user edits a comment, that person's input is marked with the new user's name and added to the original comment.

You can control whether a cell displays only the comment indicator or the indicator and the comment itself. Also, if you've just begun to review a worksheet, you can display all the comments on the sheet or move through them one at a time.

To open or close the Comments pane

- Above the right end of the ribbon, select the **Comments** button.

- On the **Review** tab, in the **Comments** group, select the **Show Comments** button.

To attach a comment to a cell

1. Identify the cell to which you want to add a comment, and then do one of the following:

   - Select the cell. Then in the **Comments** pane, select the **New** button.

   - Select the cell. Then on the **Review** tab, in the **Comments** group, select **New Comment**.

   - Right-click the cell, and then select **New Comment** on the context menu.

    TIP To display a context menu, right-click or long-press (tap and hold) the element.

2. In the comment box that opens, enter your comment.

3. To post the comment, do either of the following:

   - In the comment box, below the text entry box, select the **Post comment** button.

   - Press **Ctrl+Enter**.

To display a comment

- Point to or select the cell that includes the attached comment.

To display or hide all comments

- Open or close the **Comments** pane.

To edit a comment

1. Display the comment you want to edit.

2. In the comment bubble, select **More thread actions (...)** and then select **Edit comment**.

3. In the active comment box, edit the comment.

4. To post the comment, select the **Post comment** button or press **Ctrl+Enter**.

To reply to a comment

1. Display the comment to which you want to reply.

2. In the **Reply** box below the original comment or last reply, enter a response.

3. To post the reply, select the **Post reply** button or press **Ctrl+Enter**.

To delete a comment

■ Right-click the cell, and then select **Delete Comment** on the context menu.

Or

1. Display the comment you want to delete.

2. In the comment bubble, select **More thread actions (...)** and then select **Delete thread**.

Or

1. Select the cell that contains the comment.

2. On the **Review** tab, in the **Comments** group, select the **Delete Comment** button.

To change how Excel indicates that a cell contains a comment

1. Display the **Advanced** page of the **Excel Options** dialog.

> **TIP** To open the Excel Options dialog, select File and then at the bottom of the left pane, select Options.

2. Scroll to the **Display** section of the page.

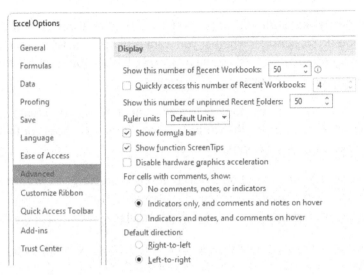

Manage how Excel displays comments

3. In the **For cells with comments, show** list, select one of the three available comment display options:

- **No comments, notes, or indicators**

- **Indicators only, and comments and notes on hover**

- **Indicators and notes, and comments on hover**

To move through worksheet comments

■ On the **Review** tab, in the **Comments** group, do either of the following:

- Select **Previous** to display the previous comment.

- Select **Next** to display the next comment.

14

Protect workbooks and worksheets

You can share Excel workbooks with other people for informational or collaborative purposes. Before you do so, consider whether you want other people to be able to modify all the workbook content or only some of it, and whether you want the workbook to be available to anyone or only specific people.

You can limit access to an entire workbook or to a worksheet by requiring that the user enter a password, either to open the workbook, to edit the workbook, or to display specific worksheets in the workbook.

You can limit access to specific content on a worksheet by protecting the worksheet and allowing users to select or modify only specific elements. Using this technique, you can prevent users from displaying or modifying formulas.

You can limit access to your workbooks or elements within workbooks by setting passwords. When you set a password for an Excel workbook, any users who want to access the workbook must enter its password first. If users don't know the password, they cannot open the workbook. If you decide you no longer want to require users to enter a password to open the workbook, you can remove the password.

> **TIP** The best passwords are long strings of random characters, but random characters are hard to remember. One reasonable method of creating hard-to-guess passwords is to string two or more words and a number together, or to string words together and replace letters with similar numbers. You can replace o with 0, I with 1, E with 3, a with @, S with $ or 5, and so on. For example, the password $uper3xcelGeek21 is 16 characters long; combines letters, numbers, and symbols; and is easy to remember. If you must create a shorter password to meet a system's constraints, avoid dictionary words and include uppercase letters, lowercase letters, numbers, and special symbols such as ! or # if they are allowed.

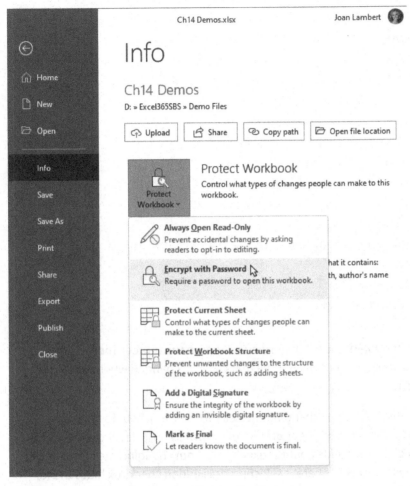

Encrypt a workbook by setting a password to open the file

If you want to allow anyone to open a workbook but want to prevent unauthorized users from editing a worksheet within that workbook, you can protect the individual worksheet. You can also set a password that a user must type in before protection can be turned off and choose which elements of the worksheet a user can change while protection is turned on. You do this from the Protect Sheet dialog.

14

*Limit the worksheet elements that a user
can edit without a password*

The checkbox at the top of the list of allowed actions in the Protect Sheet dialog mentions locked cells. A locked cell is a cell that can't be changed when worksheet protection is turned on.

You can lock or unlock a cell by changing the cell's formatting. You do this in the Format Cells dialog. When worksheet protection is turned on, selecting the Locked checkbox in the dialog prevents unauthorized users from changing the contents or formatting of the locked cell, whereas selecting the Hidden checkbox hides the formulas in the cell.

You might want to hide the formula in a cell if you retrieve sensitive data, such as customer contact information, from another workbook and don't want casual users to see the name of the workbook in a formula. This is also possible using the Format Cells dialog.

Finally, you can password-protect a cell range. For example, you might want to let users enter values in most worksheet cells but also want to protect the cells with formulas that perform calculations based on those values.

To require a password to open a workbook

1. Display the **Info** page of the Backstage view.

2. Select **Protect Workbook**, and then select **Encrypt with Password**.

3. In the **Encrypt Document** dialog, enter a password for the file.

4. Select **OK**.

5. In the **Confirm Password** dialog, re-enter the password, and then select **OK**.

To remove a password from a workbook

1. Open the password-protected workbook.

2. On the **Info** page of the Backstage view, select **Protect Workbook**, and then select **Encrypt with Password**.

3. In the **Encrypt Document** dialog, delete the existing password, and then select **OK**.

To require a password to change workbook structure

1. On the **Review** tab, in the **Protect** group, select **Protect Workbook**.

2. In the **Protect Structure and Windows** dialog, enter a password for the workbook.

3. Select **OK**.

4. In the **Confirm Password** dialog, re-enter the password.

5. Select **OK**.

To remove a password that protects a workbook's structure

1. On the **Review** tab, in the **Protect** group, select **Protect Workbook**.

2. In the **Unprotect Workbook** dialog, enter the workbook's password.

3. Select **OK**.

To protect a worksheet by setting a password

1. On the **Review** tab, in the **Protect** group, select **Protect Sheet**.

2. In the **Protect Sheet** dialog, enter a password in the **Password to unprotect sheet** box.

3. Select the checkboxes next to the actions you want to allow users to perform.

14

4. Select **OK**.

5. In the **Confirm Password** dialog, re-enter the password.

6. Select **OK**.

To remove a worksheet password

1. On the **Review** tab, in the **Protect** group, select **Unprotect Sheet**.

2. In the **Unprotect Sheet** dialog, enter the worksheet's password.

3. Select **OK**.

To lock a cell to prevent editing

1. Do either of the following to open the **Format Cells** dialog:

   - Right-click the cell you want to lock, and then select **Format Cells** on the context menu.

   - Select the cell you want to lock. Then on the **Home** tab, in the **Cells** group, select **Format**, and then select **Format Cells**.

2. In the **Format Cells** dialog, select the **Protection** tab.

3. Select the **Locked** checkbox, and then select **OK**.

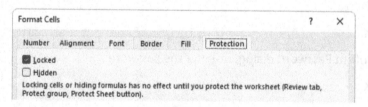

Prevent cell editing and hide formulas when you protect a sheet

To hide cell formulas

1. Right-click the cell you want to hide, and then select **Format Cells** on the context menu.

2. On the **Protection** tab, select the **Hidden** checkbox.

3. Select **OK**.

 IMPORTANT The Locked and Hidden settings take effect only when the worksheet is protected.

To require a password to edit a cell range

1. On the **Review** tab, in the **Protect** group, select **Allow Edit Ranges**.

2. For each cell range you want to protect, do the following:

   a. In the **Allow Users to Edit Ranges** dialog, select **New**.

   b. In the **New Range** dialog, in the **Title** box, enter a descriptive name for the protected cell range.

   c. In the **Refers to cells** box, enter or select the cell range you want to affect.

   d. In the **Range password** box, enter a password for the protected cell range.

   e. In the **New Range** dialog, select **OK**.

   f. In the **Confirm Password** dialog, re-enter the password, and then select **OK**.

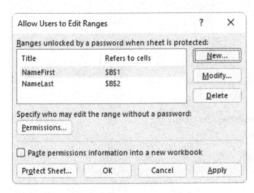

Define the cell ranges users can edit after a worksheet is protected

3. After you define all the protected cell ranges, select **Apply** or **OK** in the **Allow Users to Edit Ranges** dialog.

 IMPORTANT You must protect your worksheet for the range password settings to take effect.

14

To remove a cell range password

1. On the **Review** tab, in the **Protect** group, select **Allow Edit Ranges**.

2. In the **Allow Users to Edit Ranges** dialog, select the range you want to edit.

3. Select **Delete**, and then select **OK**.

Finalize workbooks

Distributing a workbook to other users carries many risks—including the possibility that the workbook might contain information you don't want to share with users outside your organization. With Excel, you can inspect a workbook for information you might not want to distribute to other people and create a read-only final version that prevents other people from making changes to the workbook content.

By using the Document Inspector, you can quickly locate comments and annotations, document properties and personal information, custom XML data, headers and footers, hidden rows and columns, hidden worksheets, and invisible content. You can then easily remove any hidden or personal information that the Document Inspector finds.

Check for personally identifiable information by using the Document Inspector

The Document Inspector checks your document for every category of information selected in the list. When the Document Inspector displays its results, you can select which pieces of personally identifiable information you want to remove.

When you're done making changes to a workbook, you can mark it as final. Marking a workbook as final sets the status property to Final and disables data entry and editing commands. If you later decide that you want to make more changes, you can do so, save your changes, and mark the worksheet as final again.

To remove personally identifiable information from a workbook

1. Save the workbook.

2. Display the **Info** page of the Backstage view.

3. Select **Check for Issues**, and then select **Inspect Document**.

> **TIP** If you didn't save your workbook earlier, Excel will prompt you to do so now.

4. If there is a category of content you don't want the Document Inspector to look for, clear the checkbox for that category.

5. Select **Inspect**.

6. In the results list, select the **Remove All** button next to any category of information you want to remove.

7. If necessary, select **Reinspect**, and then select **Inspect** to ensure that no personal information remains in the file.

8. Select **Close**.

To mark a workbook as final

1. Press **Ctrl+S** to save the workbook.

2. On the **Info** page of the Backstage view, select **Protect Workbook**, and then at the bottom of the menu, select **Mark as Final**.

3. In the confirmation dialog that appears, select **OK**.

4. In the informational dialog that appears, select **OK**.

> **TIP** To edit a file that has been marked as final, open the file. Then, on the message bar, select Edit Anyway.

14

Save workbook content as a PDF file

There will be times when you want to distribute information from a workbook as a PDF file so the recipients can see the information but not interact with it. You can save a workbook, or selected information from it, as a PDF file by using the functionality built into Microsoft 365. It isn't necessary to install Adobe Acrobat to perform this task.

There are two methods of saving workbook content as a PDF file. The simplest method saves the active worksheet content as a PDF file. The other method allows you to choose precisely which workbook content to include in the PDF file.

PDF files can be displayed in Adobe Acrobat or Adobe Reader. They can also be displayed in a web browser such as Microsoft Edge. This makes them a good file format for widespread distribution, as most people will be able to view the file content, and it will appear to them as you intend it to.

To save a worksheet as a PDF file

1. Display the **Save As** page of the Backstage view.

2. Browse to the folder in which you want to save the PDF file.

3. In the **Save as type** list, select **PDF (*.pdf)**.

4. The file name defaults to the same as the original workbook. If you want to change it, do so in the **File name** box.

5. Select **Save**.

To save workbook content as a PDF file

1. Do one of the following:

   - To save the entire workbook, display any worksheet.

   - To save a specific worksheet, display the worksheet.

   - To save only specific content, select the content.

2. Display the **Export** page of the Backstage view.

3. In the left pane, select **Create PDF/XPS Document**, and then in the right pane, select **Create PDF/XPS**.

4. In the **Publish as PDF or XPS** dialog, browse to the folder in which you want to save the PDF file.

   The file name defaults to the same as the original workbook and the file type to PDF (*.pdf). You can change these if you want to.

5. In the **Optimize for** area at the bottom of the dialog, do either of the following:

   - Select **Standard** to create a file of a higher quality and larger size.

   - Select **Minimum size** to create a file of lesser (but still good) quality and smaller size.

6. If you want to save something other than the worksheet in the PDF file, select **Options**. In the **Page range** and **Publish what** areas, select the appropriate options. Then select **OK**.

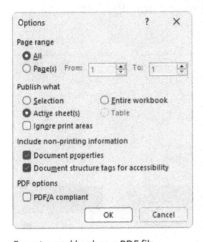

Export a workbook as a PDF file

7. In the **Publish as PDF or XPS** dialog, select **Publish**.

8. Review the published PDF file content to ensure that it looks the way you want it to.

14

Create and distribute workbook templates

Suppose you've established a design you like for your monthly sales-tracking workbook, and you want to create other workbooks with the same look and feel. You can save the workbook as a template for similar workbooks you will create in the future.

You can leave the workbook's labels to aid in data entry, but you should remove any existing data and unneeded worksheets from a workbook that you save as a template, both to avoid data-entry errors and to remove any confusion as to whether the workbook is a template.

Excel uses two template file types: Excel Template (*.xltx) and Excel Macro-Enabled Template (*.xltm). If you want to save macros in the template, choose the macro-enabled option.

> **TIP** For information about using macros in Excel workbooks, see Chapter 12, "Automate tasks and input."

When you save an Excel file as a template, Excel automatically saves it in your Custom Office Templates folder. This makes it available to you from the Personal view of the New page of the Backstage view.

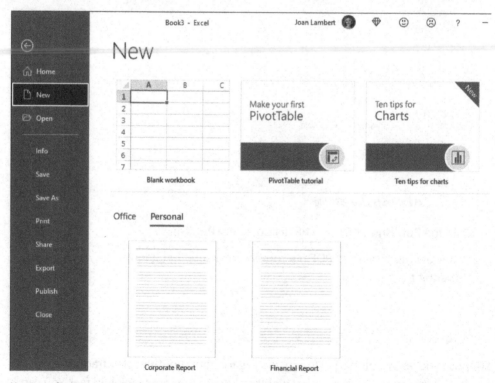

Your templates are available from the Personal view of the New page

To create a workbook based on the template, display the Personal view and then select the template. Excel creates the new file as a regular workbook (an .xlsx file) with the template's content and formatting in place.

You can distribute Excel templates for other people to use. You can email the template file as you would any other file or post the template to a shared location for people to download. Each user should save the file in their Custom Office Templates folder.

To save a workbook as a template

1. Display the **Save As** page of the Backstage view.

2. Do either of the following:

   - In the upper-right corner of the page, select the **Save as type** arrow, and then select **Excel Template (*.xltx)**.

   - In the **Other locations** list, select **Browse**. Then in the **Save As** dialog, select the **Save as type** arrow, and then select **Excel Template (*.xltx)**.

 TIP If the template contains macros that you want to be available in the files created from the template, choose Excel Macro-Enabled Template (*.xltm).

When you select a template file type, Excel automatically changes the file location to your Custom Office Templates folder.

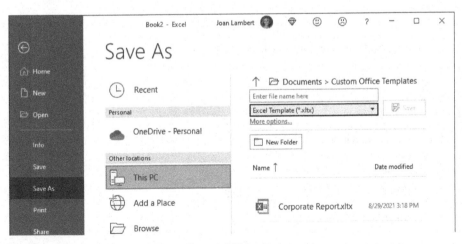

Save templates in the Custom Office Templates folder

3. In the **File name** box, enter a name for the template workbook.

4. Select **Save**.

14

To create a workbook from a custom template

1. Display the **New** page of the Backstage view.

2. In the area below the featured templates, just above the Search box, select **Personal** to display the templates in your Custom Office Templates folder.

3. Select the template from which you want to create a new workbook.

To locate your Custom Office Templates folder

- Display the **Save** page of the Excel Options dialog.

  At the bottom of the **Save workbooks** section of the page, your Custom Office Templates folder location is shown in the **Default personal templates location** box.

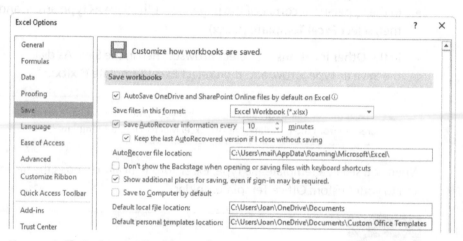

You can modify the Custom Office Templates location

Skills review

In this chapter, you learned how to:

- Manage comments

- Protect workbooks and worksheets

- Finalize workbooks

- Save workbook content as a PDF file

- Create and distribute workbook templates

Practice tasks

Before you can complete these tasks, you must copy the book's practice files to your computer. The practice files for these tasks are in the **Excel365SBS\Ch14** folder. You can save the results of the tasks in the same folder.

Manage comments

Open the **ManageComments** workbook in Excel, and then perform the following tasks:

1. Add comments to four or five cells.

2. Edit one of the comments to invite a colleague to provide input for that value.

3. Move through the comments, going forward and backward through the list.

4. Change the workbook so it displays all comments.

5. Delete a comment.

Protect workbooks and worksheets

Open the **ProtectWorkbooks** workbook in Excel, and then perform the following tasks:

1. Use the controls on the **Info** page of the Backstage view to encrypt the workbook with a password.

2. On the **Performance** worksheet, select cell **B8** and format the cell so its contents are locked and hidden.

3. Use the controls on the **Review** tab to protect the active worksheet with a password after clearing the **Select locked cells** and **Select unlocked cells** checkboxes in the dialog.

4. On the **Weights** worksheet, select cells **A3:B6** and define a protected range named **AllWeights**.

5. Protect the **Weights** worksheet by requiring users to enter a password to edit it.

Finalize workbooks

Open the **FinalizeWorkbooks** workbook in Excel, and then perform the following tasks:

1. Use the Document Inspector to inspect the workbook.

2. Remove any personally identifiable information from the file.

3. Use the tools on the **Info** page of the Backstage view to mark the file as final.

4. Close the workbook.

5. Reopen the workbook and select the **Edit Anyway** button on the message bar to work with the file.

6. Save any changes and close the workbook.

Save workbook content as a PDF file

Open the **DistributeFiles** workbook in Excel, and then perform the following tasks:

1. Export only the **Data** worksheet of the workbook as a PDF file.

2. Export the entire workbook as a PDF file.

Create and distribute workbook templates

Open the **CreateTemplate** workbook in Excel, and then perform the following tasks:

1. Add a worksheet based on an existing template, such as the Sales Report template, to the workbook.

2. Save the new workbook as a template and close it.

3. In the Backstage view, select **New**.

4. Create a new workbook based on an existing template.

Part 4

Perform advanced analysis

Perform business intelligence analysis

Organizations of all kinds generate and collect data from operations, sales, and customers. As the volume of data grows, so does the importance of generating useful insights into your operations from that data. Excel supports business intelligence analysis, which is the practice of examining data to improve business performance.

Analytical tools such as formulas, data tables, and PivotTables all provide valuable insights into your data, but their applications can be limited in size and scope. Excel for Microsoft 365 includes many advanced data analysis capabilities that were previously exclusive to enterprise customers. One technology underlying the new tools is the Excel Data Model, which you can use to create relationships among Excel tables in your workbooks. Add to this the ability to import and analyze large data sets by using Power Query and Power Pivot, and Excel for Microsoft 365 puts significant data analysis capabilities at your fingertips.

This chapter guides you through procedures related to enabling the Data Analysis add-ins and adding tables to the Excel Data Model, defining relationships between tables, analyzing data by using Power Pivot, displaying data on timelines, and importing external data by using Power Query.

In this chapter

- Manage the Excel Data Model
- Define relationships between data sources
- Manage data by using Power Pivot
- Display data on timelines
- Import data by using Power Query

> ⚠ IMPORTANT The tools and techniques described in this chapter will be available to you only after you enable the Data Analysis add-ins.

Manage the Excel Data Model

Put simply, a data model is a collection of information consisting of data from multiple sources. The Excel Data Model manages Excel tables, query tables, and other data sources as one multidimensional entity with relationships between the data sources, much like the relationships between tables in a relational database such as Access. The Excel Data Model isn't a specific file that you can open, but you can easily access and work with the data that you collect in it from Excel.

Two data analysis tools that build on the Excel Data Model are available for Excel for Microsoft 365. You can use these to manage and perform advanced analysis on large data sets.

- **Power Pivot** is available as an Excel add-in. It provides a tool with which you can populate the Excel Data Model, create and manage relationships between data sources, and create PivotTables using data from multiple sources. You must enable the Power Pivot add-in before you can use it.

> **TIP** The Power Pivot technology is also available as part of Microsoft's Power BI (Business Intelligence) service, with which you can generate powerful interactive data visualizations to inform business decisions.

- **Power Query** functionality is built into Excel. It allows you to connect to or import external data, transform a view of the data to meet the needs of your specific query, combine data from multiple sources, and load the query results into a worksheet or data model. (If this sounds familiar, it's because Power Query was available in previous versions of Excel as the Get & Transform Data tool, and that remains the ribbon group name for the Power Query functionality.) The worksheet or data model you create by using Power Query remains linked to the data source so you can refresh it with new data from time to time.

Power Pivot for Excel includes two views: Data view, which displays one table at a time in a grid like that of an Excel worksheet, and Diagram view, which displays visual representations of all the tables in the Excel Data Model and any relationships between them.

Power View data visualizations

A third data analysis tool, Power View, was available for users of earlier versions of Excel. Power View enabled users to create "charts on steroids" from within Excel. The available data visualizations included those that Excel users are familiar with from working with charts, PivotTables, and PivotCharts, as well as the ability to display table records as informative visual "cards" and to filter and pivot data through visual "tiles." Based on feedback from customers, Microsoft decided to offer the Power View technology as part of its Power BI Desktop product. Power View is not available as part of the Microsoft 365 offering; however, Power BI Desktop is currently available as a free download from the Microsoft Store. If you're interested in visual data analysis, you can have a lot of fun playing with it.

For more information about Power BI Desktop, scan this QR code

15

To enable the Power Pivot add-in

1. Display the **Add-Ins** page of the **Excel Options** dialog.

> **TIP** To open the Excel Options dialog, select File, and then at the bottom of the left pane, select Options.

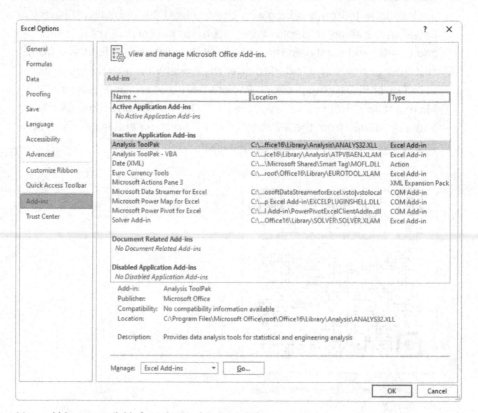

Many add-ins are available from the Excel Options dialog

2. Review the entries on this page to locate "Microsoft Power Pivot for Excel" and do either of the following:

   - If it is in the **Active Application Add-ins** section at the top of the page, then the add-in is already enabled. If it is, select **Cancel** to close the Excel Options dialog.

   - If it is in the **Inactive Application Add-ins** section, continue to the next step.

3. In the **Manage** list in the lower-left corner of the page, select **COM Add-ins**. Then select the adjacent **Go** button to open the COM Add-ins dialog.

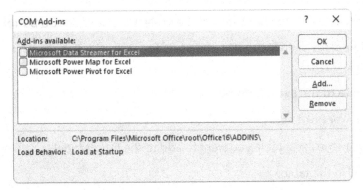

Component Object Model (COM) add-ins

> ✓ **TIP** In the COM Add-ins dialog, select the name Microsoft Power Pivot for Excel. Then look at the Location shown near the lower-left corner of the dialog. The Power Pivot add-in is already on your computer; you simply need to *enable* it—that is, to tell Excel that you want to use it.

4. Select the **Microsoft Power Pivot for Excel** checkbox, and then select **OK**.

5. Confirm that the Power Pivot tab has been added to the ribbon.

The Power Pivot tab is visible in all workbooks unless you hide it

> ✓ **TIP** After you enable Power Pivot, a Manage Data Model button becomes available in the Data Tools group on the Data tab. If only the icon is visible, pointing to it displays the tooltip *Go to the Power Pivot Window*.

15

To disable a COM add-in

1. Display the **Add-Ins** page of the **Excel Options** dialog.

2. In the **Manage** list, select **COM Add-ins**. Then select the adjacent **Go** button.

3. In the **COM Add-ins** dialog, clear the checkbox for each add-in you want to disable. Then select **OK**.

To add an Excel table to the Excel Data Model

1. Enable the Power Pivot add-in.

2. In Excel, display the Excel table you want to add to the Data Model.

3. Select any cell in the table.

4. On the **Power Pivot** tab, in the **Tables** group, select **Add to Data Model** to add the table to the Excel Data Model and display it in the Power Pivot for Excel window, in the default Data view.

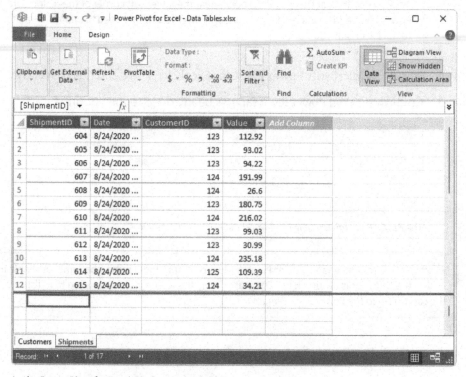

In the Power Pivot for Excel window, a sheet tab represents each data source

To automatically integrate data into the Excel Data Model

1. Display the **Data** page of the **Excel Options** dialog.

2. In the **Data options** section, select the **Prefer the Excel Data Model when creating PivotTables, QueryTables and Data Connections** checkbox. Then select **OK**.

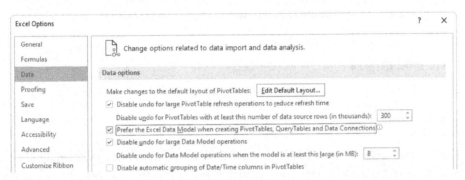

New in Excel for Microsoft 365: Data Model options on the Data page

To display the Excel Data Model

1. Do either of the following to open the **Power Pivot for Excel** window:

    - On the **Power Pivot** tab, in the **Data Model** group, select **Manage**.

    - On the **Data** tab, in the **Data Tools** group, select **Manage Data Model**.

> **TIP** As mentioned previously, after you enable Power Pivot, a *Manage Data Model* button becomes available in the Data Tools group on the Data tab. If only the icon is visible, pointing to it displays the tooltip *Go to the Power Pivot Window.*

2. In the **Power Pivot for Excel** window, select the sheet tab of the worksheet you want to display.

> **TIP** Until you add a data source to the Excel Data Model, the area of the Power Pivot for Excel window between the ribbon/formula bar and status bar is empty.

15

To switch from Power Pivot to Excel

- In the **Power Pivot for Excel** window, at the left end of the title bar, select the **Switch to Workbook** button (labeled with the Excel icon).

- On the Windows taskbar, select the **Excel** taskbar button, and then select the workbook you want to switch to.

TIP When the Power Pivot for Excel window is open, the Excel taskbar button represents both Excel and Power Pivot for Excel.

To close the Power Pivot for Excel window

- At the right end of the title bar, select the **Close** (×) button.

- On the **File** tab, select **Close**.

- Press **Ctrl+F4**.

Define relationships between data sources

One of the fundamental principles of good database design is to store data about each type of business object, such as customers, products, or orders, in a table by itself, separate from the other tables in the database. For example, you might store data about customers in one table, data about orders in a second table, and data about shipments in a third table.

Each table has one column, or field, that contains a unique value for each row, or record. This value, called the primary key, distinguishes each row of data from every other row. For example, each record in the Customers table could have a unique CustomerID field as its primary key. Each record in the Orders table could have a unique OrderID field and could reference the CustomerID field to identify the customer who placed each order. And the Shipments table could reference the CustomerID as the shipment recipient and the OrderID as the tracking number. When you use primary keys to identify unique records, it is not necessary to repeat any information within multiple tables. This saves space and prevents errors when updating information in the database.

 TIP The best keys are arbitrary numeric values. If you try to store information in a key field, you will likely run into issues of duplication that make processing your data harder, not easier.

You can create connections between tables by identifying fields they have in common. For example, consider a Customers table that has two fields—CustomerID and CustomerName—and an Orders table that has three fields—OrderID, CustomerID, and OrderPrice. The CustomerID field appears in both tables, so it can be used to establish a link, or relationship, between the two tables.

> **IMPORTANT** Before you can define relationships between data sources, you must add the data sources to the Excel Data Model.

In the Customers table, each CustomerID field value occurs exactly once, so that column is called a primary key. The CustomerID field also occurs in the Orders table, but because it's possible for a customer to place more than one order, the CustomerID field's values can repeat. When a key field appears in another table in which it doesn't distinguish each row from every other row, it's called a foreign key.

Using Power Pivot for Excel, you can create relationships between various data sources in the Excel Data Model in the same way that you do between tables in a relational database. When you create a relationship, you link the primary key field from one table to the corresponding foreign key field in another table. Although it's easier to identify matching fields if they have the same name, that isn't a requirement; they only need to contain the same data.

You can create relationships in Power Pivot for Excel by using many methods. The relationships are expressed visually in Diagram view.

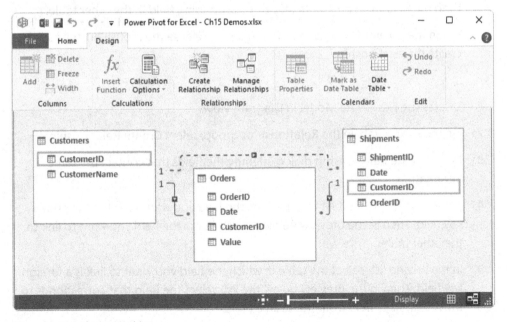

Diagram view of related tables

15

After you define a relationship in the Data Model, you can create PivotTables that use data from both Excel tables. You can also edit or delete relationships if necessary.

To display the Excel Data Model in Diagram view

■ In the **Power Pivot for Excel** window, do either of the following:

- On the **Home** tab, in the **View** group, select **Diagram View**.

- At the right end of the status bar, select the **Diagram** button.

To display the Excel Data Model in Data view

■ In the **Power Pivot for Excel** window, do either of the following:

- On the **Home** tab, in the **View** group, select **Data View**.

- Near the right end of the status bar, select the **Grid** button.

To define a relationship between tables

1. Display the Excel Data Model in **Diagram view**.

2. Identify the fields that contain the same information.

3. Drag the field from one table to the corresponding field in the other table.

4. When the pointer changes to a curved arrow, release the mouse button to create the relationship.

Or

1. Display the Excel Data Model in **Diagram view**.

2. On the **Design** tab, in the **Relationships** group, select **Create Relationship**.

3. In the **Create Relationship** dialog, identify the fields that contain the same information.

4. In the first list, select the table in which the field you want to link is the primary key field. Then in the preview below the list, select the field you want to link to the other table.

5. In the second list, select the table in which the field you want to link is a foreign key field. Then in the preview below the list, select the field that corresponds to the primary key field from the source table.

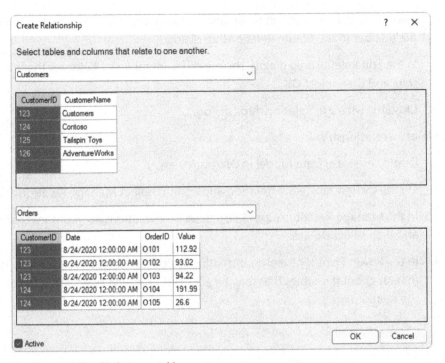

Creating a relationship between tables

6. In the **Create Relationship** dialog, select **OK**.

To edit an existing relationship

1. Display the Excel Data Model in **Diagram view**.

2. On the **Design** tab, in the **Relationships** group, select **Manage Relationships**.

3. In the **Manage Relationships** dialog, select the relationship you want to change.

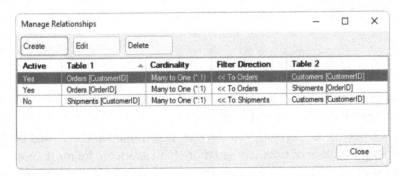

Display and edit relationships between tables in the Data Model

15

4. Select **Edit** to open the Edit Relationship dialog, which is identical other than the title bar to the Create Relationship dialog.

5. In the Edit Relationship dialog, choose different tables or fields for the relationship, and then select **OK**.

6. Close the **Manage Relationships** dialog.

To delete a relationship

1. Display the Excel Data Model in **Diagram view**.

2. On the **Design** tab, in the **Relationships** group, select **Manage Relationships**.

3. In the **Manage Relationships** dialog, select the relationship you want to delete, and then select **Delete**.

4. In the Power Pivot for Excel confirmation dialog that appears, review the information about the tables that may be affected, and then select **OK** to delete the relationship.

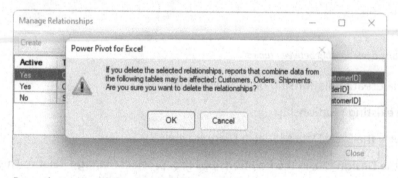

Ensure that you're deleting the correct relationship

5. Close the **Manage Relationships** dialog.

Manage data by using Power Pivot

When the Excel product team changed the underlying file format of Excel 2007 from XLS to XLSX, they let users store much more data on each worksheet. Rather than limiting each worksheet to 65,536 rows, you can now store up to 1,048,576 rows of data. In 2007, that larger number of rows seemed more than adequate for most Excel users. It still is, but the powerful business intelligence analysis tools built into Excel led users to import large data sets and to find ways to combine data collections that spanned multiple worksheets.

Originally introduced as an add-in for Excel 2010, Power Pivot is a tool you can use to work with any amount of data, as long as the total file size is less than 2 gigabytes (GB) and takes up less than 4 GB of memory. For such large data collections, you'll usually work with summaries of your data, although you can focus on specific aspects of the data by sorting and filtering.

 SEE ALSO For more information about creating filters, see "Filter data ranges and tables" in Chapter 5, "Manage worksheet data."

When you bring a data collection into Power Pivot, it attempts to identify the data type of each column. The identification is usually accurate, but some data types can cause confusion. For example, currency or accounting data columns are occasionally identified as containing regular numbers that include decimal values. If this type of mistake happens, you can change the column's data type within Power Pivot.

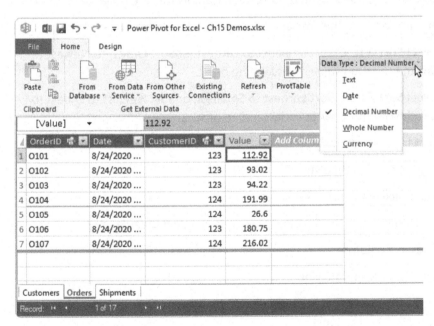

It might be necessary to change the data type of imported data

 IMPORTANT Changing the data type of a column might affect the precision of the column values and the results of calculations performed using the data.

15

Most large data sets contain raw data, such as sales amounts, and rely on a visualization or summary software program to calculate values such as sales tax, commissions, or profit. To add this type of summary to your Power Pivot data, you can define a calculated column. The formula syntax for creating a calculated column is very similar to creating a formula that refers to an Excel table column, so you already possess the skills to create them.

As with columns in Excel tables, you can rename and delete Power Pivot columns, but the real analytical power of Power Pivot comes from creating PivotTables from the large Power Pivot data sets. Creating a PivotTable from 10,000 rows of data is useful; creating a PivotTable from 10,000,000 rows can provide incredible insight.

To sort values in a column in ascending or descending order

1. In Power Pivot, display the table in Data view.

2. Select any cell in the column by which you want to sort the table.

3. On the **Home** tab, in the **Sort and Filter** group, do either of the following:

   - Select **Sort A to Z**, **Sort Smallest to Largest**, or **Sort Oldest to Newest** to sort the column's values in ascending order.

   - Select **Sort Z to A**, **Sort Largest to Smallest**, or **Sort Newest to Oldest** to sort the column's values in descending order.

To clear a sort from a sorted column

1. Display the table in Data view.

2. Select any cell in the sorted column.

3. On the **Home** tab, in the **Sort and Filter** group, select **Clear Sort**.

To filter values in a column

1. Display the table in Data view.

2. Select the filter button at the right end of the header of the column by which you want to filter the table.

Filter Power Pivot columns by creating rules or selecting specific values

3. In the filter list, do either of the following:

    - Select *DataType* **Filters**, select the type of filter rule you want to create, create the rule, and then select **OK**.

    - Select or clear the checkboxes to show or hide individual values.

4. Select **OK** to apply the filter.

To clear filters from a Power Pivot field

- On the **Home** tab, in the **Sort and Filter** group, select **Clear All Filters**.

- Select the filter button of the filtered column, and then in the filter list, select **Clear Filter from "***FieldName***"**.

To change the format of a column

1. Display the table in Data view.

2. Select a cell in the column you want to format.

3. On the **Home** tab, in the **Formatting** group, do any of the following:

- Select **Data Type**, select the new data type, and then confirm the change in the dialog.

- Select **Format**, and then select the new data format.

- Select the **Apply Currency Format**, **Apply Percentage Format**, or **Thousands Separator** button to apply that format to the column values.

- Select the **Increase Decimal** or **Decrease Decimal** button to increase or decrease the number of digits shown to the right of the decimal point.

To add a calculated column to a data source

1. Display the table in Data view and if necessary, scroll to the right to display the Add Column column to the right of the last data column.

2. Select row 1 of the **Add Column** column.

3. Enter = followed by the formula you want to create. Then add fields to the formula by selecting them.

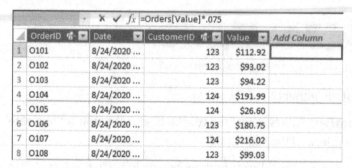

Define calculated columns

4. Press **Enter** to complete the formula and fill the calculation to the rest of the column.

To rename a column

1. Display the table in Data view.

2. Double-click the header cell of the column you want to rename.

3. Enter the new column name, and then press **Enter**.

To delete a column

1. Display the table in Data view.

2. For the column you want to delete, do either of the following:

   - Right-click the header cell and then select **Delete Columns** on the context menu.

   > **TIP** To display a context menu, right-click or long-press (tap and hold) the element.

   - Select anywhere in the column and then on the **Design** tab, in the **Columns** group, select **Delete**, and then select **Table Columns**.

To rename a table

1. Display the Excel Data Model in **Data view**.

2. Right-click the sheet tab of the table you want to rename, and then select **Rename** on the context menu.

3. Replace the selected table name, and then press **Enter**.

To delete a table from the Data Model

1. Display the Excel Data Model in **Data view**.

2. Right-click the sheet tab of the table you want to delete, and then select **Delete** on the context menu.

3. In the **Power Pivot for Excel** dialog, select **Yes** to verify that you want to delete the table and its associations.

To create a PivotTable from the Data Model

1. Display the Excel Data Model in **Data view** or **Diagram view**.

2. On the **Home** tab, select the **PivotTable** button (not the arrow).

15

3. In the **Create PivotTable** dialog, select the **New Worksheet** option, and
    then select **OK** to create a PivotTable that references all available data in
    the data model.

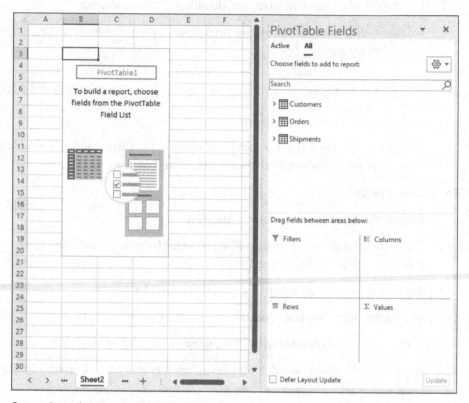

Summarize and pivot on any available data

Display data on timelines

Business data often records events at a specific point in time, whether it's a sale to an individual customer on a specific day or net profit for a quarter or a year. If your data contains a time-based value, such as the date of a sale, you can analyze the data on a timeline.

A timeline provides a graphical interface you can use to filter a PivotTable. The timeline function recognizes date values in table columns. You can filter the aggregated data by year, quarter, month, or day.

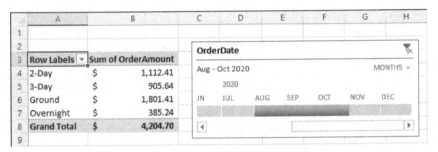

Filter data by selecting one or more contiguous time periods on the timeline

---

✅ **TIP** Timelines and slicers are built on the same design philosophy: providing a visual indication of the elements included and excluded by a filter. Timelines do for chronological data what slicers do for category data.

Within a timeline, you can select individual increments, such as days or months, or ranges of those same values. As with other objects, such as charts, you can change the appearance of your timeline, resize it, hide or display elements, and delete it when it's no longer required.

To create a timeline for a table

1. Select a cell in an Excel table that is based on a connection to an external data source or that is part of the workbook's Excel Data Model.

2. On the **Insert** tab, in the **Filters** group, select **Timeline**.

15

3. In the **Existing Connections** dialog, from either the **Connections** tab or the **Data Model** tab, select the path to the Excel table for which you want to create the timeline. Then select **Open**.

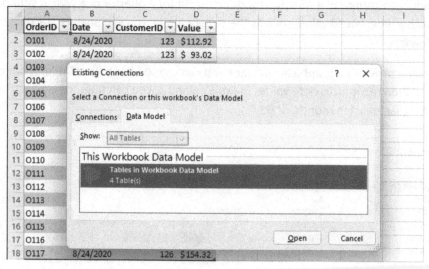

Quickly access all tables in the Excel Data Model

4. In the **Insert Timelines** dialog, select the checkbox adjacent to the field or fields you want to include in the timeline.

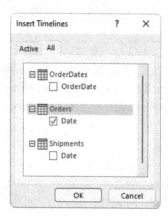

Choose from all columns that contain dates

5. Select **OK** to create the timeline.

To create a timeline for a PivotTable

1. Select a cell in the PivotTable.

2. On the **Insert** tab, in the **Filters** group, select **Timeline**.

3. In the **Insert Timelines** dialog, select the checkbox adjacent to the field or fields you want to include in the timeline. Then select **OK** to create the timeline.

To filter a PivotTable by using a timeline

1. Create a timeline for the PivotTable.

2. In the upper-right corner of the timeline, select the current time period, and then select the time period you want to display (**DAYS**, **MONTHS**, **QUARTERS**, or **YEARS**).

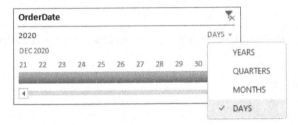

Select the filter increment for the timeline

3. In the scrolling time display, do any of the following:

   - Select the increment you want to display.

   - Select a range of increments by selecting the first increment in the range and then dragging the handle on the left or right end of the selection bar to extend it.

To clear a timeline filter

- In the timeline, at the right end of the title bar, select the **Clear Filter** button.

To change the appearance of a timeline

1. Select the timeline.

2. On the **Timeline** tool tab, in the **Timeline Styles** gallery, select the style you want to apply.

15

To resize a timeline

1. Select the timeline.

2. Drag any of the handles on the timeline to change its size, as follows:

   - Drag a handle in the middle of the top or bottom edge to make the timeline shorter or taller.

   - Drag a handle in the middle of the left or right edge to make the timeline wider or narrower.

   - Drag a handle in the corner of the timeline to change its size both horizontally and vertically.

Or

1. Select the timeline.

2. On the **Timeline** tool tab, in the **Size** group, enter or select values in the **Height** and **Width** boxes.

To hide or display timeline elements

1. Select the timeline.

2. On the **Timeline** tool tab, in the **Show** group, select or clear any of these checkboxes:

   - **Header**

   - **Selection Label**

   - **Scrollbar**

   - **Time Level**

To change a timeline caption

1. Select the timeline.

2. On the **Timeline** tool tab, in the **Timeline** group, replace the caption in the **Timeline Caption** box.

3. Press **Enter**.

To delete a timeline

- Right-click the timeline, and then select **Remove Timeline** on the context menu.

Import data by using Power Query

Power Query is a versatile tool built into Excel for Microsoft 365 that you can use to manage external data sources effectively. Power Query and Power Pivot aren't dependent on each other, but they work well together.

Using Power Query, you can create data connections to many different sources:

- **Files** These include Excel workbooks, CSV files, XML files, and text files.

- **Databases** These include Microsoft SQL Server, Access, SQL Server Analysis Services, Oracle, IBM DB2, MySQL, PostgreSQL, Sybase, and Teradata.

- **Microsoft Azure storage** These include Azure SQL Database, Azure Marketplace, Azure HDInsight, Azure Blob Storage, and Azure Table Storage.

- **Other sources** These include the web, Microsoft SharePoint lists, Hadoop files (HDFS), Facebook, Salesforce, and other sources with available Open Database Connectivity (ODBC) drivers.

Creating a query involves identifying the type of data source to which you want to connect, selecting the software from among that type's choices, and providing any necessary credentials to access the data source. Some systems require you to log on to an account to access your data, for example.

After you define the data connection, you can specify the elements of the data source that you want to import. Many Excel files and databases contain multiple tables; you can select those you want to import.

15

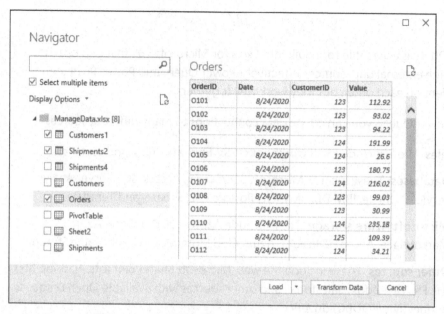

Icons adjacent to the file elements indicate their types

After you import the query data as an Excel table, you can work with it as you would any other data. You can unlock more-powerful tools by enabling the Power Pivot add-in and adding the query data table to the Excel Data Model. After the table is part of the Excel Data Model, you can define relationships between it and other tables to enhance your analysis.

Some data sources are poorly designed and don't include an index field (or primary key), which contains a unique value for each row. If that's the case, you can add an index, starting at the value of your choice and increasing in the increment you want, to provide the tool you need to create relationships between tables.

As with other Excel workbook objects, you can edit your queries after you create them. You can select which columns to include in or exclude from your results, change the query's name, edit or undo a change, and even delete your query to generate the result you want.

To create a query

1. On the **Data** tab, in the **Get & Transform Data** group, select **Get Data**, and then select the type of data source to which you want to connect.

2. In the **Import Data** dialog, browse to and select the data source you want to query, and then select **Import**.

3. In the **Navigator**, do either of the following:

    -   To query one data source, select the table or worksheet you want to query.

    -   To query multiple data sources, select the **Select multiple items** checkbox, and then select the checkbox adjacent to each table or worksheet you want to query.

4. Select **Load**.

To add query data to the Excel Data Model

1. Select any cell in the Excel table that contains the query data.

2. On the **Power Pivot** tab, in the **Tables** group, select **Add to Data Model**.

To add an index column to a query

1. Select any cell in the Excel table that contains the query data.

2. On the **Query** tool tab, in the **Edit** group, select **Edit**.

3. In the **Power Query Editor**, on the **Add Column** tab, in the **General** group, do either of the following:

    -   Select the **Index Column** button (not the arrow).

    -   Select the **Index Column** arrow (not the button), and then identify the index starting point.

Adding an index column

4. On the **Home** tab of the **Power Query Editor**, in the **Close** group, select **Close & Load**.

15

To choose columns to include in your query results

1. In the Excel workbook, select any cell in the table that contains the query data.

2. On the **Query** tool tab, select **Edit**.

3. In the **Power Query Editor**, on the **Home** tab, in the **Manage Columns** group, select **Choose Columns**.

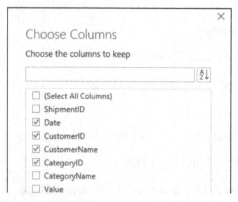

Filtering the query results

4. In the **Choose Columns** pane, clear the checkboxes next to the columns you want to remove from the query results.

5. Select **OK**.

To remove a column from the query results

1. Open the query in the **Power Query Editor**.

2. Select a cell in the column you want to remove.

3. On the **Home** tab, in the **Manage Columns** group, select **Remove Columns**.

To change the data type of a column

1. Open the query in the **Power Query Editor**.

2. Select a cell in the column you want to edit.

3. On the **Home** tab, in the **Transform** group, select **Data Type**, and then select the new data type for the column.

To change the name of a query

1. Display the query in the **Power Query Editor**.

2. If the Query Settings pane is not open, on the **View** tab, in the **Layout** group, select **Query Settings**.

3. In the **Query Settings** pane, in the **Name** box, replace the query name.

Rename and edit queries in the Query Settings pane

To undo a change to a query

1. Display the query in the **Power Query Editor** and open the **Query Settings** pane.

2. In the **Applied Steps** list, point to the change you want to delete, and then select the delete icon that appears to the left of the change.

3. In the **Delete Step** confirmation dialog, select **Delete**.

To edit a change to a query

1. Display the query in the **Power Query Editor**, and open the **Query Settings** pane.

2. In the **Applied Steps** list, point to the change you want to edit, and then select the action icon that appears to the right of the change.

3. In the dialog that appears, edit the properties of the change.

4. Select **OK**.

To close a query and return to Excel

1. In the **Power Query Editor**, on the **Home** tab, in the **Close** group, select **Close & Load**.

2. In the dialog that appears, select **Keep** to keep your changes.

To delete a query

1. In the workbook, select any cell in the table that contains the query data.

2. On the **Query** tool tab, in the **Edit** group, select **Delete**.

3. In the **Delete Query** dialog that appears, select **Delete**.

Skills review

In this chapter, you learned how to:

- Manage the Excel Data Model

- Define relationships between data sources

- Manage data by using Power Pivot

- Display data on timelines

- Import data by using Power Query

Practice tasks

Before you can complete these tasks, you must copy the book's practice files to your computer. The practice files for these tasks are in the **Excel365SBS\Ch15** folder. You can save the results of the tasks in the same folder.

Manage the Excel Data Model

Open the **DefineModel** workbook in Excel, and then perform the following tasks:

1. Enable the Power Pivot add-in.

2. Add the **Customers** table and the **Shipments** table to the Excel Data Model.

Define relationships between data sources

Open the **DefineRelationships** workbook in Excel, and then perform the following tasks:

1. The Data Model already contains the **Customers** table and the **Shipments** table. From the current workbook, add the **Categories** table to the Data Model.

2. Display the Excel Data Model in **Diagram view**.

3. Create the following relationships:

   - Between **Customers** and **Shipments** based on **CustomerID**

   - Between **Categories** and **Shipments** based on **CategoryID**

4. Close the Data Model and return to the workbook.

Manage data by using Power Pivot

Open the **AnalyzePowerPivotData** workbook in Excel, and then perform the following tasks:

1. Display the Excel Data Model in **Data view**.

2. Create a PivotTable that displays the customers' names as the row headers and the total value of their shipments in the **Values** area.

3. Change the data type of the **Value** field to **Currency**.

4. Add a calculated column that adds a three-percent surcharge to each shipment to account for increased fuel costs.

Display data on timelines

Open the **DisplayTimelines** workbook in Excel, and then perform the following tasks:

1. On the **PivotTable** worksheet, select any cell in the PivotTable.

2. Create a timeline that lets you filter the PivotTable by using the values in the **OrderDate** field.

3. Using the timeline, filter the PivotTable to display the **Sum of OrderAmount** for December 2020, then for November and December 2020, and then for the third quarter of the year.

4. Change the timeline's appearance so it has a yellow and black theme.

5. Clear the filter, and then delete the timeline.

Import data by using Power Query

Open the **CreateQuery** workbook in Excel, and then perform the following tasks:

1. Use Power Query to import the **ShipmentInfo** table from the **ManagePowerQueryData** workbook.

2. Add the query results to the Excel Data Model.

3. Remove the **CustomerID** and **CategoryID** fields from the query results.

4. In the Excel Data Model, change the query name to Shipments.

5. Save your work and return to the Excel workbook.

Create forecasts and visualizations

16

The business intelligence tools built into Excel for Microsoft 365 greatly extend the app's analytical and visualization capabilities. For example, although you have always been able to forecast future data based on current trends, you can now use an advanced technique called *exponential smoothing* to give greater weight to recent values instead of considering all historical data equally.

You can also use the Excel Data Model to create forecast worksheets, measures, key performance indicators (KPIs), and 3D maps with which to visualize your data. Forecast worksheets use exponential smoothing formulas to project a visual display of future values. Measures and KPIs summarize and evaluate business data against goals you set. Finally, 3D maps represent your data geographically, displaying static values and changes over time.

This chapter guides you through procedures related to creating forecast worksheets, forecasting data by defining and managing measures, defining and displaying KPIs, and creating 3D data maps.

> ⚠ **IMPORTANT** To complete some of the tasks in this chapter, you must enable the Power Pivot add-in. For information about Power Pivot and enabling the add-in, see **Chapter 15, "Perform business intelligence analysis."**

In this chapter

- Create forecast worksheets
- Define and manage measures
- Define and display key performance indicators
- Create 3D data maps

Create forecast worksheets

Excel for Microsoft 365 extends your ability to analyze business data by creating forecasts. Analyzing trends in Excel isn't new; you've been able to project future values based on historical data for quite some time. This topic discusses some of the forecasting functions that are available in Excel.

Linear forecasting

You can create a linear forecast by using the FORECAST.LINEAR() function, which evaluates a range of known independent variables (known x values) such as the past 24 months, and a range of known dependent variables (known y values) such as the revenue for each of those months, and projects future performance if the known trends continue. This function has the following syntax:

FORECAST.LINEAR(x, *known y values, known x values*)

The known values that you use to create a forecast worksheet must be at consistent intervals, such as every day, every Monday, the last day of each month, or the first day of each year.

You can obtain a similar outcome by extending a historical data series (selecting the historical data and dragging the fill handle). Excel analyzes the pattern of the available values and adds new values based on that analysis.

Exponential smoothing forecasting

Excel provides three functions that use exponential smoothing to forecast values and provide additional information to support those values:

- FORECAST.ETS() returns the forecasted value for a specific future target date.

- FORECAST.ETS.SEASONALITY() returns the length of the seasonal period the algorithm detects.

- FORECAST.ETS.CONFINT() returns a confidence interval for the forecast value on a specific target date. The confidence interval is the value by which the actual value will differ from the forecast, plus or minus a certain value that Excel calculates, which is a specified percentage of the time.

The FORECAST.ETS() function has the following syntax:

FORECAST.ETS(*target_date*, *values*, *timeline*, *[seasonality]*, *[data_completion]*, *[aggregation]*)

The arguments used by this function are as follows:

- *target_date* The date for which you want to predict a value, expressed as either a date/time value or a number. The *target_date* value must come after the last data point in the timeline.

- *values* The historical values Excel uses to create the forecast.

- *timeline* The dates or times Excel uses to establish the order of the *values* data. The dates in the *timeline* range must have a consistent step between them, which can't be zero.

- *seasonality* Optional. A number value indicating the presence, absence, or length of a season in the data set. A value of *1* has Excel detect seasonality automatically, *0* indicates no seasonality, and positive whole numbers up to *8,760* (the number of hours in a year) indicate to the algorithm to use patterns of this length as the seasonality period.

- *data_completion* Optional. The function allows for, and can adjust for, up to 30 percent of data missing from a time series. A value of *0* directs the algorithm to account for missing points as zeros, whereas the default value of *1* accounts for missing points by computing them as the average of the neighboring points.

- *aggregation* Optional. This argument tells the function how to aggregate multiple points that have the same time stamp. The default value of *0* directs the algorithm to use AVERAGE. Other options available in the AutoComplete list are SUM, COUNT, COUNTA, MIN, MAX, and MEDIAN.

The FORECAST.ETS.SEASONALITY() function has the same syntax and arguments as FORECAST.ETS():

FORECAST.ETS.SEASONALITY(*target_date*, *values*, *timeline*, *[seasonality]*, *[data_completion]*, *[aggregation]*)

You will often use FORECAST.ETS.SEASONALITY() and FORECAST.ETS() together, or FORECAST.ETS() by itself. The output of FORECAST.ETS.SEASONALITY() isn't very useful without a forecast.

16

The FORECAST.ETS.CONFINT() function has a similar syntax:

FORECAST.ETS.CONFINT(*target_date, values, timeline, [confidence_level],*
[seasonality], [data_completion], [aggregation])

The new argument, *confidence_level*, is an optional argument that lets you specify how certain you want the estimate to be. Smaller confidence levels allow for smaller confidence intervals because the actual result doesn't have to be within the confidence interval as often. Larger confidence levels require a larger interval to account for the greater probability of unlikely results. For example, a confidence level of 80 percent requires the actual value to be within the confidence interval (plus or minus a certain value that Excel calculates) 80 percent of the time. The default *confidence_level* value is 95 percent.

You can use the FORECAST.ETS() function to create a forecast worksheet that displays a forecast, based on historical data, in the form of a line chart or column chart. A forecast worksheet provides a striking visual summary of the exponential smoothing forecast. When creating the forecast, you can specify the start date, set seasonality, and determine how to handle missing or duplicate values.

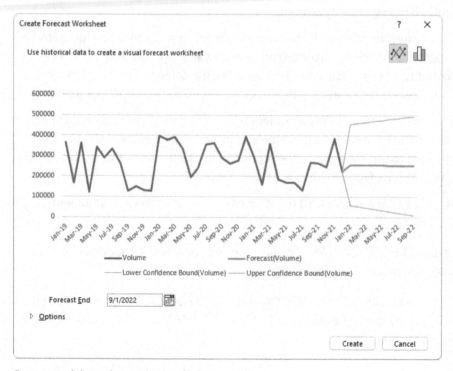

Forecast worksheets show projections for future values

To create a linear forecast by using a formula

1. On a worksheet, create a list of data that contains pairs of independent and dependent variables (known *x* values and known *y* values).

2. In a separate cell, enter a future value of *x*.

3. In another cell, create a formula with the following syntax, selecting the cells that represent each argument:

   FORECAST.LINEAR(*x, known_ys, known_xs*)

H6		f_x	=FORECAST.LINEAR(H4, MonthlyVolume[Volume], MonthlyVolume[MonthYear])						
	A	B	C	D	E	F	G	H	I
1									
2		Year ▾	Month ▾	MonthYear ▾	Volume ▾				
3		2019	January	Jan-19	367295				
4		2019	February	Feb-19	166865		Date: Jan-22		
5		2019	March	Mar-19	362315				
6		2019	April	Apr-19	121481		Forecast for date	257,133.09	
7		2019	May	May-19	345152		Confidence interval 95%		
8		2019	June	Jun-19	290746		Low forecast	257,133.09	
9		2019	July	Jul-19	332828		High forecast	257,133.09	
10		2019	August	Aug-19	260116		Seasonality		
11		2019	September	Sep-19	129790				

Referencing the data for the FORECAST.LINEAR function

4. Press **Enter** to calculate the formula results.

To create a forecast worksheet

1. In an Excel table that contains a column with date or time data (the independent variables, or known *x* values) and another column with numerical results (the dependent variables, or known *y* values), select any cell.

2. On the **Data** tab, in the **Forecast** group, select the **Forecast Sheet** button.

3. In the upper-right corner of the **Create Forecast Worksheet** dialog, select the **Create a line chart** button or the **Create a column chart** button to indicate the type of chart you want to create.

4. In the lower-left corner of the dialog, select the **Forecast End** calendar, and select an end date for the forecast.

5. Select **Create** to create the forecast worksheet.

16

To create a forecast worksheet with advanced options

1. In an Excel table that contains a column with date or time data (the independent variables, or known *x* values) and another column with numerical results (the dependent variables, or known *y* values), select any cell.

2. On the **Data** tab, in the **Forecast** group, select the **Forecast Sheet** button.

3. In the **Create Forecast Worksheet** dialog, select the chart type and forecast end date, and then select **Options** to expand the dialog.

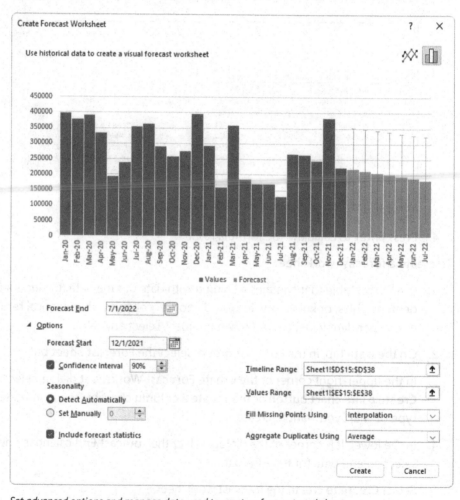

Set advanced options and manage data used to create a forecast worksheet

4. Using the tools in the **Options** area of the **Create Forecast Worksheet** dialog, do any of the following:

    - Identify the cell range that contains the timeline values.

    - Identify the cell range that contains the numerical values.

    - Select a new forecast start date.

    - Change the confidence interval.

    - Set seasonality manually or automatically.

    - Include or exclude forecast statistics.

    - Select a method for filling in missing values.

    - Select a method for aggregating multiple values for the same time period.

5. Select **Create** to create the forecast worksheet.

To calculate a forecast value by using exponential smoothing

1. Create a list of data that contains pairs of independent variables (*timeline*) and dependent variables (*values*).

2. In a separate cell, enter a future date (*target_date*).

3. In another cell, create a formula with the following syntax, selecting the cells that represent each argument:

    FORECAST.ETS(*target_date, values, timeline, [seasonality], [data_completion], [aggregation]*)

4. Press **Enter** to calculate the formula results.

To calculate the confidence interval for a forecast by using exponential smoothing

1. Create a list of data that contains pairs of independent variables (*timeline*) and dependent variables (*values*).

2. In a separate cell, enter a future date (*target_date*).

3. In another cell, create a formula with the following syntax:

    FORECAST.ETS.CONFINT(*target_date, values, timeline, [confidence_level], [seasonality], [data_completion], [aggregation]*)

4. Press **Enter** to calculate the formula results.

16

To calculate the length of a seasonally repetitive pattern in time series data

1. Create a list of data that contains pairs of independent variables (*timeline*) and dependent variables (*values*).

2. In a separate cell, enter a future date (*target_date*).

3. In another cell, create a formula with the following syntax:

   FORECAST.ETS.SEASONALITY(*target_date, values, timeline, [seasonality], [data_completion], [aggregation]*)

4. Press **Enter** to calculate the formula results.

Define and manage measures

You can use Power Pivot to analyze huge data collections that include millions or even hundreds of millions of rows of values. Although the details are important, it's also valuable to examine your data in aggregate. This type of aggregate summary, such as the average of values in a column, is called a *measure*.

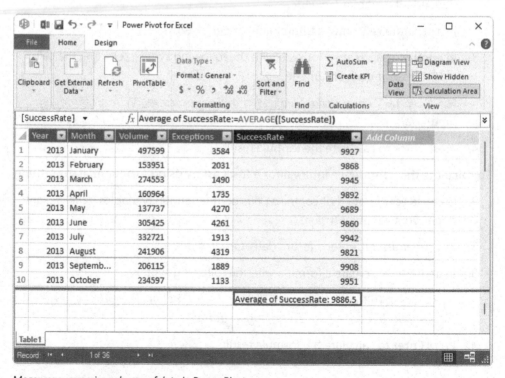

Measures summarize columns of data in Power Pivot

SEE ALSO For more information about using Power Pivot to analyze data, see "Manage data by using Power Pivot" in Chapter 15, "Perform business intelligence analysis."

There are two main ways to define a measure in Power Pivot. The first is to use a version of AutoSum, which calculates a SUM, AVERAGE, MEDIAN, or other summary of a Power Pivot column. The other method is to create a calculated column manually. Regardless of the technique you use to create the measure, you can edit it if necessary.

To create a measure by using AutoSum

1. Open a workbook in which you have added at least one Excel table to the Excel Data Model.

2. On the **Power Pivot** tab, in the **Data Model** group, select **Manage** to display the Power Pivot for Excel window.

3. Display the Data Model in Data view. If the Calculation Area below the grid is closed, select the **Calculation Area** button in the **View** group on the Power Pivot **Home** tab to display it.

4. In the Calculation Area, select the first cell below the column on which you want to base the measure.

5. On the **Home** tab, in the **Calculations** group, do either of the following:

   • Select the **AutoSum** button to create a measure by using the SUM function.

   • Select the **AutoSum** arrow, and then in the list, select the function with which you want to summarize the data.

To create a calculated column

1. In the **Power Pivot for Excel** window, display an Excel table that is part of the Data Model.

2. Select the first blank cell in the **Add Column** column.

3. Enter = followed by the formula.

 TIP To refer to a field in the Excel table, enclose the field name in square brackets—for example, *[Exceptions]*.

16

To edit a measure

1. Open the workbook that contains the Data Model with the measure.

2. In Power Pivot, display the Data Model and the Calculation Area in Data view.

3. In the Calculation Area, select the cell that contains the measure.

4. In the formula bar, change the text of the measure's formula.

5. Press **Enter** to commit the change.

To delete a measure

1. Open the workbook that contains the Data Model with the measure.

2. In Power Pivot, display the Data Model and the Calculation Area in Data view.

3. In the Calculation Area, select the cell that contains the measure.

4. Press **Delete**, and then in the **Confirm** dialog, select **Delete from Model**.

Define and display key performance indicators

Businesses of all sizes can evaluate their results by using measures, which convey overall business performance by summarizing operations data. The next step in this analysis is to compare results from a specific part of the business, whether for a department or for the entire company's overall performance for a month, to determine whether the company is meeting its goals.

One common way to measure business performance is by using key performance indicators (KPIs). A KPI is a measure that the company's officials have determined reflects the underlying health and efficiency of the organization. A shipping company might set KPIs for maintaining a low level of package-handling errors. A charitable organization could set a KPI for maximizing the return of its donation income to their clients through services and direct support.

KPIs are most often implemented through a dashboard that summarizes organizational performance. In Excel for Microsoft 365, you add KPIs to your workbooks by creating PivotTables based on data stored in the Data Model.

Row Labels	Sum of SuccessRate	Average of SuccessRate Status
2021		
January	9927 ✅	
February	9868 ✅	
March	9945 ✅	
April	9892 ✅	
May	9689 ✅	
June	9860 ✅	
July	8196 ⏸	
August	5039 ❌	
September	9908 ✅	
October	9951 ✅	
November	9958 ✅	
December	9952 ✅	

A PivotTable that includes a KPI created in Power Pivot

In some cases, high values are good, whereas in other cases low values are preferred. For example, minimizing package-handling errors and maximizing operating profit would represent success for a shipping company. For a manufacturing firm that wants to reduce variance in the items they fabricate for their customers, variance from the target value in either direction, high or low, would indicate a fault in the process.

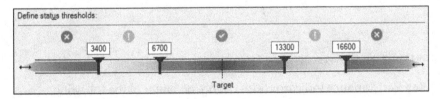

A KPI that warns of variance in either direction from the target value

To create a KPI

1. Open a workbook in which you have added at least one measure to the Data Model.

2. In Power Pivot, display the **Data Model** and the **Calculation Area** in **Data** view.

16

3. In the **Calculation Area**, right-click the cell that contains the measure you want to use as the basis for your KPI, and then on the context menu, select **Create KPI**.

 TIP To display a context menu, right-click or long-press (tap and hold) the element.

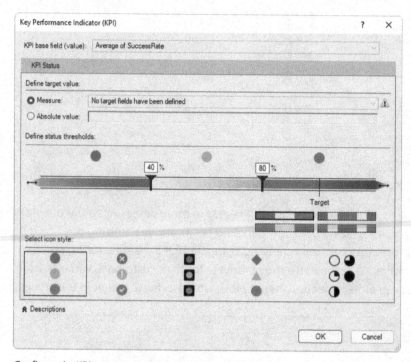

Configure the KPI to meet your organization's specific needs

4. In the **Key Performance Indicator (KPI)** dialog, do either of the following:

   - Select **Measure** and then select the measure to use as the comparison for the KPI.

   - Select **Absolute Value** and enter the target value in the adjacent box.

5. In the **Define status thresholds** section of the dialog, select the **Target** pattern that you want to use to represent the distribution of good, neutral, and bad values in the data set. Then do either of the following:

   - Drag the sliders to indicate where the bad, neutral, and good zones start.

   - Select in the box above a slider and enter a value that defines where the zone starts.

6. In the **Select icon style** section, select the icon set you want to apply to the KPI.

7. Select **OK** to create the KPI.

To use a KPI in a PivotTable

1. On the **Data** tab, in the **Data Tools** group, select **Manage Data Model**.

2. In the **Power Pivot for Excel** window, on the **Home** tab, select the **PivotTable** button (not the arrow).

3. In the **Create PivotTable** dialog, select **New Worksheet**, and then select **OK**.

4. In the **PivotTable Fields** pane, select the name of the Excel table that contains the data you want to use in the PivotTable.

5. Add fields to the **Rows** and **Columns** areas to organize the data, and then add the field that contains the data to the **Values** area.

6. At the bottom of the field list, expand the field name of the measure you used to create your KPI.

7. Drag the **Status** field of the measure to the **Values** area.

To edit a KPI

1. Open the workbook that contains the KPI and its associated measure.

2. In Power Pivot, display the Data Model and the Calculation Area in Data view.

3. In the Calculation Area, right-click the cell that contains the measure that is the basis of the KPI, and then select **Edit KPI Settings**.

4. In the **Key Performance Indicator (KPI)** dialog, change the KPI settings. Then select **OK** to update the KPI.

To delete a KPI

1. Open the workbook that contains the KPI and its associated measure.

2. In Power Pivot, display the Data Model and the Calculation Area in Data view.

3. In the Calculation Area, right-click the cell that contains the measure that is the basis of the KPI, and then select **Delete KPI**.

4. In the **Confirm** dialog, select **Delete from Model**.

16

Create 3D data maps

Much of the business data you collect will refer to geographic entities such as countries, regions, cities, or states. In Excel for Microsoft 365, you can plot such data on a three-dimensional map by using the built-in Power Map facilities. Excel examines the data source and adds the fields corresponding to recognized geographic entities to the map.

Summarize data geographically on a 3D map

After you create the map, you can add data fields to its layout, change the fields used in the visualization, and supplement the map with a two-dimensional line or column chart of the data. If the data includes multiple geographic data levels such as country or region, state or province, county, and city, you can specify the geographic level of analysis that the map displays. You can then copy an image of the map to the Office Clipboard to use in a data presentation.

 SEE ALSO For information about creating a 2D map chart of geographic statistics in Excel, see "Create specialized charts" in Chapter 9, "Create charts and graphics."

If the data source associated with a 3D map includes a date or time component, such as years, months, days, specific dates, or specific times, you can create an animated tour that shows how the data changes over time. You can save the animated tour as a video for use in a data presentation.

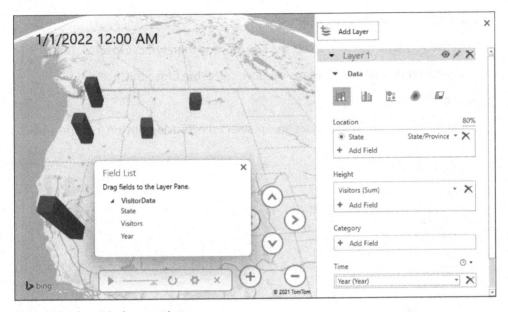

Animate the change in data over time

 TIP After you close the 3D Maps window, Excel adds a text box to the data source worksheet to indicate that a 3D Maps tour of the workbook data is available.

To create a 3D map

1. Select a cell in the Excel table that contains the data you want to map.

2. On the **Insert** tab, in the **Tours** group, select the **3D Map** button (not the arrow).

3. In the **3D Maps** window, on the **Home** tab, in the **View** group, select **Field List** to display the **Field List** pane.

4. Drag the field that contains geographic information from the **Field List** to the **Location** box.

16

5. Drag the field that contains the summary data from the **Field List** to the **Height** box.

6. If the data contains category data, such as a company, drag the category data field from the **Field List** to the **Category** box.

To return to the main Excel workbook

- In the **3D Maps** window, select the **File** tab, and then select **Close**.

- On the title bar of the **3D Maps** window, select the **Close** button.

To launch a 3D map

1. On the **Insert** tab, in the **Tours** group, select the **3D Map** button (not the arrow).

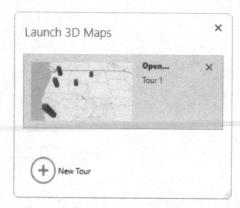

Select an existing 3D map to launch

2. In the **Launch 3D Maps** window, select the tour you want to launch.

To summarize mapped data in a chart

1. Launch the 3D map you want to summarize.

2. On the **Home** tab, in the **Insert** group, select **2D Chart**.

3. If you want to change the chart type, point to the chart, select the **Change the chart type** button that appears in the upper-right corner of the chart, and then select the new chart type.

To change the geographic level of a 3D map

1. Launch the 3D map you want to edit.

2. On the **Home** tab, in the **View** group, select **Layer Pane** to display the **Layer** pane.

3. If the Field List pane is closed, select **Field List**.

4. In the **Location** box, select the geographical type.

5. In the list that appears, select the geographic level at which you want to summarize the data.

To animate geographic data over time

1. Create a 3D map that includes summary and location data.

2. Display the **Layer** pane and the **Field List** pane.

3. Drag a field that contains time data from the **Field List** to the **Time** box on the **Layer** pane.

> **IMPORTANT** The field you add to the Time box must be formatted as a Date or Time data type.

4. In the **Time** list, select the time period that the field represents.

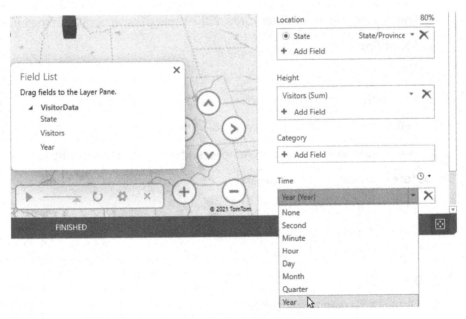

Specify the time period

5. On the map, select **Play Tour**.

16

To filter 3D map data

1. Launch the 3D map you want to edit.

2. Display the **Layer** pane.

3. In the **Layer** pane, expand the **Filters** section, select **Add Filter**, and then select the field by which you want to filter the map.

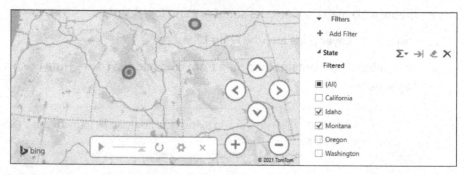

Apply a filter to focus the map on specific data

4. Use the controls in the **Filters** area of the **Layer** pane to configure the filter.

5. Select **Apply Filter**.

To remove a 3D map filter

1. Launch the 3D map from which you want to remove the filter.

2. In the **Layer** pane, display the available filters.

3. Point to the filter you want to remove, and then select **Delete Filter**.

To capture a screenshot of a 3D map

1. Launch the 3D map.

2. On the **Home** tab, in the **Tour** group, select **Capture Screen** to copy an image of the map to the Clipboard.

To play a 3D map tour as a video

1. Display a 3D map tour that has a time component.

2. On the **Home** tab, in the **Tour** group, select **Play Tour**.

3. When the tour finishes playing, point to the bottom of the screen to display the control bar, and then select the **Go Back to Edit View** button.

To save a 3D map tour as a video

1. Display a 3D map tour that has a time component.

2. On the **Home** tab, in the **Tour** group, select **Create Video**.

3. In the **Create Video** dialog, select the video quality and resolution you want. Then select **Create**.

4. In the **Save Movie** dialog, navigate to the folder where you want to save the video.

5. In the **File name** box, enter a name for the video file.

6. Select **Save**.

To delete a 3D map

1. Open the workbook that contains the map.

2. On the **Insert** tab, in the **Tours** group, select the **3D Map** button (not the arrow).

3. In the **Launch 3D Maps** dialog, point to the 3D map tour you want to delete, and then select the **Delete this Tour** button that appears in the upper-right corner of the tour.

4. In the **Delete Tour** dialog, select **Yes** to confirm that you want to delete the tour.

5. Close the **Launch 3D Maps** dialog.

Skills review

In this chapter, you learned how to:

- Create forecast worksheets

- Define and manage measures

- Define and display key performance indicators

- Create 3D data maps

16

Practice tasks

Before you can complete these tasks, you must copy the book's practice files to your computer. The practice files for these tasks are in the **Excel365SBS\Ch16** folder. You can save the results of the tasks in the same folder.

Create forecast worksheets

Open the **CreateForecastSheets** workbook in Excel, and then perform the following tasks:

1. In cell **H6**, create a formula that uses exponential smoothing to forecast the value for **January 2022** (found in cell **H4**) based on the values in the **MonthYear** and **Volume** columns in the Excel table.

2. Using the same inputs, calculate the 95-percent confidence interval (the default value) for your forecast in cell **H7**.

3. In cell **H10**, calculate the length of the season implied by the data used in the previous two formulas.

4. Create a forecast worksheet based on the data in the **MonthlyVolume** table on **Sheet1**.

5. If necessary, edit the forecast worksheet so its **Timeline Range** is cells **D2:D38** and the **Values Range** is cells **E2:E38**.

6. Change the forecast worksheet's **Confidence Interval** to 90 percent.

Define and manage measures

> ⚠️ **IMPORTANT** You must enable the Power Pivot add-in before you can complete this practice task. For information about Power Pivot and enabling the add-in, see **Chapter 15, "Perform business intelligence analysis."**

Open the **DefineMeasures** workbook in Excel, and then perform the following tasks:

1. Display the Data Model.

2. Create a measure for the **Exceptions** field that finds the sum of the **Exceptions** values.

3. Create a measure for the **SuccessRate** field that finds the sum of the **SuccessRate** values.

4. Delete the measure that finds the sum of the **Exceptions** values.

5. Edit the measure that finds the sum of the **SuccessRate** values so that it finds the average of those values.

Define and display key performance indicators

> ⚠️ **IMPORTANT** You must enable the Power Pivot add-in before you can complete this practice task. For information about Power Pivot and enabling the add-in, see **Chapter 15, "Perform business intelligence analysis."**

Open the **CreateKPIs** workbook in Excel, and then perform the following tasks:

1. Open Power Pivot and display the Data Model.

2. Create a KPI named **Status** based on the **Average of SuccessRate** measure with the following characteristics:

   - An absolute value of 9925

   - A green lower limit of 9900

   - A yellow lower limit of 9825

   - The black-bordered traffic-light icon set

3. From Power Pivot, create a PivotTable on a new worksheet.

4. In the **PivotTable Fields** pane, add the **Year** and **Month** columns to the **Rows** area, and add the **Success Rate** and **Status** fields to the **Values** area.

Create 3D data maps

Open the **CreateMaps** workbook in Excel, and then perform the following tasks:

1. Create a 3D map based on the data in the **VisitorData** Excel table. Show the visitors by state.

2. Add the **Year** field to the **Time** area, and then play the tour.

3. Create and save a video based on the tour you created.

4. Add a 2D Clustered Column chart that summarizes your data to the map.

Keyboard shortcuts

Throughout this book, we provide information about how to perform tasks quickly and efficiently by using keyboard shortcuts. You can use the following keyboard shortcuts when working in Excel and other Microsoft 365 apps.

In this appendix

- Excel keyboard shortcuts
- Excel function key commands
- Microsoft 365 app keyboard shortcuts

 TIP In the keyboard shortcut tables, keys you press at the same time are separated by a plus sign (+), and keys you press sequentially are separated by a comma (,).

Excel for Microsoft 365 keyboard shortcuts

This section provides a comprehensive list of keyboard shortcuts built into Excel for Microsoft 365. You can use these keyboard shortcuts to:

- Perform common tasks
- Access and manage the ribbon
- Navigate among worksheet cells
- Select cell ranges
- Format cells

Perform common tasks

Action	Keyboard shortcut
Open a workbook.	Ctrl+O
Save a workbook.	Ctrl+S
Close a workbook.	Ctrl+W
Copy.	Ctrl+C
Cut.	Ctrl+X
Paste.	Ctrl+V
Undo.	Ctrl+Z
Redo.	Ctrl+Y
Zoom in.	Ctrl+Alt+= or Ctrl+scroll the mouse wheel up
Zoom out.	Ctrl+Alt+Minus or Ctrl+scroll the mouse wheel down
Choose a fill color.	Alt+H, H
Apply bold formatting.	Ctrl+B
Center-align cell contents.	Alt+H, A, C
Add borders.	Alt+H, B
Delete the selected rows.	Alt+H, D, R
Delete the selected columns.	Alt+H, D, C
Hide the selected rows.	Ctrl+9
Hide the selected columns.	Ctrl+0
Open a context menu.	Shift+F10 or, on a Windows keyboard, the Context key (between the right Alt and right Ctrl keys)

Access and manage the ribbon

Action	Keyboard shortcut
Go to the Search field on the ribbon.	Alt+Q
Go to the File tab to access Backstage view.	Alt+F
Go to the Home tab.	Alt+H
Go to the Insert tab.	Alt+N
Go to Page Layout tab.	Alt+P
Go to the Formulas tab.	Alt+M
Go to the Data tab	Alt+A
Go to the Review tab.	Alt+R
Go to the View tab.	Alt+W
Expand or collapse the ribbon.	Ctrl+F1
Select the active tab on the ribbon and activate the access keys.	Alt or F10
Move the focus to commands on the ribbon.	Tab key or Shift+Tab
Move down, up, left, or right, respectively, among the items on the Ribbon.	Arrow keys
Activate a selected button.	Spacebar or Enter
Open the list for a selected command.	Down arrow key
Open the menu for a selected button.	Alt+Down arrow key
When a menu or submenu is open, move to the next command.	Down arrow key
Move to the submenu when a main menu is open or selected.	Left arrow key

Navigate among worksheet cells

Action	Keyboard shortcut
Move to the previous cell in a worksheet or the previous option in a dialog.	Shift+Tab
Move one cell up in a worksheet.	Up arrow key
Move one cell down in a worksheet.	Down arrow key
Move one cell left in a worksheet.	Left arrow key
Move one cell right in a worksheet.	Right arrow key
Move to the edge of the current data region in a worksheet.	Ctrl+Arrow key
Enter the End mode, move to the next non-blank cell in the same column or row as the active cell, and turn off End mode. If the cells are blank, move to the last cell in the row or column.	End, Arrow key
Move to the last cell on a worksheet, to the lowest used row of the rightmost used column.	Ctrl+End
Extend the selection of cells to the last used cell on the worksheet (lower-right corner).	Ctrl+Shift+End
Move to the cell in the upper-left corner of the window when Scroll Lock is turned on.	Home+Scroll Lock
Move to the beginning of a worksheet.	Ctrl+Home
Move one screen down in a worksheet.	Page Down
Move to the next sheet in a workbook.	Ctrl+Page Down
Move one screen to the right in a worksheet.	Alt+Page Down
Move one screen up in a worksheet.	Page Up
Move one screen to the left in a worksheet.	Alt+Page Up
Move to the previous sheet in a workbook.	Ctrl+Page Up
Move one cell to the right in a worksheet. Or, in a protected worksheet, move between unlocked cells.	Tab key
Open the list of validation choices on a cell that has data validation option applied to it.	Alt+Down arrow key

Action	Keyboard shortcut
Cycle through floating shapes, such as text boxes or images.	Ctrl+Alt+5, then the Tab key repeatedly
Exit the floating shape navigation and return to the normal navigation.	Esc
Scroll horizontally.	Ctrl+Shift, then scroll the mouse wheel up to go left or down to go right

Select cell ranges

Action	Keyboard shortcut
Extend the selection one cell to the right.	Shift+Right arrow
Extend the selection one cell to the left.	Shift+Left arrow
Extend the selection up one cell.	Shift+Up arrow
Extend the selection down one cell.	Shift+Down arrow
Extend the selection to the last non-blank cell in the row.	Ctrl+Shift+Right arrow
Extend the selection to the first non-blank cell in the row.	Ctrl+Shift+Left arrow
Extend the selection to the first non-blank cell in the column.	Ctrl+Shift+Up arrow
Extend the selection to the last non-blank cell in the column.	Ctrl+Shift+Down arrow
Select the entire active region.	Ctrl+*
Extend the selection to the beginning of the row.	Shift+Home
Extend the selection to the beginning of the worksheet.	Ctrl+Shift+Home
Extend the selection to the end of the worksheet.	Ctrl+Shift+End
Extend the selection down one screen.	Shift+Page Down
Extend the selection up one screen.	Shift+Page Up
Select the visible cells in the current selection.	Alt+;

Format cells

Action	Keyboard shortcut
Open the Format Cells dialog.	Ctrl+1
Format fonts in the Format Cells dialog.	Ctrl+Shift+F or Ctrl+Shift+P
Edit the active cell and put the insertion point at the end of its contents. Or, if editing is turned off for the cell, move the insertion point into the formula bar. If editing a formula, toggle Point mode off or on so you can use arrow keys to create a reference.	F2
Insert a note.	Shift+F2
Open and edit a cell note.	Shift+F2
Insert a threaded comment.	Ctrl+Shift+F2
Open and reply to a threaded comment.	Ctrl+Shift+F2
Open the Insert dialog to insert blank cells.	Ctrl++
Open the Delete dialog to delete selected cells.	Ctrl+-
Enter the current time.	Ctrl+:
Enter the current date.	Ctrl+;
Switch between displaying cell values or formulas in the worksheet.	Ctrl+`
Copy a formula from the cell above the active cell into the cell or the formula bar.	Ctrl+'
Move the selected cells.	Ctrl+X
Copy the selected cells.	Ctrl+C
Paste content at the insertion point, replacing any selection	Ctrl+V
Open the Paste Special dialog.	Ctrl+Alt+V
Italicize text or remove italic formatting.	Ctrl+I or Ctrl+3
Bold text or remove bold formatting.	Ctrl+B or Ctrl+2
Underline text or remove underline.	Ctrl+U or Ctrl+4

Action	Keyboard shortcut
Apply or remove strikethrough formatting.	Ctrl+5
Switch between hiding objects, displaying objects, and displaying placeholders for objects.	Ctrl+6
Apply an outline border to the selected cells.	Ctrl+&
Remove the outline border from the selected cells.	Ctrl+Shift+underline (_)
Display or hide the outline symbols.	Ctrl+8
Use the Fill Down command to copy the contents and format of the topmost cell of a selected range into the cells below.	Ctrl+D
Apply the General number format.	Ctrl+~
Apply the Number format with two decimal places, thousands separator, and minus sign (–) for negative values.	Ctrl+!
Apply the Currency format with two decimal places (negative numbers in parentheses).	Ctrl+$
Apply the Percentage format with no decimal places.	Ctrl+%
Apply the Scientific number format with two decimal places.	Ctrl+^
Apply the Date format with the day, month, and year.	Ctrl+#
Apply the Time format with the hour and minute, and AM or PM.	Ctrl@
Open the Insert hyperlink dialog.	Ctrl+K
Check spelling in the active worksheet or selected range.	F7
Display the Quick Analysis options for selected cells that contain data.	Ctrl+Q
Display the Create Table dialog.	Ctrl+L or Ctrl+T
Open the Workbook Statistics dialog.	Ctrl+Shift+G

Excel function key commands

Key	Description
F1	F1 alone: displays the Excel Help task pane. Ctrl+F1: displays or hides the ribbon. Alt+F1: creates an embedded chart of the data in the current range. Alt+Shift+F1: inserts a new worksheet.
F2	F2 alone: edits the active cell and puts the insertion point at the end of its contents. Or, if editing is turned off for the cell, moves the insertion point into the formula bar. If editing a formula, toggles Point mode off or on so you can use arrow keys to create a reference. Shift+F2: adds or edits a cell note. Ctrl+F2: displays the print preview area on the Print tab in the Backstage view.
F3	F3 alone: displays the Paste Name dialog. Available only if names have been defined in the workbook. Shift+F3: displays the Insert Function dialog.
F4	F4 alone: repeats the last command or action, if possible. When a cell reference or range is selected in a formula, F4 cycles through all the various combinations of absolute and relative references. Ctrl+F4: closes the selected workbook window. Alt+F4: closes Excel.
F5	F5 alone: displays the Go To dialog. Ctrl+F5: restores the window size of the selected workbook window.
F6	F6 alone: switches between the worksheet, ribbon, task pane, and Zoom controls. In a worksheet that has been split , F6 includes the split panes when switching between panes and the ribbon area. Shift+F6: switches between the worksheet, Zoom controls, task pane, and ribbon. Ctrl+F6: switches between 2 Excel windows. Ctrl+Shift+F6: switches between all Excel windows.

Key	Description
F7	F7 alone: opens the Spelling dialog to check spelling in the active worksheet or selected range.
	Ctrl+F7: performs the Move command on the workbook window when it is not maximized. Use the arrow keys to move the window, and when finished, press Enter or Esc to cancel.
F8	F8 alone: turns extend mode on or off. In extend mode, Extended Selection appears in the status line, and the arrow keys extend the selection.
	Shift+F8: enables you to add a non-adjacent cell or range to a selection of cells by using the arrow keys.
	Ctrl+F8: performs the Size command when a workbook is not maximized.
	Alt+F8: displays the Macro dialog to create, run, edit, or delete a macro.
F9	F9 alone: calculates all worksheets in all open workbooks.
	Shift+F9: calculates the active worksheet.
	Ctrl+Alt+F9: calculates all worksheets in all open workbooks, regardless of whether they have changed since the last calculation.
	Ctrl+Alt+Shift+F9: rechecks dependent formulas, and then calculates all cells in all open workbooks, including cells not marked as needing to be calculated.
	Ctrl+F9: minimizes a workbook window to an icon.
F10	F10 alone: Turns key tips on or off. (Pressing Alt does the same thing.)
	Shift+F10: displays the shortcut menu for a selected item.
	Alt+Shift+F10: displays the menu or message for an Error Checking button.
	Ctrl+F10: maximizes or restores the selected workbook window.
F11	F11 alone: Creates a chart of the data in the current range in a separate Chart sheet.
	Shift+F11: inserts a new worksheet.
	Alt+F11: opens the Microsoft Visual Basic For Applications Editor, in which you can create a macro by using Visual Basic for Applications (VBA).
F12	F12 alone: displays the Save As dialog.

Microsoft 365 app keyboard shortcuts

The following keyboard shortcuts are available in all the primary Microsoft 365 apps, including Excel. You can use these keyboard shortcuts to:

- Display and use windows
- Work in dialogs
- Use the Backstage view
- Navigate the ribbon
- Change the keyboard focus without using the mouse
- Move around in and work in tables
- Access and use panes and galleries
- Access and use available actions
- Find and replace content
- Get Help

Display and use windows

Action	Keyboard shortcut
Switch to the next window.	Alt+Tab
Switch to the previous window.	Alt+Shift+Tab
Close the active window.	Ctrl+W or Ctrl+F4
Restore the size of the active window after you maximize it.	Alt+F5
Move to a pane from another pane in the app window (clockwise direction). If pressing F6 does not display the pane that you want, press Alt to put the focus on the ribbon, and then press Ctrl+Tab to move to the pane.	F6 or Shift+F6
Switch to the next open window.	Ctrl+F6
Switch to the previous window.	Ctrl+Shift+F6
Maximize or restore a selected window.	Ctrl+F10
Copy a picture of the screen to the Clipboard.	Print Screen
Copy a picture of the selected window to the Clipboard.	Alt+Print Screen

Use dialogs

Action	Keyboard shortcut
Move to the next option or option group.	Tab
Move to the previous option or option group.	Shift+Tab
Switch to the next tab in a dialog.	Ctrl+Tab
Switch to the previous tab in a dialog.	Ctrl+Shift+Tab
Move between options in an open drop-down list or between options in a group of options.	Arrow keys
Perform the action assigned to the selected button. Select or clear the selected checkbox.	Spacebar
Select an option. Select or clear a checkbox.	Alt+the underlined letter
Open a selected drop-down list.	Alt+Down Arrow
Select an option from a drop-down list.	First letter of the list option
Close a selected drop-down list. Cancel a command and close a dialog.	Esc
Run the selected command.	Enter

Use edit boxes within dialogs

An edit box is a blank box in which you enter or paste an entry.

Action	Keyboard shortcut
Move to the beginning of the entry.	Home
Move to the end of the entry.	End
Move one character to the left or right.	Left arrow or Right arrow
Move one word to the left.	Ctrl+Left arrow
Move one word to the right.	Ctrl+Right arrow
Select or cancel selection one character to the left.	Shift+Left arrow
Select or cancel selection one character to the right.	Shift+Right arrow
Select or cancel selection one word to the left.	Ctrl+Shift+Left arrow

Action	Keyboard shortcut
Select or cancel selection one word to the right.	Ctrl+Shift+Right arrow
Select from the insertion point to the beginning of the entry.	Shift+Home
Select from the insertion point to the end of the entry.	Shift+End

Use the Open and Save As dialogs

Action	Keyboard shortcut
Open the Open dialog.	Ctrl+F12 or Ctrl+O
Open the Save As dialog.	F12
Open the selected folder or file.	Enter
Open the folder one level above the selected folder.	Backspace
Delete the selected folder or file.	Delete
Display a shortcut menu for a selected item such as a folder or file.	Shift+F10
Move forward through options.	Tab
Move back through options.	Shift+Tab
Open the Look In list.	F4 or Alt+I
Refresh the file list.	F5

Use the Backstage view

Action	Keyboard shortcut
Display the Open page of the Backstage view.	Ctrl+O
Display the Save As page of the Backstage view (when saving a file for the first time).	Ctrl+S
Continue saving a Microsoft 365 file (after giving the file a name and location).	Ctrl+S
Display the Save As or Save A Copy page of the Backstage view (after initially saving a file).	Alt+F+A
Close the Backstage view.	Esc

TIP You can use dialogs instead of Backstage view pages by selecting the Don't Show The Backstage When Opening Or Saving Files With Keyboard Shortcuts checkbox on the Save page of the Excel Options dialog. Set this option in any Microsoft 365 app to enable it in all Microsoft 365 apps.

Navigate the ribbon

Follow these steps:

1. Press **Alt** to display the KeyTips over each feature in the current view.

2. Press the letter shown in the KeyTip over the feature that you want to use.

 TIP To cancel the action and hide the KeyTips, press Alt.

Change the keyboard focus without using the mouse

Action	Keyboard shortcut
Select the active tab of the ribbon and activate the access keys.	Alt or F10: press either of these keys again to move back to the document and cancel the access keys
Move to another tab of the ribbon.	F10 to select the active tab, and then Left arrow or Right arrow
Expand or collapse the ribbon.	Ctrl+F1
Display the shortcut menu for the selected item.	Shift+F10
Move the focus to select each of the following areas of the window: Active tab of the ribbon Any open panes Status bar at the bottom of the window Your workbook	F6

Action	Keyboard shortcut
Move the focus to each command on the ribbon, forward or backward, respectively.	Tab or Shift+Tab
Move among the items on the ribbon.	Arrow keys
Activate the selected command or control on the ribbon.	Spacebar or Enter
Display the selected menu or gallery on the ribbon.	Spacebar or Enter
Activate a command or control on the ribbon so that you can modify a value.	Enter
Finish modifying a value in a control on the ribbon, and move focus back to the document.	Enter
Get help on the selected command or control on the ribbon.	F1

Move around in and work in tables

Action	Keyboard shortcut
Move to the next cell.	Tab
Move to the preceding cell.	Shift+Tab
Move to the next row.	Down arrow
Move to the preceding row.	Up arrow
Start a new paragraph.	Enter
Add a new row at the bottom of the table.	Tab at the end of the last row

Access and use panes and galleries

Action	Keyboard shortcut
Move to a pane from another pane in the app window.	F6
When a menu is active, move to a pane.	Ctrl+Tab
When a pane is active, select the next or previous option in the pane.	Tab or Shift+Tab

Display the full set of commands on the pane menu.	Ctrl+Spacebar
Perform the action assigned to the selected button.	Spacebar or Enter
Open a drop-down menu for the selected gallery item.	Shift+F10
Select the first or last item in a gallery.	Home or End
Scroll up or down in the selected gallery list.	Page Up or Page Down
Close a pane.	Ctrl+Spacebar, C
Open the Clipboard.	Alt+H, F, O

Access and use available actions

Action	Keyboard shortcut
Display the shortcut menu for the selected item.	Shift+F10
Display the menu or message for an available action or for the AutoCorrect Options button or the Paste Options button	Alt+Shift+F10
Move between options in a menu of available actions	Arrow keys
Perform the action for the selected item on a menu of available actions.	Enter
Close the available actions menu or message.	Esc

Find and replace content

Action	Keyboard shortcut
Open the Find dialog.	Ctrl+F
Open the Replace dialog.	Ctrl+H
Repeat the last Find action.	Shift+F4

Get Help

Action	Keyboard shortcut
Open the Help window.	F1
Return to the Help table of contents.	Alt+Home
Select the next item in the Help window.	Tab
Select the previous item in the Help window.	Shift+Tab
Perform the action for the selected item.	Enter
Select the next hidden text or hyperlink, including Show All or Hide All at the top of a Help topic.	Tab
Select the previous hidden text or hyperlink.	Shift+Tab
Perform the action for the selected Show All, Hide All, hidden text, or hyperlink.	Enter
Move back to the previous Help topic (Back button).	Alt+Left arrow or Backspace
Move forward to the next Help topic (Forward button).	Alt+Right arrow
Scroll small amounts up or down, respectively, within the currently displayed Help topic.	Up arrow, Down arrow
Scroll larger amounts up or down, respectively, within the currently displayed Help topic.	Page Up, Page Down
Stop the last action (Stop button).	Esc
Print the current Help topic. If the cursor is not in the current Help topic, press F6 and then press Ctrl+P.	Ctrl+P
In a table of contents in tree view, select the next or previous item, respectively.	Up arrow, Down arrow
In a table of contents in tree view, expand or collapse the selected item, respectively.	Left arrow, Right arrow

Glossary

3-D reference A pattern for referring to the workbook, worksheet, and cell from which a value should be read.

absolute reference A cell reference, such as =$B$3, that does not change when you copy a formula containing the reference to another cell. See also *relative reference*.

active cell The cell that is currently selected and open for editing.

add-in A utility that adds specialized functionality to an app such as Excel but does not operate as an independent app.

alignment The way a cell's contents are arranged within that cell (for example, centered).

arguments The specific data a function requires to calculate a value.

aspect ratio The relationship between an image's width and height.

auditing The process of examining a worksheet for errors.

AutoCalculate The Excel functionality that displays summary calculations on the status bar for a selected cell range.

AutoComplete The Excel functionality that completes data entry for a cell based on similar values in other cells in the same column.

AutoFill The Excel functionality that extends a series of values based on the contents of a single cell.

AutoFilter An Excel tool you can use to create filters.

AutoRepublish The Excel technology that maintains a link between a web document and the worksheet on which the web document is based and updates the web document whenever the original worksheet is saved.

Backstage view A view that gathers workbook-management tasks into a single location. You access the Backstage view by selecting the File tab.

bin A value range used to summarize frequencies in a histogram chart. See also *histogram*.

box-and-whisker A chart type that visualizes average, median, minimum, and maximum values for one or more data series.

browser An app with which users view web documents.

button A user interface element that invokes a command; a content control that can be inserted on a worksheet and configured to run a macro when selected. See also *option button*.

category axis The horizontal reference line of a chart or graph, which usually depicts category or time data. Also called the *x-axis*.

cell A box formed by the intersection of a row and column in a worksheet or a table, in which you enter text or numeric data or a formula.

cell range A group of cells.

cell reference The letter and number combination, such as C16, that identifies the row and column intersection of a cell.

cell style A built-in format that can be applied to a cell.

chart A visual summary of worksheet data, also called a *graph*.

checkbox A worksheet control, depicted as a square, that can be selected or cleared to turn an option on or off.

circular reference A formula that contains a reference either to itself or to a cell that uses the formula's result.

color scale A type of conditional format that changes the color of a cell's fill to reflect the value in the cell. See also *conditional format*.

column Vertically aligned worksheet cells labeled and referenced in Excel by a letter.

combo box A worksheet control that lets users enter or select a value from a defined list.

combo chart A chart that combines two visualization styles into a single graphic.

conditional format A format that is applied only when cell contents meet certain criteria.

conditional formula A formula that calculates a value by using one of two or more different expressions, depending on whether a third expression is true or false.

confidence interval The range of values within which future values will fall a specified percentage of the time (for example, "plus or minus 3 percent with 95 percent confidence").

context menu A menu of commands related to specific content or a specific user interface element that appears when you right-click the content or element.

contextual tab See *tool tab*.

control group A set of checkboxes or option buttons within which only one control can be selected at a time.

data bar A horizontal line within a cell that indicates the relative magnitude of the cell's value.

data consolidation Summarizing data from a set of similar cell ranges.

data table A defined cell range that applies a set of alternative input values to a single formula. See also *What-If Analysis*.

delimiter A character in a text file that separates values from each other.

dependent A cell with a formula that uses the value from a particular cell. See also *precedent*.

digital certificate A file that contains a unique string of characters that can be combined with another file, such as an Excel workbook, to create a verifiable signature for that file.

digital signature An electronic, encrypted, stamp of authentication that verifies the authorship and integrity of the content of a file, such as an Excel workbook.

distribute To share a file with other users.

Document Inspector An Office feature that detects and optionally removes hidden properties and personal information from a workbook.

embed To save a file as part of another file, as opposed to linking one file to another. See also *link*.

error code A brief message that appears in a worksheet cell, describing a problem with a formula or a function.

Excel table An Excel object with which you can store and refer to data based on the name of the table and the names of its columns and rows.

exponential smoothing The process of creating a forecast by giving recent values in a data series more weight than older values.

Extensible Markup Language See *XML*.

field A column of data used to create a PivotTable.

fill handle The square at the lower-right corner of a cell that can be dragged to indicate other cells that should hold values in the series defined by the active cell.

FillSeries The Excel functionality that allows you to create a data series by defining the starting value, the rule for calculating the next value, and the length of the series.

filter A rule that Excel uses to determine which worksheet rows to display.

footer An area of a worksheet that appears below the worksheet content when you print the worksheet or display it in Layout view. See also *header*.

foreign key A value in a data list or Excel table that uniquely identifies a row in another table. See also *primary key*.

format A predefined set of characteristics that can be applied to cell contents.

formula An operation performed within a cell that returns a value. A formula always begins with an equal sign (=), which is often followed by a function, and may include values, operators, and references to other cells, cell ranges, or table elements.

Formula AutoComplete The Excel functionality with which you can enter a formula quickly by selecting functions, named ranges, and table references that appear when you begin to type the formula into a cell.

Formula bar A text box above the worksheet grid in which you can enter and edit cell content The Insert Function button to the left of the formula bar provides assistance with building formulas.

function A predefined formula.

Goal Seek A What-If Analysis tool that determines the input value necessary to produce a specified result from a calculation.

graph A visual summary of worksheet data, also called a *chart*.

header An area of a worksheet that appears above the worksheet content when you print the worksheet or view it in Layout view. See also *footer*.

histogram A chart type that represents the distribution of values by counting the number of occurrences within specified ranges. See also *bin*; *Pareto*.

HTML *Hypertext Markup Language*, a markup language that uses tags to mark elements in a document to indicate how web browsers, such as Microsoft Edge, should display these elements to the user and how they should respond to user actions. See also *XML*.

hyperlink A connection from an anchor, such as text or a graphic, that connects you to a target such as a file, a location in a file, or a website. By default, text hyperlinks in Office files are formatted as colored and underlined text. When you point to a hyperlink, the pointer shape changes to a hand.

Hypertext Markup Language See *HTML*.

icon set A conditional format that uses distinct visual indicators to designate how a value compares to a set of criteria.

key performance indicator (KPI) A metric by which an organization is deemed to be meeting, exceeding, or falling short of its goals. See also *measure*.

landscape mode A display and printing mode whereby columns run parallel to the short edge of a sheet of paper.

link A formula that has a cell show the value from another cell; a connection to an external data source. See also *embed*; *hyperlink*.

list box A worksheet control in which you select a value from a specified set of values.

Live Preview An Office feature that temporarily displays the result of an operation, such as pasting data or applying a cell style, without implementing the change.

locked cell A cell that cannot be modified if its worksheet is protected.

macro A recording of a series of VBA commands performed in a Word, Excel, or PowerPoint file that can be played and performed with a click or keyboard shortcut. See also *Visual Basic for Applications (VBA)*.

mailto hyperlink A special type of hyperlink with which a user creates an email message to a particular email address.

measure A summary of data, such as an average or sum, stored in a PowerPivot worksheet column. See also *key performance indicator (KPI)*.

Merge And Center An operation that combines a contiguous group of cells into a single cell.

named range A group of related cells defined by a single name.

OneDrive An online service, accessed through a Microsoft account, with which a user can store data online in the cloud.

option button A worksheet control, depicted as a circle, that can be selected or cleared to turn an option on or off.

Pareto A type of chart that combines a histogram with a line chart to show the progressive contribution of categories to a whole. See also *histogram*.

Paste Options A button that appears after you paste an item from the Clipboard into your workbook, and that provides options for how the item appears in the workbook.

Pick From List The Excel functionality that you can use to enter a value into a cell by choosing the value from the set of values already entered in cells in the same column.

pivot To reorganize the contents of a PivotTable.

PivotChart A chart, which can be linked to a PivotTable, that can be reorganized dynamically to emphasize different aspects of the underlying data.

PivotTable A dynamic worksheet that can be reorganized by a user.

portrait mode A display and printing mode whereby columns run parallel to the long edge of a sheet of paper.

precedent A cell that is used in a formula. See also *dependent*.

primary key A field or group of fields with values that distinguish a row of data from all other rows. See also *foreign key*.

property A file detail, such as an author name or project code, that helps identify the file.

Quick Access Toolbar A customizable toolbar that displays commands of your choice above or below the ribbon.

Quick Analysis menu A selection of tools with which a user can summarize data quickly by using formulas and charts.

range A group of related cells.

recommended chart A chart, designed by the Excel app, that summarizes a selected data range.

recommended PivotTable A PivotTable, designed by the Excel app, that summarizes a selected data range.

refresh To update the contents of one document when the contents of another document are changed.

relationship A link between two tables, based on a common field, that allows the contents of the tables to be combined.

relative reference A cell reference in a formula, such as =B3, that refers to a cell that is a specific distance away from the cell that contains the formula. For example, if the formula =B3 were in cell C3, copying the formula to cell C4 would cause the formula to change to =B4. See also *absolute reference*.

ribbon A user interface design introduced in Microsoft Office 2007 that organizes commands into logical groups on separate tabs.

row Horizontally aligned worksheet cells labeled and referenced in Excel by a number.

scale The percentage of actual size at which a worksheet is printed or displayed.

Scenarios A What-If Analysis tool that enables you to switch between data sets to display the impact on worksheet data.

schema A defined structure an app can use to interpret the contents of an XML file.

search filter A filter in which you enter a string of characters to instruct Excel to display every value within an Excel table, data set, or PivotTable that contains that character string.

selection filter A mechanism for selecting the specific values to be displayed in a data list, Excel table, or PivotTable.

series axis The third axis in a three-dimensional coordinate system, used in charts or graphs to represent depth. Also called the *z-axis*.

sharing Making a workbook available for more than one user to open and modify.

sheet tab The indicator for selecting a worksheet, located at the bottom of the workbook window.

shortcut menu See *context menu*.

Slicer An Excel tool with which you can filter an Excel table, data list, or PivotTable while indicating which items are displayed and which are hidden.

Solver An Excel add-in that finds the optimal value for one cell by varying the results of other cells.

sort To reorder a data range or table based on one or more criteria such as text, numbers, dates, cell fill color or text color.

sparkline A compact chart that summarizes data visually within a single worksheet cell.

spin button A content control in which users can enter a value or increase or decrease a value in set increments by selecting arrows on the control.

subtotal A partial total for related data in a worksheet.

sunburst A chart, shaped as a circle, that depicts the magnitude of values within a data set by using a combination of color, size, and position.

template A file that can contain predefined content and formatting, and that serves as the basis for new workbooks.

theme A set of unified design elements that combine color, fonts, and effects, and that can be applied to a workbook or saved as part of a template.

timeline A worksheet control that lets users filter the contents of a PivotTable based on time increments.

tool tab A ribbon tab containing groups of commands that are pertinent only to a specific type of workbook element such as a table. Tool tabs appear only when relevant content is selected.

Top 10 filter A filter by which a user can specify the top or bottom number of items, or top or bottom percentage of items, to display in a worksheet.

tracer arrow An arrow that indicates the formulas to which a cell contributes its value (a dependent arrow) or the cells from which a formula derives its value (a precedent arrow).

treemap A square chart that depicts the magnitude of values within a data set by using a combination of color, size, and position.

trendline A projection of future data (such as sales) based on past performance.

validation rule A test that data must pass to be entered into a cell without generating a warning message.

value axis The vertical reference line of a chart or graph, which usually depicts value data. Also called the *y-axis*.

Visual Basic for Applications (VBA) An event-driven programming language that is built into Microsoft Office.

watch The display of a cell's contents in a separate window even when the cell is not visible in the Excel workbook.

waterfall A chart that uses columns to depict increases and decreases of a value over time based on transactional data.

What-If Analysis The process of changing the values of specific worksheet cells to determine the impact of the changes on other calculations. Excel includes three What-If Analysis tools: *data tables*, *Goal Seek*, and *Scenarios*.

workbook The basic Excel document, consisting of one or more worksheets.

worksheet A page in an Excel workbook.

x-axis The horizontal reference line of a chart or graph, which usually depicts category or time data. Also called the *category axis*.

XML *Extensible Markup Language*, a format for delivering rich, structured data in a standard, consistent way. XML tags describe a file's content, whereas HTML tags describe a file's appearance. XML is *extensible* because it allows designers to create their own customized tags. See also *HTML*.

y-axis The vertical reference line of a chart or graph, which usually depicts value data. Also called the *value axis*.

z-axis The third axis in a three-dimensional coordinate system, used in charts or graphs to represent depth. Also called the *series axis*.

Index

Numbers

Symbols

A

B

C